Ethics of Research with Human Subjects

Selected Policies and Resources

Edited by

**Jeremy Sugarman,
Anna C. Mastroianni,
and Jeffrey P. Kahn**

While the authors and the publisher have made every effort to ensure that the documents, policies, directives, and resources set forth in this volume, together with the editorial notations, were accurate at the time of publication, these materials may be modified in the future. This volume is intended as a reference guide to selected policies and resources related to research with human subjects. Neither the authors nor the publisher are offering specific medical or legal advice.

University Publishing Group, Inc.
Frederick, Maryland 21701
1-800-654-8188

Copyright © 1998 by University Publishing Group.

All rights reserved. No part of this publication may be reproduced, stored in a retrieval system, or transmitted, in any form, or by any means, electronic, mechanical, photocopying, recording or otherwise, without the prior permission of University Publishing Group.
Printed in the United States of America

ISBN 1-55572-057-9

Preface

In our own research and teaching we have sometimes found it difficult to locate relevant policies and useful resources bearing on the ethics of research with human subjects. The fact that three colleagues from different disciplines within bioethics (medicine, law, and philosophy—all with interest and degrees in public health) faced these similar challenges made us realize that a compilation of these materials could be useful in many settings. In the process of reviewing policies and resources for this volume, we learned much about the richness of the materials available to help grapple with some of the complex ethical issues related to research with human subjects. We hope that easy access to these materials will ultimately enhance both the knowledge of and sensitivity to these issues. In addition, we hope to prompt scholarship and analysis by identifying some of the areas in which policy direction remains absent or reference materials are limited.

This project could not have been successfully undertaken without the hard work of the staffs of the Program in Medical Ethics at Duke University and in the Center for Bioethics at the University of Minnesota. In particular, we would like to thank Janet Malek and Amy Ferlazzo at Duke, and Robert Koepp, Carmel Barth, and Julie Vangelof at Minnesota.

Jeremy Sugarman, M.D., M.P.H., M.A.
Anna C. Mastroianni, J.D., M.P.H.
Jeffrey P. Kahn, Ph.D., M.P.H.
May 1998

Contents

Preface	iii
Introduction	1
Finding Aids	
1 Location of Documents and Policies in this Volume	3
2 Policies Listed by Federal Agency	6
3 Documents Cited form the Code of Federal Regulations	8

Part 1 *Landmark Documents*

Overview of Part 1	11
The Nuremberg Code	12
World Medical Association Declaration of Helsinki	14
The Belmont Report	19

Part 2 *Selected Major Policies*

Overview of Part 2	33
General Federal Policies	
The Common Rule	35
DHHS—Basic Policy for Protection of Human Research Subjects	53
DHHS—Research Activities which may be Reviewed through	
Expedited Review Procedures	71
FDA—Protection of Human Subjects	74
FDA—Institutional Review Boards	86
FDA—Clinical Investigations which may be Reviewed through	
Expedited Review Procedures Set Forth in FDA Regulations	100
FDA—Financial Disclosure by Clinical Investigators	102
Policies for Subject Populations	
General	
FDA—Reporting of Demographic Subgroups	108
Racial and Ethnic Groups	
NIH—Guidelines on the Inclusion of Women and Minorities	
as Subjects in Clinical Research	115
CDC/ATSDR—Policy on the Inclusion of Women and Racial	
and Ethnic Minorities in Externally Awarded Research	132

Women
    *NIH—Guidelines on the Inclusion of Women and Minorities
       as Subjects in Clinical Research*   142
    *CDC/ATSDR—Policy on the Inclusion of Women and Racial
       and Ethnic Minorities in Externally Awarded Research*   143
    *FDA—Guideline for the Study and Evaluation of Gender
       Differences in the Clinical Evaluation of Drugs*   144
    *DHHS—Additional Protections Pertaining to Research,
       Development, and Related Activities Involving Fetuses,
       Pregnant Women, and Human In Vitro Fertilization*   153
Embryos and Fetuses
    Ban on Federal Funding for Embryo and Related Research   159
    *DHHS—Additional Protections Pertaining to Research,
       Development, and Related Activities Involving Fetuses,
       Pregnant Women, and Human In Vitro Fertilization*   161
Minors
    *DHHS—Additional DHHS Protections for Children Involved
       as Subjects in Research*   162
    *NIH—Policy and Guidelines on the Inclusion of Children
       as Participants in Research Involving Human Subjects*   167
Older Persons
    *FDA—Guideline for the Study of Drugs Likely to be Used
       in the Elderly*   176

Research in Particular Settings
Prisons
    *DHHS—Additional Protections Pertaining to Biomedical
       and Behavioral Research Involving Prisoners as Subjects*   187
International
    *USAID—Procedures for Protection of Human Subjects
       in Research Supported by USAID*   191
    *CIOMS—International Ethical Guidelines for Biomedical
       Research Involving Human Subjects*   200
    World Medical Association Declaration of Helsinki   208

Waivers of Informed Consent
Emergency Research
    *DHHS—Waiver of Informed Consent Requirements in
       Certain Emergency Research*   209
    *FDA—Waiver of Informed Consent in Certain
       Emergency Research*   214

Military Exigencies
    FDA—Determinations that Informed Consent is not
        Feasible for Military Exigencies   216

Part 3 Selected Bibliography

Overview of Part 3   227

General Resources   229
History   230
Subject Populations   232
   Racial and Ethnic Groups   232
   Women   233
   Embryos and Fetuses   234
   Minors   236
      General   236
      Adolescents   237
   Older Persons   238
   Students   238
   Healthy Volunteers   238
Research in Particular Settings   239
   Prisons   239
   International   239
   Institutions   240
Waivers of Informed Consent   241
   Emergency Research   241
   Military Settings   241
Other Issues   242
   Genetics   242
   Subjects with Diminished Capacity   243
   Compensation   244
      Incentives   244
      Injury   244

Appendices
   List of Abbreviations   245
   Relevant Web Sites   246

Introduction

Research policies include statutes, regulations, guidelines, and other policy directives. They can play an important role in the process of research with human subjects as well as in facilitating understanding of the ethics of this research. For instance, by consolidating directives, policies can help assure that important matters are considered and rules followed in the conduct of research. As such, they are crucial to the success of the research enterprise. At the same time, they also are an indication of a common understanding of standards for ethical behavior, an important consideration in scholarship regarding research ethics.

Over the last decade, we have witnessed an explosion in the promulgation of policies regarding research with human subjects, making it difficult to get a clear view of the larger picture of research ethics. For instance, where research policies once emphasized the protection of research subjects through processes such as informed consent and careful assessments of the risks to subjects, they now increasingly emphasize issues of justice such as the inclusion of subjects in research. This increase in the number of policies, as well as their shifting emphases, can also make it difficult to keep up with current requirements. This book was designed to help mitigate some of these difficulties associated with policies regarding research with human subjects. Accordingly, this book should be useful for IRB members and administrators, scholars, students, researchers, and those responsible for research oversight in various settings.

This book is divided into three parts. Part 1: Landmark Documents, contains materials that have in some way influenced policy development related to research with human subjects. Part 2: Selected Major Policies, presents important policies relating to this research. These include policies that address general issues arising in the context of research with human subjects, as well as those addressing particular subject populations and research settings. Part 3: Selected Bibliography, provides citations to resources that are intended to amplify understanding of policies for human subjects research and, perhaps more importantly, address gaps where policy guidance is lacking.

Three finding aids are included to assist in the location of relevant materials. Finding Aid 1 is designed to facilitate locating particular policies in this volume according to category (for example, Landmark Documents, General Federal Policies, and so on), title, and citation. Finding Aid 2 lists policies by federal agency or department. Finding Aid 3 provides citations to the *Code of Federal Regulations* and titles for relevant policies. Finally, lists of abbreviations and useful web sites for related materials are provided as appendices.

Each part of this volume represents a selection of important and useful documents. This volume as a whole, however, is certainly not intended to be an exhaustive compendium of policies related to research with human subjects. There may exist other relevant federal policies as well as policies promulgated at state, local, or institutional levels. In addition, it is important to emphasize that the policies reproduced in this volume may be modified in the future; it is essential that users of this book maintain current and accurate versions of the policies in this volume. To facilitate this task, we have included contact information at the beginning of each of the relevant policies in this collection. Further, we strongly encourage readers to consult with persons in their institutions charged with oversight of research with human subjects about interpretations of these policies and the identification of other state, local, or institutional policies that may be relevant.

We acknowledge at the outset that policies are not synonymous with, nor do they necessarily correlate with, right conduct, but they certainly can play a role in encouraging the ethical conduct of research. It is our hope that providing these documents in an accessible form and providing additional bibliographic guidance will enhance understanding of the ethical issues arising in research with human subjects.

Finding Aids
1 Location of Documents and Policies in this Volume

Type of Document		Title	Source	Page
Landmark document		The Nuremberg Code	"Permissible Medical Experiments," *Trials of War Criminals before the Nuernberg Military Tribunals under Control Council Law No. 10*, 1949	12
		World Medical Association Declaration of Helsinki	World Medical Association, Inc. 48th General Assembly, Somerset West, Republic of South Africa, October 1996	14
		The Belmont Report	Report of the National Commission for the Protection of Human Subjects of Biomedical and Behavioral Research, DHEW, 18 April 1979	19
General policy for	16 federal agencies & depts.	The Common Rule	56 *Fed. Reg.* 28012, 18 June 1991	35
	DHHS	Basic Policy for Protection of Human Research Subjects	45 *CFR* 46, Subpart A, last rev. 28 June 1991	53
		Research Activities which may be Reviewed through Expedited Review Procedures	46 *Fed. Reg.* 8392, 26 January 1981	71
	FDA	Protection of Human Subjects	21 *CFR* 50, last rev. 23 July 1997	74
		Institutional Review Boards	21 *CFR* 56, last rev. 2 October 1996	86
		Clinical Investigations which may be Reviewed through Expedited Review Procedures Set Forth in FDA Regulations	46 *Fed. Reg.* 8980, 27 January 1998	100
		Financial Disclosure by Clinical Investigators	21 *CFR* 54, last rev. 2 February 1998	102
Policies regarding subject populations	General	FDA—Reporting of Demographic Subgroups	63 *Fed. Reg.* 6854, 11 February 1998, to be codified at 21 *CFR* 312.33, 314.50	108
	Racial & ethnic groups	NIH—Guidelines on the Inclusion of Women and Minorities as Subjects in Clinical Research	59 *Fed. Reg.* 14508, 28 March 1994	115

Finding Aid 1, Continued

Type of Document		Title	Source	Page
Policies regarding subject populations	Racial & ethnic groups	CDC/ATSDR— Policy on the Inclusion of Women and Racial and Ethnic Minorities in Externally Awarded Research	60 *Fed. Reg.* 47947, 15 September 1995	132
	Women	NIH—Guidelines on the Inclusion of Women and Minorities as Subjects in Clinical Research	59 *Fed. Reg.* 14508, 28 March 1994	115
		CDC/ATSDR—Policy on the Inclusion of Women and Racial and Ethnic Minorities in Externally Awarded Research	60 *Fed. Reg.* 47947, 15 September 1995	132
		FDA—Guideline for the Study and Evaluation of Gender Differences in the Clinical Evaluation of Drugs	58 *Fed. Reg.* 39409, 22 July 1993	144
		DHHS—Additional Protections Pertaining to Research, Development, and Related Activities Involving Fetuses, Pregnant Women, and Human In Vitro Fertilization	45 *CFR* 46, Subpart B, last rev. 1 June 1994	153
	Embryos and fetuses	Ban on Federal Funding for Embryo and Related Research	Public Law 105-78, 513, 1997	159
		DHHS—Additional Protections Pertaining to Research, Development, and Related Activities Involving Fetuses, Pregnant Women, and Human In Vitro Fertilization	45 *CFR* 46, Subpart B, last rev. 1 June 1994	153
	Minors	DHHS—Additional DHHS Protections for Children Involved as Subjects in Research	45 *CFR* 46, Subpart D, last rev. 28 June 1991	162
		NIH—Policy and Guidelines on the Inclusion of Children as Participants in Research Involving Human Subjects	*NIH Guide for Grants and Contracts*, vol. 27, 6 March 1998	167
	Older persons	FDA—Guideline for the Study of Drugs Likely to be Used in the Elderly	*Guidance for Industry*, FDA, November 1989	176
Research in particular settings	Prisons	DHHS—Additional Protections Pertaining to Biomedical and Behavioral Research Involving Prisoners as Subjects	45 *CFR* 46, Subpart C, last rev. 26 January 1981	187

Finding Aid 1, Continued

Type of Document		Title	Source	Page
Research in particular settings	International	USAID—Procedures for Protection for Human Subjects in Research Supported by USAID	*USAID/General Notice PPC and G* 19 April 1995, available from USAID	191
		CIOMS—International Ethical Guidelines for Biomedical Research Involving Human Subjects	CIOMS, in collaboration with WHO, Geneva, 1993	200
		World Medical Association Declaration of Helsinki	World Medical Association, Inc. 48th General Assembly, Somerset West, Republic of South Africa, October 1996	14
Waivers of informed consent	Emergency research	DHHS—Waiver of Informed Consent Requirements in Certain Emergency Research	61 *Fed. Reg.* 51531, 2 October 1996	209
		FDA—Waiver of Informed Consent in Certain Emergency Research	61 *Fed. Reg.* 51498, 2 October 1996, codified at 21 *CFR* Parts 50, 56, 312, 314, 601, 812, and 814	214
	Military exigencies	FDA—Determinations that Informed Consent is not Feasible for Military Exigencies	55 *Fed. Reg.* 52814, 21 December 1990, codified at 21 *CFR* 50.23 (d)	216

The information presented in this finding aid is current as of 1 May 1998.

6 Finding Aids

2 Policies Listed by Federal Agency

Federal Agency/Dept.		Title	Source	Page
DHHS		Basic Policy for Protection of Human Research Subjects	45 *CFR* 46, Subpart A, last rev. 28 June 1991	53
		Research Activities which may be Reviewed through Expedited Review Procedures	46 *Fed. Reg.* 8392, 26 January 1981	71
		Additional Protections Pertaining to Research, Development, and Related Activities Involving Fetuses, Pregnant Women and Human In Vitro Fertilization	45 *CFR* 46, Subpart B, last rev. 1 June 1994	153
		Additional DHHS Protections for Children Involved as Subjects in Research	45 *CFR* 46, Subpart D, last rev. 28 June 1991	162
		Additional Protections Pertaining to Biomedical and Behavioral Research Involving Prisoners as Subjects	45 *CFR* 46, Subpart C, last rev. 26 January 1981	187
		Waiver of Informed Consent Requirements in Certain Emergency Research	61 *Fed. Reg.* 51531, 2 October 1996	209
	NIH	Guidelines on the Inclusion of Women and Minorities as Subjects in Clinical Research	59 *Fed. Reg.* 14508, 28 March 1994	115
		Policy and Guidelines on the Inclusion of Children as Participants in Research Involving Human Subjects	*NIH Guide for Grants and Contracts*, vol. 27, 6 March 1998	167
	CDC/ ATSDR	Policy on the Inclusion of Women and Racial and Ethnic Minorities in Externally Awarded Research	60 *Fed. Reg.* 47947, 15 September 1995	132

Finding Aid 2, Continued

Federal Agency/Dept.		Title	Source	Page
DHHS	FDA	Protection of Human Subjects	21 *CFR* 50, last rev. 23 July 1997	74
		Institutional Review Boards	21 *CFR* 56, last rev. 2 October 1996	86
		Clinical Investigations which may be Reviewed through Expedited Review Procedures Set Forth in FDA Regulations	46 *Fed. Reg.* 8980, 27 January 1981	100
		Financial Disclosure by Clinical Investigators	21 *CFR* 54, last rev. 2 February 1998	102
		Reporting of Demographic Subgroups	63 *Fed. Reg.* 6854, 11 February 1998, to be codified at 21 *CFR* 312.33, 314.50	108
		Guideline for the Study and Evaluation of Gender Differences in the Clinical Evaluation of Drugs	58 *Fed. Reg.* 39409, 22 July 1993	144
		Guideline for the Study of Drugs Likely to be Used in the Elderly	*Guidance for Industry*, November 1989, available from the FDA	176
		Waiver of Informed Consent Requirements in Certain Emergency Research	61 *Fed. Reg.* 51498, 2 October 1996, codified at 21 *CFR* Parts 50, 56, 312, 314, 601, 812, and 814	215
		Determinations that Informed Consent is not Feasible for Military Exigencies	55 *Fed. Reg.* 52814, 21 December 1990, codified at 21 *CFR* 50.23 (d)	216
USAID		Procedures for the Protection of Human Subjects in Research Supported by USAID	*USAID/General Notice PPC and G* 19 April 1995, available from USAID	191

The information presented in this finding aid is current as of 1 May 1998.

3 Policies Cited from the Code of Federal Regulations

Citation	Title	Page
21 *CFR* 50	FDA—Protection of Human Subjects	74
21 *CFR* 50.3(n), 50.24, 56.109(c), 56.109(d)	FDA—Waiver of Informed Consent in Certain Emergency Research	214
21 *CFR* 50.23(d)	FDA—Determinations that Informed Consent is not Feasible for Military Exigencies	216
21 *CFR* 54	FDA—Financial Disclosure by Clinical Investigators	102
21 *CFR* 56	FDA—Institutional Review Boards	86
21 *CFR* 312.33 and 314.50	FDA—Reporting of Demographic Subgroups	108
45 *CFR* 46, Subpart A	DHHS—Basic Policy for Protection of Human Research Subjects	53
45 *CFR* 46, Subpart B	DHHS—Additional Protections Pertaining to Research, Development, and Related Activities Involving Fetuses, Pregnant Women, and Human In Vitro Fertilization	153
45 *CFR* 46, Subpart C	DHHS—Additional DHHS Protections for Children Involved as Subjects in Research	162
45 *CFR* 46, Subpart D	DHHS—Additional Protections Pertaining to Biomedical and Behavioral Research Involving Prisoners as Subjects	187

The information presented in this finding aid is current as of 1 May 1998.

Part 1
Landmark Documents

Overview of Part 1

Part 1 contains a selection of some of the most important documents in the history and evolution of policies regarding research with human subjects. *The Nuremberg Code* and the *Declaration of Helsinki*, as international codes of conduct, are viewed as espousing important guidelines for the ethical conduct of research. Similarly, the influence of *The Belmont Report* is due to its ethical analysis of research with human subjects and its enumeration of important ethical principles at stake in the conduct of research.

These documents should be considered landmarks not only for the thinking they represent, but also for the thinking they subsequently prompted. It was this thinking that played a role in the development and refinement of the policies that make up Part 2 of this volume. The documents in this section can therefore be read with an appreciation of their role in the evolution of the current standards and policies for the ethical conduct of research with human subjects.

The Nuremberg Code

Excerpted from: "Permissable Medical Experiments," Trials of War Criminals before the Nuernberg Military Tribunals under Control Council Law No. 10: Nuernberg, October 1946-1949, vol. 2 (Washington, D.C.: U.S. Government Printing Office, n.d.), 181-182.

1. The voluntary consent of the human subject is absolutely essential. This means that the person involved should have legal capacity to give consent; should be so situated as to be able to exercise free power of choice without the intervention of any element of force, fraud, deceit, duress, overreaching, or other ulterior form of constraint or coercion; and should have sufficient knowledge and comprehension of the elements of the subject matter involved as to enable him to make an understanding and enlightened decision. This latter element requires that before the acceptance of an affirmative decision by the experimental subject there should be made known to him the nature, duration, and purpose of the experiment; the method and means by which it is to be conducted; all inconveniences and hazards reasonably to be expected; and their effects upon his health or person which may possibly come from his participation in the experiment.

The duty and responsibility for ascertaining the quality of the consent rests upon each individual who initiates, directs, or engages in the experiment. It is a personal duty and responsibility which may not be delegated to another with impunity.

2. The experiment should be such as to yield fruitful results for the good of society, unprocurable by other methods or means of study, and not random and unnecessary in nature.

3. The experiment should be so designed and based on the results of animal experimentation and a knowledge of the natural history of the disease or other problem under study that the anticipated results will justify the performance of the experiment.

4. The experiment should be so conducted as to avoid all unnecessary physical and mental suffering and injury.

5. No experiment should be conducted where there is an *a priori* reason to believe that death or disabling injury will occur, except perhaps, in those experiments where the experimental physicians also serve as subjects.

6. The degree of risk to be taken should never exceed that determined by the humanitarian importance of the problem to be solved by the experiment.

7. Proper preparations should be made and adequate facilities provided to protect the experimental subject against even remote possibilities of injury, disability or death.

8. The experiment should be conducted only by scientifically qualified persons. The highest degree of skill and care should be required through all stages of the experiment of those who conduct or engage in the experiment.

9. During the course of the experiment the human subject should be at liberty to bring the experiment to an end if he has reached the physical or mental state where continuation of the experiment seems to him to be impossible.

10. During the course of the experiment the scientist in charge must be prepared to terminate the experiment at any stage, if he has probable cause to believe, in the exercise of the good faith, superior skill, and careful judgment required of him, that a continuation of the experiment is likely to result in injury, disability, or death to the experimental subject.

World Medical Association Declaration of Helsinki
Recommendations Guiding Physicians in Biomedical Research Involving Human Subjects

Adopted by the 18th World Medical Assembly
Helsinki, Finland, June 1964

and amended by the
29th World Medical Assembly, Tokyo, Japan, October 1975
35th World Medical Assembly, Venice, Italy, October 1983
41st World Medical Assembly, Hong Kong, September 1989
and the
48th General Assembly,
Somerset West, Republic of South Africa, October 1996

Reprinted in full with permission from the World Medical Association, Inc., B.P. 63-01212 Ferney-Voltaire Cedex, France. Telephone (04) 50 40 75 75; Fax (04) 50 49 59 37.

INTRODUCTION

It is the mission of the physician to safeguard the health of the people. His or her knowledge and conscience are dedicated to the fulfillment of this mission.

The Declaration of Geneva of the World Medical Association binds the physician with the words, "The health of my patient will be my first consideration," and the International Code of Medical Ethics declares that, "A physician shall act only in the patient's interest when providing medical care which might have the effect of weakening the physical and mental condition of the patient."

The purpose of biomedical research involving human subjects must be to improve diagnostic, therapeutic and prophylactic procedures and the understanding of the aetiology and pathogenesis of disease.

In current medical practice most diagnostic, therapeutic or prophylactic procedures involve hazards. This applies especially to biomedical research.

Medical progress is based on research which ultimately must rest in part on experimentation involving human subjects.

In the field of biomedical research a fundamental distinction must be recognized between medical research in which the aim is essentially diagnostic or therapeutic for a patient, and medical research, the essential object of which is purely scientific and without implying direct diagnostic or therapeutic value to the person subjected to the research.

Special caution must be exercised in the conduct of research which may affect the environment, and the welfare of animals used for research must be respected.

Because it is essential that the results of laboratory experiments be applied to human beings to further scientific knowledge and to help suffering humanity, the World Medical Association has prepared the following recommendations as a guide to every physician in biomedical research involving human subjects. They should be kept under review in the future. It must be stressed that the standards as drafted are only a guide to physicians all over the world. Physicians are not relieved from criminal, civil and ethical responsibilities under the laws of their own countries.

I. BASIC PRINCIPLES

1. Biomedical research involving human subjects must conform to generally accepted scientific principles and should be based on adequately performed laboratory and animal experimentation and on a thorough knowledge of the scientific literature.
2. The design and performance of each experimental procedure involving human subjects should be clearly formulated in an experimental protocol which should be transmitted for consideration, comment and guidance to a specially appointed committee independent of the investigator and the sponsor provided that this independent committee is in conformity with the laws and regulations of the country in which the research experiment is performed.
3. Biomedical research involving human subjects should be conducted only by scientifically qualified persons and under the supervision of a clinically competent medical person. The responsibility for the human subject must always rest with a medically qualified person

and never rest on the subject of the research, even though the subject has given his or her consent.
4. Biomedical research involving human subjects cannot legitimately be carried out unless the importance of the objective is in proportion to the inherent risk to the subject.
5. Every biomedical research project involving human subjects should be preceded by careful assessment of predictable risks in comparison with foreseeable benefits to the subject or to others. Concern for the interests of the subject must always prevail over the interests of science and society.
6. The right of the research subject to safeguard his or her integrity must always be respected. Every precaution should be taken to respect the privacy of the subject and to minimize the impact of the study on the subject's physical and mental integrity and on the personality of the subject.
7. Physicians should abstain from engaging in research projects involving human subjects unless they are satisfied that the hazards involved are believed to be predictable. Physicians should cease any investigation if the hazards are found to outweigh the potential benefits.
8. In publication of the results of his or her research, the physician is obliged to preserve the accuracy of the results. Reports of experimentation not in accordance with the principles laid down in this Declaration should not be accepted for publication.
9. In any research on human beings, each potential subject must be adequately informed of the aims, methods, anticipated benefits and potential hazards of the study and the discomfort it may entail. He or she should be informed that he or she is at liberty to abstain from participation in the study and that he or she is free to withdraw his or her consent to participation at any time. The physician should then obtain the subject's freely-given informed consent, preferably in writing.
10. When obtaining informed consent for the research project the physician should be particularly cautious if the subject is in a dependent relationship to him or her or may consent under duress. In that case the informed consent should be obtained by a physician who is not engaged in the investigation and who is completely independent of this official relationship.

11. In case of legal incompetence, informed consent should be obtained from the legal guardian in accordance with national legislation. Where physical or mental incapacity makes it impossible to obtain informed consent, or when the subject is a minor, permission from the responsible relative replaces that of the subject in accordance with national legislation.
Whenever the minor child is in fact able to give a consent, the minor's consent must be obtained in addition to the consent of the minor's legal guardian.
12. The research protocol should always contain a statement of the ethical considerations involved and should indicate that the principles enunciated in the present Declaration are complied with.

II. MEDICAL RESEARCH COMBINED WITH PROFESSIONAL CARE (Clinical Research)

1. In the treatment of the sick person, the physician must be free to use a new diagnostic and therapeutic measure, if in his or her judgment it offers hope of saving life, reestablishing health or alleviating suffering.
2. The potential benefits, hazards and discomfort of a new method should be weighed against the advantages of the best current diagnostic and therapeutic methods.
3. In any medical study, every patient—including those of a control group, if any—should be assured of the best proven diagnostic and therapeutic method. This does not exclude the use of inert placebo in studies where no proven diagnostic or therapeutic method exists.
4. The refusal of the patient to participate in a study must never interfere with the physician-patient relationship.
5. If the physician considers it essential not to obtain informed consent, the specific reasons for this proposal should be stated in the experimental protocol for transmission to the independent committee (I, 2).
6. The physician can combine medical research with professional care, the objective being the acquisition of new medical knowledge, only to the extent that medical research is justified by its potential diagnostic or therapeutic value for the patient.

III. NON-THERAPEUTIC BIOMEDICAL RESEARCH INVOLVING HUMAN SUBJECTS (Non-Clinical Biomedical Research)

1. In the purely scientific application of medical research carried out on a human being, it is the duty of the physician to remain the protector of the life and health of that person on whom biomedical research is being carried out.
2. The subjects should be volunteers—either healthy persons or patients for whom the experimental design is not related to the patient's illness.
3. The investigator or the investigating team should discontinue the research if in his/her or their judgment it may, if continued, be harmful to the individual.
4. In research on man, the interest of science and society should never take precedence over considerations related to the wellbeing of the subject.

The Belmont Report

Ethical Principles and Guidelines for the Protection of Human Subjects of Research

Report of the National Commission for the Protection of Human Subjects of Biomedical and Behavioral Research, Department of Health, Education, and Welfare. 18 April 1979.

Scientific research has produced substantial social benefits. It has also posed some troubling ethical questions. Public attention was drawn to these questions by reported abuses of human subjects in biomedical experiments, especially during the Second World War. During the Nuremberg War Crime Trials, the Nuremberg code was drafted as a set of standards for judging physicians and scientists who had conducted biomedical experiments on concentration camp prisoners. This code became the prototype of many later codes[1] intended to assure that research involving human subjects would be carried out in an ethical manner.

The codes consist of rules, some general, others specific, that guide the investigators or the reviewers of research in their work. Such rules often are inadequate to cover complex situations; at times they come into conflict, and they are frequently difficult to interpret or apply. Broader ethical principles will provide a basis on which specific rules may be formulated, criticized and interpreted.

Three principles, or general prescriptive judgments, that are relevant to research involving human subjects are identified in this statement. Other principles may also be relevant. These three are comprehensive, however, and are stated at a level of generalization that should assist scientists, subjects, reviewers and interested citizens to understand the ethical issues inherent in research involving human subjects. These principles cannot always be applied so as to resolve beyond dispute particular ethical problems. The objective is to provide an analytical framework that will guide the resolution of ethical problems arising from research involving human subjects.

This statement consists of a distinction between research and practice, a discussion of the three basic ethical principles, and remarks about the application of these principles.

A. Boundaries Between Practice and Research

It is important to distinguish between biomedical and behavioral research, on the one hand, and the practice of accepted therapy on the other, in order to know what activities ought to undergo review for the protection of human subjects of research. The distinction between research and practice is blurred partly because both often occur together (as in research designed to evaluate a therapy) and partly because notable departures from standard practice are often called "experimental" when the terms "experimental" and "research" are not carefully defined.

For the most part, the term "practice" refers to interventions that are designed solely to enhance the well being of an individual patient or client and that have a reasonable expectation of success. The purpose of medical or behavioral practice is to provide diagnosis, preventive treatment or therapy to particular individuals.[2] By contrast, the term "research" designates an activity designed to test an hypothesis, permit conclusions to be drawn, and thereby to develop or contribute to generalizable knowledge (expressed, for example, in theories, principles, and statements of relationships). Research is usually described in a formal protocol that sets forth an objective and a set of procedures designed to reach that objective.

When a clinician departs in a significant way from standard or accepted practice, the innovation does not, in and of itself, constitute research. The fact that a procedure is "experimental," in the sense of new, untested or different, does not automatically place it in the category of research. Radically new procedures of this description should, however, be made the object of formal research at an early stage in order to determine whether they are safe and effective. Thus, it is the responsibility of medical practice committees, for example, to insist that a major innovation be incorporated into a formal research project.[3]

Research and practice may be carried on together when research is designed to evaluate the safety and efficacy of a therapy. This need not cause any confusion regarding whether or not the activity requires review; the general rule is that if there is any element of research in an activity, that activity should undergo review for the protection of human subjects.

B. Basic Ethical Principles

The expression "basic ethical principles" refers to those general judgments that serve as a basic justification for the many particular ethical prescriptions and evaluations of human actions. Three basic principles, among those generally accepted in our cultural tradition, are particularly relevant to the ethics of research involving human subjects: The principles of respect for persons, beneficence and justice.

1. Respect for Persons.—Respect for persons incorporates at least two ethical convictions: first, that individuals should be treated as autonomous agents, and second, that persons with diminished autonomy are entitled to protection. The principle of respect for persons thus divides into two separate moral requirements: The requirement to acknowledge autonomy and the requirement to protect those with diminished autonomy.

An autonomous person is an individual capable of deliberation about personal goals and of acting under the direction of such deliberation. To respect autonomy is to give weight to autonomous persons' considered opinions and choices while refraining from obstructing their actions unless they are clearly detrimental to others. To show lack of respect for an autonomous agent is to repudiate that person's considered judgments, to deny an individual the freedom to act on those considered judgments, or to withhold information necessary to make a considered judgment, when there are no compelling reasons to do so.

However, not every human being is capable of self-determination. The capacity for self-determination matures during an individual's life, and some individuals lose this capacity wholly or in part because of illness, mental disability, or circumstances that severely restrict liberty. Respect for the immature and the incapacitated may require protecting them as they mature or while they are incapacitated.

Some persons are in need of extensive protection, even to the point of excluding them from activities which may harm them; other persons require little protection beyond making sure they undertake activities freely and with awareness of possible adverse consequences. The extent of protection afforded should depend upon the risk of harm and the likelihood of benefit. The judgment that any individual lacks autonomy should be periodically reevaluated and will vary in different situations.

In most cases of research involving human subjects, respect for persons demands that subjects enter into the research voluntarily and with adequate information. In some situations, however, application of the principle is not obvious. The involvement of prisoners as subjects of research provides an instructive example. On the one hand, it would seem that the principle of respect for persons requires that prisoners not be deprived of the opportunity to volunteer for research. On the other hand, under prison conditions they may be subtly coerced or unduly influenced to engage in research activities for which they would not otherwise volunteer. Respect for persons would then dictate that prisoners be protected. Whether to allow prisoners to "volunteer" or to "protect" them presents a dilemma. Respecting persons, in most hard cases, is often a matter of balancing competing claims urged by the principle of respect itself.

2. *Beneficence.*—Persons are treated in an ethical manner not only by respecting their decisions and protecting them from harm, but also by making efforts to secure their well being. Such treatment falls under the principle of beneficence. The term "beneficence" is often understood to cover acts of kindness or charity that go beyond strict obligation. In this document, beneficence is understood in a stronger sense, as an obligation. Two general rules have been formulated as complementary expressions of beneficent actions in this sense: (1) do not harm and (2) maximize possible benefits and minimize possible harms.

The Hippocratic maxim "do no harm" has long been a fundamental principle of medical ethics. Claude Bernard extended it to the realm of research, saying that one should not injure one person regardless of the benefits that might come to others. However, even avoiding harm requires learning what is harmful; and, in the process of obtaining this information, persons may be exposed to risk of harm. Further, the Hippocratic Oath requires physicians to benefit their patients "according to their best judgment." Learning what will in fact benefit may require exposing persons to risk. The problem posed by these imperatives is to decide when it is justifiable to seek certain benefits despite the risks involved, and when the benefits should be foregone because of the risks.

The obligations of beneficence affect both individual investigators and society at large, because they extend both to particular research projects and to the entire enterprise of research. In the case of particular projects, investigators and members of their institutions are obliged to give forethought to the maximization of benefits and the reduction of risk that might occur from the research investigation. In the case of scientific research in general, members of the larger society are obliged to recognize the longer term benefits and risks that may result from the improvement of knowledge and from the development of novel medical, psychotherapeutic, and social procedures.

The principle of beneficence often occupies a well-defined justifying role in many areas of research involving human subjects. An example is found in research involving children. Effective ways of treating childhood diseases and fostering healthy development are benefits that serve to justify research involving children—even when individual research subjects are not direct beneficiaries. Research also makes is possible to avoid the harm that may result from the application of previously accepted routine practices that on closer investigation turn out to be dangerous. But the role of the principle of beneficence is not always so unambiguous. A difficult ethical problem remains, for example, about research that presents more than minimal risk without immediate prospect of direct benefit to the children involved. Some have argued that such research is inadmissible, while others have pointed out that this limit would rule out much research promising great benefit to children in the future. Here again, as with all hard cases, the different claims covered by the principle of beneficence may come into conflict and force difficult choices.

3. Justice.—Who ought to receive the benefits of research and bear its burdens? This is a question of justice, in the sense of "fairness in distribution" or "what is deserved." An injustice occurs when some benefit to which a person is entitled is denied without good reason or when some burden is imposed unduly. Another way of conceiving the principle of justice is that equals ought to be treated equally. However, this statement requires explication. Who is equal and who is unequal? What considerations justify departure from equal distribution? Almost all commentators allow that distinctions based on experience, age, deprivation, competence, merit and position do sometimes constitute criteria justifying differential treatment for certain purposes. It is necessary, then, to explain in what respects people should be treated equally. There are several widely accepted formulations of just ways to distribute burdens and benefits. Each formulation mentions some relevant property on the basis of which burdens and benefits should be distributed. These formulations are (1) to each person an equal share, (2) to each person according to individual need, (3) to each person according to individual effort, (4) to each person according to societal contribution, and (5) to each person according to merit.

Questions of justice have long been associated with social practices such as punishment, taxation and political representation. Until recently these questions have not generally been associated with scientific research. However, they are foreshadowed even in the earliest reflections on the ethics of research involving human subjects. For example, during the 19th and early 20th centuries the burdens of serving as research subjects fell largely upon poor ward patients, while the benefits of improved medical care flowed primarily to private patients. Subsequently, the exploitation of unwilling prisoners as research subjects in Nazi concentration camps was condemned as a particularly flagrant injustice. In this country, in the 1940's, the Tuskegee syphilis study used disadvantaged, rural black men to study the untreated course of a disease that is by no means confined to that population. These subjects were deprived of demonstrably effective treatment in order not to interrupt the project, long after such treatment became generally available.

Against this historical background, it can be seen how conceptions of justice are relevant to research involving human subjects. For example, the selection of research subjects needs to be scrutinized in order to determine whether some classes (e.g., welfare patients, particular racial and ethnic minorities, or persons confined to institutions) are being systematically selected simply because of their easy availability, their compromised position, or their manipulability, rather than for reasons directly related to the problem being studied. Finally, whenever research supported by public funds leads to the development of therapeutic devices and procedures, justice demands both that these not provide advantages only to those who can afford them and that such research should not unduly involve persons from groups unlikely to be among the beneficiaries of subsequent applications of the research.

C. Applications

Applications of the general principles to the conduct of research leads to consideration of the following requirements: Informed consent, risk/benefit assessment, and the selection of subjects of research.

1. Informed Consent.—Respect for persons requires that subjects, to the degree that they are capable, be given the opportunity to choose what shall or shall not happen to them. This opportunity is provided when adequate standards for informed consent are satisfied.

While the importance of informed consent is unquestioned, controversy prevails over the nature and possibility of an informed consent. Nonetheless, there is widespread agreement that the consent process can be analyzed as containing three elements: information, comprehension and voluntariness.

Information. Most codes of research establish specific items for disclosure intended to assure that subjects are given sufficient information. These items generally include: the research procedure, their purposes, risks and anticipated benefits, alternative procedures (where therapy is involved), and a statement offering the subject the opportunity to ask questions and to withdraw at any time from the research. Additional items have been proposed, including how subjects are selected, the person responsible for the research, etc.

However, a simple listing of items does not answer the question of what the standard should be for judging how much and what sort of information should be provided. One standard frequently invoked in medical practice, namely the information commonly provided by practitioners in the field or in the locale, is inadequate since research takes place precisely when a common understanding does not exist. Another standard, currently popular in malpractice law, requires the practitioner to reveal the information that reasonable persons would wish to know in order to make a decision regarding their care. This, too, seems insufficient since the research subject, being in essence a volunteer, may wish to know considerably more about risks gratuitously undertaken than do patients who deliver themselves into the hand of a clinician for needed care. It may be that a standard of "the reasonable volunteer" should be proposed: The extent and nature of information should be such that persons, knowing that the procedure is neither necessary for their care nor perhaps fully understood, can decide whether they wish to participate in the furthering of knowledge. Even when some direct benefit to them is anticipated, the subjects should understand clearly the range of risk and the voluntary nature of participation.

A special problem of consent arises where informing subjects of some pertinent aspect of the research is likely to impair the validity of the research. In many cases, it is sufficient to indicate to subjects that they are being invited to participate in research of which some features will not be revealed until the research is concluded. In all cases of research involving incomplete disclosure, such research is justified only if it is clear that (1) incomplete disclosure is truly necessary to accomplish the goals of the research, (2) there are no undisclosed risks to subjects that are more than minimal, and (3) there is an adequate plan for debriefing subjects, when appropriate, and for dissemination of research results to them. Information about risks should never be withheld for the purpose of eliciting the cooperation of subjects, and truthful answers should always be given to direct questions about the research. Care should be taken to distinguish cases in which disclosure would destroy or invalidate the research from cases in which disclosure would simply inconvenience the investigator.

Comprehension. The manner and context in which information is conveyed is as important as the information itself. For example, presenting information in a disorganized and rapid fashion, allowing too little time for consideration or curtailing opportunities for questioning, all may adversely affect a subject's ability to make an informed choice.

Because the subject's ability to understand is a function of intelligence, rationality, maturity and language, it is necessary to adapt the presentation of the information to the subject's capacities. Investigators are responsible for ascertaining that the subject has comprehended the information. While there is always an obligation to ascertain that the information about risk to subjects is complete and adequately comprehended, when the risks are more serious, that obligation increases. On occasion, it may be suitable to give some oral or written tests of comprehension.

Special provision may need to be made when comprehension is severely limited—for example, by conditions of immaturity or mental disability. Each class of subjects that one might consider as incompetent (e.g., infants and young children, mentally disabled patients, the terminally ill and the comatose) should be considered on its own terms. Even for these persons, however, respect requires giving them the opportunity to choose to the extent they are able, whether or not to participate in research. The objections of these subjects to involvement should be honored, unless the research entails providing them a therapy unavailable elsewhere. Respect for persons also requires seeking the permission of other parties in order to protect the subjects from harm. Such persons are thus respected both by acknowledging their own wishes and by the use of third parties to protect them from harm.

The third parties chosen should be those who are most likely to understand the incompetent subject's situation and to act in that person's best interest. The person authorized to act on behalf of the subject should be given an opportunity to observe the research as it proceeds in order to be able to withdraw the subject from the research, if such action appears in the subject's best interest.

Voluntariness. An agreement to participate in research constitutes a valid consent only if voluntarily given. This element of informed consent requires conditions free of coercion and undue influence. Coercion occurs when an overt threat of harm is intentionally presented by one person to another in order to obtain compliance. Undue influence, by contrast, occurs through an offer of an excessive, unwarranted, inappropriate or improper reward or other overture in order to obtain compliance. Also, inducements that would ordinarily be acceptable may become undue influences if the subject is especially vulnerable.

Unjustifiable pressures usually occur when persons in positions of authority or commanding influence—especially where possible sanctions are involved—urge a course of action for a subject. A continuum of such influencing factors exists, however, and it is impossible to state precisely where justifiable persuasion ends and undue influence begins. But undue influence would include actions such as manipulating a person's choice through the controlling influence of a close relative and threatening to withdraw health services to which an individual would otherwise be entitled.

2. *Assessment of Risks and Benefits.*—The assessment of risks and benefits requires a careful arrayal of relevant data, including, in some cases, alternative ways of obtaining the benefits sought in the research. Thus, the assessment presents both an opportunity and a responsibility to gather systematic and comprehensive information about proposed research. For the investigator, it is a means to examine whether the proposed research is properly designed. For a review committee, it is a method for determining whether the risks that will be presented to subjects are justified. For prospective subjects, the assessment will assist the determination whether or not to participate.

The Nature and Scope of Risks and Benefits. The requirement that research be justified on the basis of a favorable risk/benefit assessment bears a close relation to the principle of beneficence, just as the moral requirement that informed consent be obtained is derived primarily from the principle of respect for persons. The term "risk" refers to a possibility that harm may occur. However, when expressions such as "small risk" or "high risk" are used, they usually refer (often ambiguously) both to the chance (probability) of experiencing a harm and the severity (magnitude) of the envisioned harm.

The term "benefit" is used in the research context to refer to something of positive value related to health or welfare. Unlike "risk," "benefit" is not a term that expresses probabilities. Risk is properly contrasted to probability of benefits, and benefits are properly contrasted with harms rather than risks of harm. Accordingly, so-called risk benefit assessments are concerned with the probabilities and magnitudes of possible harms and anticipated benefits. Many kinds of possible harms and benefits need to be taken into account. There are, for example, risks of psychological harm, physical harm, legal harm, social harm and economic harm and the corresponding benefits. While the most likely types of harms to research subjects are those of psychological or physical pain or injury, other possible kinds should not be overlooked.

Risks and benefits of research may affect the individual subjects, the families of the individual subjects, and society at large (or special groups of subjects in society). Previous codes and Federal regulations have required that risks to subjects be outweighed by the sum of both the anticipated benefit to the subject, if any, and the anticipated benefit to society in the form of knowledge to be gained from the research. In balancing these different elements, the risks and benefits affecting the immediate research subject will normally carry special weight. On the other hand, interests other than those of the subject may on some occasions be sufficient by themselves to justify the risks involved in the research, so long as the subjects' rights have been protected. Beneficence thus requires that we protect against risk of harm to subjects and also that we be concerned about the loss of the substantial benefits that might be gained from research.

The Systematic Assessment of Risks and Benefits. It is commonly said that benefits and risks must be "balanced" and shown to be "in a favorable ratio." The metaphorical character of these terms draws attention to the difficulty of making precise judgments. Only on rare occasions will quantitative techniques be available for the scrutiny of research protocols. However, the idea of systematic, nonarbitrary analysis of risks and benefits should be emulated insofar as possible. This ideal requires those making decisions about the justifiability of research to be thorough in the accumulation and assessment of information about all aspects of the research, and to consider alternatives systematically. This procedure renders the assessment of research more rigorous and precise, while making communication between review board members and investigators less subject to misinterpretation, misinformation and conflicting judgments. Thus, there should first be a determination of the validity of the presuppositions of the research; then the nature, probability and magnitude of risk should be distinguished with as much clarity as possible. The method of ascertaining risks should be explicit, especially where there is no alternative to the use of such vague categories as small or slight risk. It should also be determined whether an investigator's estimates of the probability of harm or benefits are reasonable, as judged by known facts or other available studies.

Finally, assessment of the justifiability of research should reflect at least the following considerations: (i) Brutal or inhumane treatment of human subjects is never morally justified; (ii) Risks should be reduced to those necessary to achieve the research objective. It should be determined whether it is in fact necessary to use human subjects at all. Risk can perhaps never be entirely eliminated, but it can often be reduced by careful attention to alternative procedures; (iii) When research involves significant risk of serious impairment, review committees should be extraordinarily insistent on the justification of the risk (looking usually to the likelihood of benefit to the subject or, in some rare cases. to the manifest voluntariness of the participation); (iv) When vulnerable populations are involved in research, the appropriateness of involving them should itself be demonstrated. A number of variables go into such judgments, including the nature and degree of risk, the condition of the particular population involved, and the nature and level of the anticipated benefits; and (v)

Relevant risks and benefits must be thoroughly arrayed in documents and procedures used in the informed consent process.

3. *Selection of Subjects.*—Just as the principle of respect for persons finds expression in the requirements for consent. and the principle of beneficence in risk, benefit assessment, the principle of justice gives rise to moral requirements that there be fair procedures and outcomes in the selection of research subjects.

Justice is relevant to the selection of subjects of research at two levels: the social and the individual. Individual justice in the selection of subjects would require that researchers exhibit fairness: Thus, they should not offer potentially beneficial research only to some patients who are in their favor or select only "undesirable" persons for risky research. Social justice requires that distinction be drawn between classes of subjects that ought, and ought not, to participate in any particular kind of research, based on the ability of members of that class to bear burdens and on the appropriateness of placing further burdens on already burdened persons. Thus, it can be considered a matter of social justice that there is an order of preference in the selection of classes of subjects (e.g., adults before children) and that some classes of potential subjects (e.g., the institutionalized mentally infirm or prisoners) may be involved as research subjects, if at all, only on certain conditions.

Injustice may appear in the selection of subjects, even if individual subjects are selected fairly by investigators and treated fairly in the course of research. Thus injustice arises from social, racial, sexual and cultural biases institutionalized in society. Thus, even if individual researchers are treating their research subjects fairly, and even if IRBs are taking care to assure that subjects are selected fairly within a particular institution, unjust social patterns may nevertheless appear in the overall distribution of the burdens and benefits of research. Although individual institutions or investigators may not be able to resolve a problem that is pervasive in their social setting, they can consider distributive justice in selecting research subjects.

Some populations, especially institutionalized ones, are already burdened in many ways by their infirmities and environments. When research is proposed that involves risks and does not include a therapeutic component, other less burdened classes of persons should be called upon first to accept these risks of research, except where the research is directly related to the specific conditions of the class involved. Also, even though public funds for research may often flow in the same directions as public funds for health care, it seems unfair that populations dependent on public health care constitute a pool of preferred research subjects if more advantaged populations are likely to be the recipients of the benefits.

One special instance of injustice results from the involvement of vulnerable subjects. Certain groups, such as racial minorities, the economically disadvantaged, the very sick, and the institutionalized may continually be sought as research subjects, owing to their ready availability in settings where research is conducted. Given their dependent status and their frequently compromised capacity for free consent, they should be protected against the danger of being involved in research solely for administrative convenience, or because they are easy to manipulate as a result of their illness or socioeconomic condition.

NOTES

1. Since 1945, various codes for the proper and responsible conduct of human experimentation in medical research have been adopted by different organizations. The best known of these codes are the Nuremberg Code of 1948, the Helsinki Declaration of 1964 (revised in 1975), and the 1971 Guidelines (codified into Federal Regulations in 1974) issued by the U.S. Department of Health, Education, and Welfare Codes for the conduct of social and behavioral research have also been adopted, the best known being that of the American Psychological Association, published in 1973.

2. Although practice usually involves interventions designed solely to enhance the well being of a particular individual, interventions are sometimes applied to one individual for the enhancement of the well-being of another (e.g., blood donation, skin grafts, organ transplants) or an intervention may have the dual purpose of enhancing the well-being of a particular individual, and, at the same time, providing some benefit to others (e.g., vaccination, which protects both the person who is vaccinated and society generally). The fact that some forms of practice have elements other than immediate benefit to the individual receiving an intervention, however, should not confuse the general distinction between research and practice. Even when a procedure applied in practice may benefit some other person, it remains an intervention designed to enhance the well-being of a particular individual or groups of individuals; thus, it is practice and need not be reviewed as research.

3. Because the problems related to social experimentation may differ substantially from those of biomedical and behavioral research, the Commission specifically declines to make any policy determination regarding such research at this time. Rather, the Commission believes that the problem ought to be addressed by one of its successor bodies.

Part 2
Selected Major Policies

Overview of Part 2

In this part, we have collected and reproduced major policies concerning the ethical conduct of research with human subjects. Among other topics, these policies address informed consent, assessment of risks and benefits, and considerations of justice. We have chosen to use the term "policy" generically to encompass statutes, regulations, guidelines and other policy directives. While each type of policy carries different legal import, our purpose in selecting and presenting them in this fashion is to provide sources of available guidance in the ethical conduct of research, rather than legal direction.

We have divided the policies into several sections for ease of reference. In the first section are federal policies that apply to most research with human subjects. The Model Federal Policy for the Protection of Human Subjects, known as "The Common Rule," applies to 16 federal agencies and departments of the U.S. government. Particular restatements of "The Common Rule" and other pertinent policies are provided for both the Department of Health and Human Services (DHHS) and the Food and Drug Administration (FDA). In the second section are policies that are specific to population subgroups (for example, women, racial and ethnic groups). Policies collected for specific population subgroups may be issued by different federal agencies. Read together, they give a sense of the status of policy thinking on issues related to particular subject populations. In the third section are policies regarding research in particular settings, including prison and international settings. Lastly, we include policies permitting a waiver of informed consent. These permitted waivers are recognized in certain emergency situations and in military exigencies.

How does one determine which policy applies to a particular situation? The answer depends on the funding or oversight agency, the subject population, the research setting, and whether any exceptions are applicable. More than one policy can apply to a particular research project. Federally funded research as well as non-federally funded research performed at an institution with a multiple project assurance (MPA) will be subject to "The Common Rule." Other policies will apply depending on the answers to a series of questions that basically follow the organizational structure of this part:

- Does the research project involve a population subgroup, that is, women, women of childbearing potential, pregnant women, a racial or ethnic group, children, fetuses?
- Does the research take place in a unique research setting, that is, prison, a foreign country?
- Do any exceptions to obtaining informed consent apply, that is, emergency research, military exigency?
- What is the federal funding source or regulatory oversight body, for example, National Institutes of Health (NIH), Food and Drug Administration (FDA), Centers for Disease Control and Prevention (CDC)?

This compendium is not intended to be complete survey of available policy guidance on research with human subjects. The agencies noted herein, as well as other federal agencies, may have adopted relevant policies that are not reflected in this volume. In addition, policies may have been adopted at the state, local, or institutional levels and guidelines may also have been prepared by professional organizations.

The editors took various steps to make these policies accessible and current. Each policy was checked to confirm that it was current as of 1 May 1998; the date of the last known revision to the policy is noted in the heading. For easy reference, contact information is provided for each policy so that the reader can confirm if there have been any revisions. Where available, we have provided web site addresses to assist readers in locating information about particular policies. Editors' notes throughout indicate if revisions were known to be under consideration at the time of this volume's publication, and where such proposed revisions can be found. For the reader's convenience, the effective date of the policy is noted where it was known to be after the date of this volume's publication. In addition, we have extracted summary comments from *Federal Register* announcements of new policies where we thought they would provide useful background information.

Unless otherwise noted, these documents have been copied from publicly available sources. The editors are not responsible for errors in printing or any consequences resulting from reliance on these documents. This compendium of documents is not intended to provide legal guidance or advice, but rather to reproduce available guidance documents in a convenient and accessible format.

The Common Rule

56 Federal Register *28012. 18 June 1991.*
Contact: *Office for Protection from Research Risks, National Institutes of Health, 6100 Executive Blvd., Suite 3B01, Rockville, Md. 20892-7507; Telephone: (301) 496-7005.*

[This policy was adopted by the federal agencies identified below and incorporated into the relevant sections of the *Code of Federal Regulations* (*CFR*). Each agency's rules are codified in titles of the *CFR* devoted to each particular agency. For example, the Department of Health and Human Services's version of the Common Rule is found at title 45, part 46, subpart A of the *CFR* (reproduced in this volume), and the Agency for International Development's version of the rule is found at title 22, part 225 of the *CFR*. The FDA adopted a modified version of the Common Rule, codified at 21 Code of Federal Regulations parts 50 and 56 of the CFR (reproduced in this volume).

The agencies and departments that have adopted the Common Rule are as follows: Department of Agriculture; Department of Energy; National Aeronautics and Space Administration; Department of Commerce; Consumer Product Safety Commission; International Development Cooperation Agency, Agency for International Development; Department of Housing and Urban Development; Department of Justice; Department of Defense; Department of Education; Department of Veterans Affairs; Environmental Protection Agency; Department of Health and Human Services; National Science Foundation; Department of Transportation.—The Editors]

§__.101 **To what does this policy apply?**
(a) Except as provided in paragraph (b) of this section, this policy applies to all research involving human subjects conducted, supported or otherwise subject to regulation by any federal department or agency which takes appropriate administrative action to make the policy applicable to such research. This includes research conducted by federal civilian employees or military personnel, except that each department or agency

head may adopt such procedural modifications as may be appropriate from an administrative standpoint. It also includes research conducted, supported, or otherwise subject to regulation by the federal government outside the United States.

(1) Research that is conducted or supported by a federal department or agency, whether or not it is regulated as defined in §__.102(e), must comply with all sections of this policy.

(2) Research that is neither conducted nor supported by a federal department or agency but is subject to regulation as defined in §__.102(e) must be reviewed and approved, in compliance with §__.101, §__.102, and §__.107 through §__.117 of this policy, by an institutional review board (IRB) that operates in accordance with the pertinent requirements of this policy.

(b) Unless otherwise required by department or agency heads, research activities in which the only involvement of human subjects will be in one or more of the following categories are exempt from this policy:

(1) Research conducted in established or commonly accepted educational settings, involving normal educational practices, such as: (i) research on regular and special education instructional strategies; or (ii) research on the effectiveness of or the comparison among instructional techniques, curricula, or classroom management methods.

(2) Research involving the use of educational tests (cognitive, diagnostic, aptitude, achievement), survey procedures, interview procedures or observation of public behavior, unless:

(i) Information obtained is recorded in such a manner that human subjects can be identified, directly or through identifiers linked to the subjects; and (ii) any disclosure of the human subjects' responses outside the research could reasonably place the subjects at risk of criminal or civil liability or be damaging to the subjects' financial standing, employability, or reputation.

(3) Research involving the use of educational tests (cognitive, diagnostic, aptitude, achievement), survey procedures, interview procedures, or observation of public behavior that is not exempt under paragraph (b)(2) of this section, if: (i) The human subjects are elected or appointed public officials or candidates for public office; or (ii) federal statute(s) require(s) without exception that the confidentiality of the personally identifiable information will be maintained throughout the research and thereafter.

(4) Research, involving the collection or study of existing data, documents, records, pathological specimens, or diagnostic specimens, if these sources are publicly available or if the information is recorded by

the investigator in such a manner that subjects cannot be identified, directly or through identifiers linked to the subjects.

(5) Research and demonstration projects which are conducted by or subject to the approval of department of agency heads, and which are designed to study, evaluate, or otherwise examine: (i) Public benefit or service programs; (ii) procedures for obtaining benefits or services under those programs; (iii) possible changes in or alternatives to those programs or procedures; or (iv) possible changes in methods or levels of payment for benefits or services under those programs.

(6) Taste and food quality evaluation and consumer acceptance studies; (i) if wholesome foods without additives are consumed; or (ii) if a food is consumed that contains a food ingredient at or below the level and for a use found to be safe, or agricultural chemical or environmental contaminant at or below the level found to be safe, by the Food and Drug Administration or approved by the Environmental Protection Agency or the Food Safety and Inspection Service of the U.S. Department of Agriculture.

(c) Department or agency heads retain final judgment as to whether a particular activity is covered by this policy.

(d) Department or agency heads may require that specific research activities or classes of research activities conducted, supported, or otherwise subject to regulation by the department or agency but not otherwise covered by this policy, comply with some or all of the requirements of this policy.

(e) Compliance with this policy requires compliance with pertinent federal laws or regulations which provide additional protections for human subjects.

(f) This policy does not affect any state or local laws or regulations which may otherwise be applicable and which provide additional protections for human subjects.

(g) This policy does not affect any foreign laws or regulations which may otherwise be applicable and which provide additional protections to human subjects of research.

(h) When research covered by this policy takes place in foreign countries, procedures normally followed in the foreign countries to protect human subjects may differ from those set forth in this policy. [An example is a foreign institution which complies with guidelines consistent with the World Medical Assembly Declaration (Declaration of Helsinki amended 1989) issued either by sovereign states or by an organization whose function for the protection of human research subjects is internationally recognized.] In these circumstances, if a department or agency head determines that the procedures prescribed by the institution afford protections that are at least equivalent to those provided in this policy, the department or agency head may approve the substitution of the foreign procedures in lieu of the procedural requirements provided in this policy. Except when otherwise required by statute, Executive Order, or the department or agency head, notices of these actions as they occur will be published in the **Federal Register** or will be otherwise published as provided in department or agency procedures.

(i) Unless otherwise required by law, department or agency heads may waive the applicability of some or all of the provisions of this policy to specific research activities or classes of research activities otherwise covered by this policy. Except when otherwise required by statute or Executive Order, the department or agency head shall forward advance notices of these actions to the Office for Protection from Research Risks, Department of Health and Human Services (HHS), and shall also publish them in the **Federal Register** or in such a manner as provided in department or agency procedures. Institutions with HHS-approved assurances on file will abide by provisions of title 45 CFR part 46 subparts A-D. Some of the other Departments and Agencies have incorporated all provisions of title 45 CFR part 46 into their policies and procedures as well. However, the exemptions at 45 CFR part 46.101(b) do not apply to research involving prisoners, fetuses, pregnant women, or human in vitro fertilization, subparts B and C. The exemption at 45 CFR part 46.101(b)(2), for research involving survey or interview procedures or observation of public behavior, does not apply to research with children, subpart D, except for research involving observations of public behavior when the investigator(s) do not participate in the activities being observed.

§ __.102 **Definitions.**

(a) *Department or agency head* means the head of any federal department or agency and any other officer or employee of any department or agency to whom authority has been delegated.

(b) *Institution* means any public or private entity or agency (including federal, state, and other agencies).

(c) *Legally authorized representative* means an individual or judicial or other body authorized under applicable law to consent on behalf of a prospective subject to the subject's participation in the procedure(s) involved in the research.

(d) *Research* means a systematic investigation, including research development, testing and evaluation, designed to develop or contribute to generalizable knowledge. Activities which meet this definition constitute research for purposes of this policy, whether or not they are conducted or supported under a program which is considered research for other purposes. For example, some demonstration and service programs may include research activities.

(e) *Research subject to regulation,* and similar terms are intended to encompass those research activities for which a federal department or agency has specific responsibility for regulating as a research activity, (for example, Investigational New Drug requirements administered by the Food and Drug Administration). It does not include research activities which are incidentally regulated by a federal department or agency solely as part of the department's or agency's broader responsibility to regulate certain types of activities whether research or non-research in nature (for example, Wage and Hour requirements administered by the Department of Labor).

(f) *Human subject* means a living individual about whom an investigator (whether professional or student) conducting research obtains (1) data through intervention or interaction with the individual, or (2) identifiable private information. Intervention includes both physical procedures by which data are gathered (for example, venipuncture) and manipulations of the subject or the subject's environment that are performed for research purposes. Interaction includes communication or interpersonal contact between investigator and subject. "Private information" includes information about behavior that occurs in a context in which an individual can reasonably expect that no observation or recording is taking place, and information which has been provided for specific purposes by an individual and which the individual can reasonably expect will not be made public (for example, a medical record). Private information must be individually identifiable (i.e., the identity of the subject is or may readily be ascertained by the investigator or associated with the information) in order for obtaining the information to constitute research involving human subjects.

(g) *IRB* means an institutional review board established in accord with and for the purposes expressed in this policy.

(h) *IRB approval* means the determination of the IRB that the research has been reviewed and may be conducted at an institution within the constraints set forth by the IRB and by other institutional and federal requirements.

(i) *Minimal risk* means that the probability and magnitude of harm or discomfort anticipated in the research are not greater in and of themselves than those ordinarily encountered in daily life or during the performance of routine physical or psychological examinations or tests.

(j) *Certification* means the official notification by the institution to the supporting department or agency, in accordance with the requirements of this policy, that a research project or activity involving human subjects has been reviewed and approved by an IRB in accordance with an approved assurance.

§ __.103 Assuring compliance with this policy—research conducted or supported by any Federal Department or Agency.

(a) Each institution engaged in research which is covered by this policy and which is conducted or supported by a federal department or agency shall provide written assurance satisfactory to the department or agency head that it will comply with the requirements set forth in this policy. In lieu of requiring submission of an assurance, individual department or agency heads shall accept the existence of a current assurance, appropriate for the research in question, on file with the Office for Protection from Research Risks, HHS, and approved for Federalwide use by that office. When the existence of an HHS-approved assurance is accepted in lieu of requiring submission of an assurance, reports (except certification) required by this policy to be made to department and agency heads shall also be made to the Office for Protection from Research Risks, HHS.

(b) Departments and agencies will conduct or support research covered by this policy only if the institution has an assurance approved as provided in this section, and only if the institution has certified to the department or agency head that the research has been reviewed and approved by an IRB provided for in the assurance, and will be subject to continuing review by the IRB. Assurances applicable to federally supported or conducted research shall at a minimum include:

(1) A statement of principles governing the institution in the discharge of its responsibilities for protecting the rights and welfare of human subjects of research conducted at or sponsored by the institution, regardless of whether the research is subject to federal regulation. This may include an appropriate existing code, declaration, or statement of ethical principles, or a statement formulated by the institution itself. This requirement does not preempt provisions of this policy applicable to department- or agency-supported or regulated research and need not be applicable to any research exempted or waived under § __.101 (b) or (i).

(2) Designation of one or more IRBs established in accordance with the requirements of this policy, and for which provisions are made

for meeting space and sufficient staff to support the IRB's review and recordkeeping duties.

(3) A list of IRB members identified by name; earned degrees; representative capacity; indications of experience such as board certifications, licenses, etc., sufficient to describe each member's chief anticipated contributions to IRB deliberations; and any employment or other relationship between each member and the institution; for example: full-time employee, part-time employee, member of governing panel or board, stockholder, paid or unpaid consultant. Changes in IRB membership shall be reported to the department or agency head, unless in accord with §__.103(a) of this policy, the existence of an HHS-approved assurance is accepted. In this case, change in IRB membership shall be reported to the Office for Protection from Research Risks, HHS.

(4) Written procedures which the IRB will follow: (i) for conducting its initial and continuing review of research and for reporting its findings and actions to the investigator and the institution; (ii) for determining which projects require review more often than annually and which projects need verification from sources other than the investigators that no material changes have occurred since previous IRB review; and (iii) for ensuring prompt reporting to the IRB of proposed changes in a research activity, and for ensuring that such changes in approved research, during the period for which IRB approval has already been given, may not be initiated without IRB review and approval except when necessary to eliminate apparent immediate hazards to the subject.

(5) Written procedures for ensuring prompt reporting to the IRB, appropriate institutional officials, and the department or agency head of: (i) any unanticipated problems involving risks to subjects or others or any serious or continuing noncompliance with this policy or the requirements or determinations of the IRB; and (ii) any suspension or termination of IRB approval.

(c) The assurance shall be executed by an individual authorized to act for the institution and to assume on behalf of the institution the obligations imposed by this policy and shall be filed in such form and manner as the department or agency head prescribes.

(d) The department or agency head will evaluate all assurances submitted in accordance with this policy through such officers and employees of the department or agency and such experts or consultants engaged for this purpose as the department or agency head determines to be appropriate. The department or agency head's evaluation will take into consideration the adequacy of the proposed IRB in light of the anticipated scope of the institution's research activities and the types of subject populations likely to be involved, the appropriateness of the proposed initial and continuing review procedures in light of the probable risks, and the size and complexity of the institution.

(e) On the basis of this evaluation, the department or agency head may approve or disapprove the assurance, or enter into negotiations to develop an approvable one. The department or agency head may limit the period during which any particular approved assurance or class of approved assurances shall remain effective or otherwise condition or restrict approval.

(f) Certification is required when the research is supported by a federal department or agency and not otherwise exempted or waived under §__.101 (b) or (i). An institution with an approved assurance shall certify that each application or proposal for research covered by the assurance and by §__.103 of this Policy has been reviewed and approved by the IRB. Such certification must be submitted with the application or proposal or by such later date as may be prescribed by the department or agency to which the application or proposal is submitted. Under no condition shall research covered by §__.103 of the Policy be supported prior to receipt of the certification that the research has been reviewed and approved by the IRB. Institutions without an approved assurance covering the research shall certify within 30 days after receipt of a request for such a certification from the department or agency, that the application or proposal has been approved by the IRB. If the certification is not submitted within these time limits, the application or proposal may be returned to the institution. (Approved by the Office of Management and Budget under Control Number 9999-0020.)

§__.104-106 [Reserved]

§__.107 IRB membership.

(a) Each IRB shall have at least five members, with varying backgrounds to promote complete and adequate review of research activities commonly conducted by the institution. The IRB shall be sufficiently qualified through the experience and expertise of its members, and the diversity of the members, including consideration of race, gender, and cultural backgrounds and sensitivity to such issues as community attitudes, to promote respect for its advice and counsel in safeguarding the rights and welfare of human subjects. In addition to possessing the professional competence necessary to review specific research activities, the IRB shall be able to ascertain the acceptability of proposed research in terms of institutional commitments and regulations, applicable law, and standards of professional conduct and practice. The IRB shall therefore include persons knowledgeable in these areas. If an IRB regularly reviews research that involves a vulnerable category of subjects, such as children, prisoners, pregnant women, or handicapped or mentally disabled persons, consideration shall be given to the inclusion of one or more individuals who are knowledgeable about and experienced in working with these subjects.

(b) Every nondiscriminatory effort will be made to ensure that no IRB consists entirely of men or entirely of women, including the institution's consideration of qualified persons of both sexes, so long as no selection is made to the IRB on the basis of gender. No IRB may consist entirely of members of one profession.

(c) Each IRB shall include at least one member whose primary concerns are in scientific areas and at least one member whose primary concerns are in nonscientific areas.

(d) Each IRB shall include at least one member who is not otherwise affiliated with the institution and who is not part of the immediate family of a person who is affiliated with the institution.

(e) No IRB may have a member participate in the IRB's initial or continuing review of any project in which the member has a conflicting interest, except to provide information requested by the IRB.

(f) An IRB may, in its discretion, invite individuals with competence in special areas to assist in the review of issues which require expertise beyond or in addition to that available on the IRB. These individuals may not vote with the IRB.

§__.108 IRB functions and operations.

In order to fulfill the requirements of this policy each IRB shall:

(a) Follow written procedures in the same detail as described in §__.103(b)(4) and, to the extent required by, §__.103(b)(5).

(b) Except when an expedited review procedure is used (see §__.110), review proposed research at convened meetings at which a majority of the members of the IRB are present, including at least one member whose primary concerns are in nonscientific areas. In order for the research to be approved, it shall receive the approval of a majority of those members present at the meeting.

§__.109 IRB review of research.

(a) An IRB shall review and have authority to approve, require modifications in (to secure approval), or disapprove all research activities covered by this policy.

(b) An IRB shall require that information given to subjects as part of informed consent is in accordance with §__.116. The IRB may require that information, in addition to that specifically mentioned in §__.116, be given to the subjects when in the IRB's judgment the information would meaningfully add to the protection of the rights and welfare of subjects.

(c) An IRB shall require documentation of informed consent or may waive documentation in accordance with §__.117.

(d) An IRB shall notify investigators and the institution in writing of its decision to approve or disapprove the proposed research activity, or of modifications required to secure IRB approval of the research activity. If the IRB decides to disapprove a research activity, it shall include in its written notification a statement of the reasons for its decision and give the investigator an opportunity to respond in person or in writing.

(e) An IRB shall conduct continuing review of research covered by this policy at intervals appropriate to the degree of risk, but not less than once per year, and shall have authority to observe or have a third party observe the consent process and the research. (Approved by the Office of Management and Budget under Control Number 9999-0020.)

§__.110 Expedited review procedures for certain kinds of research involving no more than minimal risk, and for minor changes in approved research.

(a) The Secretary, HHS, has established, and published as a Notice in the **Federal Register**, a list of categories of research that may be reviewed by the IRB through an expedited review procedure. The list will be amended, as appropriate after consultation with other departments and agencies, through periodic republication by the Secretary, HHS, in the **Federal Register**. A copy of the list is available from the Office for Protection from Research Risks, National Institutes of Health, HHS, Bethesda, Maryland 20892.

(b) An IRB may use the expedited review procedure to review either or both of the following:

(1) Some or all of the research appearing on the list and found by the reviewer(s) to involve no more than minimal risk,

(2) Minor changes in previously approved research during the period (of one year or less) for which approval is authorized. Under an expedited review procedure, the review may be carried out by the IRB chairperson or by one or more experienced reviewers designated by the chairperson from among members of the IRB. In reviewing the research, the reviewers may exercise all of the authorities of the IRB except that the reviewers may not disapprove the research. A research activity may be disapproved only after review in accordance with the non-expedited procedure set forth in §__.108(b).

(c) Each IRB which uses an expedited review procedure shall adopt a method for keeping all members advised of research proposals which have been approved under the procedure.

(d) The department or agency head may restrict, suspend, terminate, or choose not to authorize an institution's or IRB's use of the expedited review procedure.

§__.111 Criteria for IRB approval of research.

(a) In order to approve research covered by this policy the IRB shall determine that all of the following requirements are satisfied:

(1) Risks to subjects are minimized: (i) By using procedures which are consistent with sound research design and which do not unnecessarily expose subjects to risk; and (ii) whenever appropriate, by using procedures already being performed on the subjects for diagnostic or treatment purposes.

(2) Risks to subjects are reasonable in relation to anticipated benefits, if any, to subjects, and the importance of the knowledge that may reasonably be expected to result. In evaluating risks and benefits, the IRB should consider only those risks and benefits that may result from the research (as distinguished from risks and benefits of therapies subjects would receive even if not participating in the research). The IRB should not consider possible long-range effects of applying knowledge gained in the research (for example, the possible effects of the research on public policy) as among those research risks that fall within the purview of its responsibility.

(3) Selection of subjects is equitable. In making this assessment the IRB should take into account the purposes of the research and the setting in which the research will be conducted and should be particularly cognizant of the special problems of research involving vulnerable populations, such as children, prisoners, pregnant women, mentally

disabled persons, or economically or educationally disadvantaged persons.

(4) Informed consent will be sought from each prospective subject or the subject's legally authorized representative, in accordance with, and to the extent required by §__.116.

(5) Informed consent will be appropriately documented, in accordance with, and to the extent required by §__.117.

(6) When appropriate, the research plan makes adequate provision for monitoring the data collected to ensure the safety of subjects.

(7) When appropriate, there are adequate provisions to protect the privacy of subjects and to maintain the confidentiality of data.

(b) When some or all of the subjects are likely to be vulnerable to coercion or undue influence, such as children, prisoners, pregnant women, mentally disabled persons, or economically or educationally disadvantaged persons, additional safeguards have been included in the study to protect the rights and welfare of these subjects.

§__.112 Review by institution.

Research covered by this policy that has been approved by an IRB may be subject to further appropriate review and approval or disapproval by officials of the institution. However, those officials may not approve the research if it has not been approved by an IRB.

§__.113 Suspension or termination of IRB approval of research.

An IRB shall have authority to suspend or terminate approval of research that is not being conducted in accordance with the IRB's requirements or that has been associated with unexpected serious harm to subjects. Any suspension or termination of approval shall include a statement of the reasons for the IRB's action and shall be reported promptly to the investigator, appropriate institutional officials, and the department or agency head. (Approved by the Office of Management and Budget under Control Number 9999-0020.)

§__.114 Cooperative research.

Cooperative research projects are those projects covered by this policy which involve more than one institution. In the conduct of cooperative research projects, each institution is responsible for safeguarding the rights and welfare of human subjects and for complying with this policy. With the approval of the department or agency head, an institution participating in a cooperative project may enter into a joint review arrangement, rely upon the review of another qualified IRB, or make similar arrangements for avoiding duplication of effort.

§__.115 IRB records.

(a) An institution, or when appropriate an IRB, shall prepare and maintain adequate documentation of IRB activities, including the following:

(1) Copies of all research proposals reviewed, scientific evaluations, if any, that accompany the proposals, approved sample consent documents, progress reports submitted by investigators, and reports of injuries to subjects.

(2) Minutes of IRB meetings which shall be in sufficient detail to show attendance at the meetings; actions taken by the IRB; the vote on these actions including the number of members voting for, against, and abstaining; the basis for requiring changes in or disapproving research; and a written summary of the discussion of controverted issues and their resolution.

(3) Records of continuing review activities.

(4) Copies of all correspondence between the IRB and the investigators.

(5) A list of IRB members in the same detail as described is §__.103(b)(3).

(6) Written procedures for the IRB in the same detail as described in §__.103(b)(4) and §__.103(b)(5).

(7) Statements of significant new findings provided to subjects, as required by §__.116(b)(5).

(b) The records required by this policy shall be retained for at least 3 years, and records relating to research which is conducted shall be retained for at least 3 years after completion of the research. All records shall be accessible for inspection and copying by authorized representatives of the department or agency at reasonable times and in a reasonable manner. (Approved by the Office of Management and Budget under Control Number 9999-0020.)

§__.116 General requirements for informed consent.

Except as provided elsewhere in this policy, no investigator may involve a human being as a subject in research covered by this policy unless the investigator has obtained the legally effective informed consent of the subject or the subject's legally authorized representative. An investigator shall seek such consent only under circumstances that provide the prospective subject or the representative sufficient opportunity to consider whether or not to participate and that minimize the possibility of coercion or undue influence. The information that is given to the subject or the representative shall be in language understandable to the subject or the representative. No informed consent, whether oral or written, may include any exculpatory language through which the subject or the representative is made to waive or appear to waive any of the subject's legal rights, or releases or appears to release the investigator, the sponsor, the institution or its agents from liability for negligence.

(a) Basic elements of informed consent. Except as provided in paragraph (c) or (d) of this section, in seeking informed consent the following information shall be provided to each subject:

(1) A statement that the study involves research, an explanation of the purposes of the research and the expected duration of the subject's participation, a description of the procedures to be followed, and identification of any procedures which are experimental;

(2) A description of any reasonably foreseeable risks or discomforts to the subject;

(3) A description of any benefits to the subject or to others which may reasonably be expected from the research;

(4) A disclosure of appropriate alternative procedures or courses of treatment, if any, that might be advantageous to the subject;

(5) A statement describing the extent, if any, to which confidentiality of records identifying the subject will be maintained;

(6) For research involving more than minimal risk, an explanation as to whether any compensation and an explanation as to whether any medical treatments are available if injury occurs and, if so, what they consist of, or where further information may be obtained;

(7) An explanation of whom to contact for answers to pertinent questions about the research and research subjects' rights, and whom to contact in the event of a research-related injury to the subject; and

(8) A statement that participation is voluntary, refusal to participate will involve no penalty or loss of benefits to which the subject is otherwise entitled, and the subject may discontinue participation at any time without penalty or loss of benefits to which the subject is otherwise entitled.

(b) Additional elements of informed consent. When appropriate, one or more of the following elements of information shall also be provided to each subject:

(1) A statement that the particular treatment or procedure may involve risks to the subject (or to the embryo or fetus, if the subject is or may become pregnant) which are currently unforeseeable;

(2) Anticipated circumstances under which the subject's participation may be terminated by the investigator without regard to the subject's consent;

(3) Any additional costs to the subject that may result from participation in the research;

(4) The consequences of a subject's decision to withdraw from the research and procedures for orderly termination of participation by the subject;

(5) A statement that significant new findings developed during the course of the research which may relate to the subject's willingness to continue participation will be provided to the subject; and

(6) The approximate number of subjects involved in the study.

(c) An IRB may approve a consent procedure which does not include, or which alters, some or all of the elements of informed consent set forth above, or waive the requirement to obtain informed consent provided the IRB finds and documents that:

(1) The research or demonstration project is to be conducted by or subject to the approval of state or local government officials and is designed to study, evaluate, or otherwise examine: (i) Public benefit of service programs; (ii) procedures for obtaining benefits or services under those programs; (iii) possible changes in or alternatives to those programs or procedures; or (iv) possible changes in methods or levels of payment for benefits or services under those programs; and

(2) The research could not practicably be carried out without the waiver or alteration.

(d) An IRB may approve a consent procedure which does not include, or which alters, some or all of the elements of informed consent set forth in this section, or waive the requirements to obtain informed consent provided the IRB finds and documents that:

(1) The research involves no more than minimal risk to the subjects;

(2) The waiver or alteration will not adversely affect the rights and welfare of the subjects;

(3) The research could not practicably be carried out without the waiver or alteration; and

(4) Whenever appropriate, the subjects will be provided with additional pertinent information after participation.

(e) The informed consent requirements in this policy are not intended to preempt any applicable federal, state, or local laws which require additional information to be disclosed in order for informed consent to be legally effective.

(f) Nothing in this policy is intended to limit the authority of a physician to provide emergency medical care, to the extent the physician is permitted to do so under applicable federal, state, or local law.

(Approved by the Office of Management and Budget under Control Number 9999-0020.)

§__.117 Documentation of informed consent.

(a) Except as provided in paragraph (c) of this section, informed consent shall be documented by the use of a written consent form approved by the IRB and signed by the subject or the subject's legally authorized representative. A copy shall be given to the person signing the form.

(b) Except as provided in paragraph (c) of this section, the consent form may be either of the following:

(1) A written consent document that embodies the elements of informed consent required by §__.116. This form may be read to the subject or the subject's legally authorized representative, but in any event, the investigator shall give either the subject or the representative adequate opportunity to read it before it is signed; or

(2) A short form written consent document stating that the elements of informed consent required by §__.116 have been presented orally to the subject or the subject's legally authorized representative. When this method is used, there shall be a witness to the oral presentation. Also, the IRB shall approve a written summary of what is to be said to the subject or the representative. Only the short form itself is to be signed by the subject or the representative. However, the witness shall sign both the short form and a copy of the summary, and the person actually obtaining consent shall sign a copy of the summary. A copy of the summary shall be given to the subject or the representative, in addition to a copy of the short form.

(c) An IRB may waive the requirement for the investigator to obtain a signed consent form for some or all subjects if it finds either:

(1) That the only record linking the subject and the research would be the consent document and the principal risk would be potential harm resulting from a breach of confidentiality. Each subject will be asked whether the subject wants documentation linking the subject with the research, and the subject's wishes will govern; or

(2) That the research presents no more than minimal risk of harm to subjects and involves no procedures for which written consent is normally required outside of the research context. In cases in which the documentation requirement is waived, the IRB may require the investigator to provide subjects with a written statement regarding the research. (Approved by the Office of Management and Budget under Control Number 9999-0020.)

§__.118 Applications and proposals lacking definite plans for involvement of human subjects.

Certain types of applications for grants, cooperative agreements, or contracts are submitted to departments or agencies with the knowledge that subjects may be involved within the period of support, but definite plans would not normally be set forth in the application or proposal. These include activities such as institutional type grants when selection of specific projects is the institution's responsibility; research training grants in which the activities involving subjects remain to be selected; and projects in which human subject's involvement will depend upon completion of instruments, prior animal studies, or purification of compounds. These applications need not be reviewed by an IRB before an award may be made. However, except for research exempted or waived under §__.101 (b) or (i), no human subjects may be involved in any project supported by these awards until the project has been reviewed and approved by the IRB, as provided in this policy, and certification submitted, by the institution, to the department or agency.

§__.119 Research undertaken without the intention of involving human subjects.

In the event research is undertaken without the intention of involving human subjects, but it is later proposed to involve human subjects in the research, the research shall first be reviewed and approved by an IRB, as provided in this policy, a certification submitted, by the institution, to the department or agency, and final approval given to the proposed change by the department or agency.

§__.120 Evaluation and disposition of applications and proposals for research to be conducted or supported by a Federal Department or Agency.

(a) The department or agency head will evaluate all applications and proposals involving human subjects submitted to the department or agency through such officers and employees of the department or agency and such experts and consultants as the department or agency head determines to be appropriate. This evaluation will take into consideration the risks to the subjects, the adequacy of protection against these risks, the potential benefits of the research to the subjects and others, and the importance of the knowledge gained or to be gained.

(b) On the basis of this evaluation, the department or agency head may approve or disapprove the application or proposal, or enter into negotiations to develop an approvable one.

§__ 121 [Reserved]

§__.122 Use of Federal funds.
Federal funds administered by a department or agency may not be expended for research involving human subjects unless the requirements of this policy have been satisfied.

§__.123 Early termination of research support; evaluation of applications and proposals.
(a) The department or agency head may require that department or agency support for any project be terminated or suspended in the manner prescribed in applicable program requirements, when the department or agency head finds an institution has materially failed to comply with the terms of this policy.

(b) In making decisions about supporting or approving applications or proposals covered by this policy the department or agency head may take into account, in addition to all other eligibility requirements and program criteria, factors such as whether the applicant has been subject to a termination or suspension under paragraph (a) of this section and whether the applicant or the person or persons who would direct or has have directed the scientific and technical aspects of an activity has have, in the judgment of the department or agency head, materially failed to discharge responsibility for the protection of the rights and welfare of human subjects (whether or not the research was subject to federal regulation).

§__.124 Conditions.
With respect to any research project or any class of research projects the department or agency head may impose additional conditions prior to or at the time of approval when in the judgment of the department or agency head additional conditions are necessary for the protection of human subjects.

DHHS—Basic Policy for Protection of Human Research Subjects

45 Code of Federal Regulations 46, Subpart A. Last revised 28 June 1991. Contact: Office for Protection from Research Risks, National Institutes of Health, 6100 Executive Blvd., Suite 3B01, Rockville, Md. 20892-7507; Telephone: (301) 496-7005.

§ 46.101 To what does this policy apply?

(a) Except as provided in paragraph (b) of this section, this policy applies to all research involving human subjects conducted, supported or otherwise subject to regulation by any federal department or agency which takes appropriate administrative action to make the policy applicable to such research. This includes research conducted by federal civilian employees or military personnel, except that each department or agency head may adopt such procedural modifications as may be appropriate from an administrative standpoint. It also includes research conducted, supported, or otherwise subject to regulation by the federal government outside the United States.

(1) Research that is conducted or supported by a federal department or agency, whether or not it is regulated as defined in §46.102(e), must comply with all sections of this policy.

(2) Research that is neither conducted nor supported by a federal department or agency but is subject to regulation as defined in §46.102(e) must be reviewed and approved, in compliance with §46.101, §46.102, and §46.107 through §46.117 of this policy, by an institutional review board (IRB) that operates in accordance with the pertinent requirements of this policy.

(b) Unless otherwise required by department or agency heads, research activities in which the only involvement of human subjects will be in one or more of the following categories are exempt from this policy:

(1) Research conducted in established or commonly accepted educational settings, involving normal educational practices, such as (i)

research on regular and special education instructional strategies, or (ii) research on the effectiveness of or the comparison among instructional techniques, curricula, or classroom management methods.

(2) Research involving the use of educational tests (cognitive, diagnostic, aptitude, achievement), survey procedures, interview procedures or observation of public behavior, unless: (i) Information obtained is recorded in such a manner that human subjects can be identified, directly or through identifiers linked to the subjects; and (ii) any disclosure of the human subjects' responses outside the research could reasonably place the subjects at risk of criminal or civil liability or be damaging to the subjects' financial standing, employability, or reputation.

(3) Research involving the use of educational tests (cognitive, diagnostic, aptitude, achievement), survey procedures, interview procedures, or observation of public behavior that is not exempt under paragraph (b)(2) of this section, if: (i) The human subjects are elected or appointed public officials or candidates for public office; or (ii) federal statute(s) require(s) without exception that the confidentiality of the personally identifiable information will be maintained throughout the research and thereafter.

(4) Research, involving the collection or study of existing data, documents, records, pathological specimens, or diagnostic specimens, if these sources are publicly available or if the information is recorded by the investigator in such a manner that subjects cannot be identified, directly or through identifiers linked to the subjects.

(5) Research and demonstration projects which are conducted by or subject to the approval of department or agency heads, and which are designed to study, evaluate, or otherwise examine: (i) Public benefit or service programs; (ii) procedures for obtaining benefits or services under those programs; (iii) possible changes in or alternatives to those programs or procedures; or (iv) possible changes in methods or levels of payment for benefits or services under those programs.

(6) Taste and food quality evaluation and consumer acceptance studies, (i) if wholesome foods without additives are consumed or (ii) if a food is consumed that contains a food ingredient at or below the level and for a use found to be safe, or agricultural chemical or environmental contaminant at or below the level found to be safe, by the Food and Drug Administration or approved by the Environmental Protection Agency or the Food Safety and Inspection Service of the U.S. Department of Agriculture.

(c) Department or agency heads retain final judgment as to whether a particular activity is covered by this policy.

(d) Department or agency heads may require that specific research activities or classes of research activities conducted, supported, or otherwise subject to regulation by the department or agency but not otherwise covered by this policy, comply with some or all of the requirements of this policy.

(e) Compliance with this policy requires compliance with pertinent federal laws or regulations which provide additional protections for human subjects.

(f) This policy does not affect any state or local laws or regulations which may otherwise be applicable and which provide additional protections for human subjects.

(g) This policy does not affect any foreign laws or regulations which may otherwise be applicable and which provide additional protections to human subjects of research.

(h) When research covered by this policy takes place in foreign countries, procedures normally followed in the foreign countries to protect human subjects may differ from those set forth in this policy. [An example is a foreign institution which complies with guidelines consistent with the World Medical Assembly Declaration (Declaration of Helsinki amended 1989) issued either by sovereign states or by an organization whose function for the protection of human research subjects is internationally recognized.] In these circumstances, if a department or agency head determines that the procedures prescribed by the institution afford protections that are at least equivalent to those provided in this policy, the department or agency head may approve the substitution of the foreign procedures in lieu of the procedural requirements provided in this policy. Except when otherwise required by statute, Executive Order, or the department or agency head, notices of these actions as they occur will be published in the FEDERAL REGISTER or will be otherwise published as provided in department or agency procedures. (i) Unless otherwise required by law, department or agency heads may waive the applicability of some or all of the provisions of this policy to specific research activities or classes of research activities otherwise covered by this policy. Except when otherwise required by statute or Executive Order, the department or agency head shall forward advance notices of these actions to the Office for Protection from Research Risks, Department of Health and Human Services (HHS), and shall also publish them in the FEDERAL

REGISTER or in such other manner as provided in department or agency procedures.

§46.102 Definitions.

(a) *Department or agency head* means the head of any federal department or agency and any other officer or employee of any department or agency to whom authority has been delegated.

(b) *Institution* means any public or private entity or agency (including federal, state, and other agencies).

(c) *Legally authorized representative* means an individual or judicial or other body authorized under applicable law to consent on behalf of a prospective subject to the subject's participation in the procedure(s) involved in the research.

(d) *Research* means a systematic investigation, including research development, testing and evaluation, designed to develop or contribute to generalizable knowledge. Activities which meet this definition constitute research for purposes of this policy, whether or not they are conducted or supported under a program which is considered research for other purposes. For example, some demonstration and service programs may include research activities.

(e) *Research subject to regulation*, and similar terms are intended to encompass those research activities for which a federal department or agency has specific responsibility for regulating as a research activity, (for example, Investigational New Drug requirements administered by the Food and Drug Administration). It does not include research activities which are incidentally regulated by a federal department or agency solely as part of the department's or agency's broader responsibility to regulate certain types of activities whether research or non-research in nature (for example, Wage and Hour requirements administered by the Department of Labor).

(f) *Human subject* means a living individual about whom an investigator (whether professional or student) conducting research obtains (1) Data through intervention or interaction with the individual, or (2) Identifiable private information.

Intervention includes both physical procedures by which data are gathered (for example, venipuncture) and manipulations of the subject or the subject's environment that are performed for research purposes. Interaction includes communication or interpersonal contact between investigator and subject. *Private information* includes information about behavior that occurs in a context in which an individual can reasonably expect that no observation or recording is taking place, and information which has been provided for specific purposes by an individual and which the individual can reasonably expect will not be made public (for example, a medical record). Private information must be individually identifiable (i.e., the identity of the subject is or may readily be ascertained by the investigator or associated with the information) in order for obtaining the information to constitute research involving human subjects.

(g) *IRB* means an institutional review board established in accord with and for the purposes expressed in this policy.

(h) *IRB approval* means the determination of the IRB that the research has been reviewed and may be conducted at an institution within the constraints set forth by the IRB and by other institutional and federal requirements.

(i) *Minimal risk* means that the probability and magnitude of harm or discomfort anticipated in the research are not greater in and of themselves than those ordinarily encountered in daily life or during the performance of routine physical or psychological examinations or tests.

(j) *Certification* means the official notification by the institution to the supporting department or agency, in accordance with the requirements of this policy, that a research project or activity involving human subjects has been reviewed and approved by an IRB in accordance with an approved assurance.

§46.103 Assuring compliance with this policy—research conducted or supported by any Federal Department or Agency.

(a) Each institution engaged in research which is covered by this policy and which is conducted or supported by a federal department or agency shall provide written assurance satisfactory to the department or agency head that it will comply with the requirements set forth in this policy. In lieu of requiring submission of an assurance, individual department or agency heads shall accept the existence of a current assurance, appropriate for the research in question, on file with the Office for Protection from Research Risks, HHS, and approved for Federalwide use by that office. When the existence of an HHS-approved assurance is accepted in lieu of requiring submission of an assurance, reports (except certification) required by this policy to be made to department and agency heads shall also be made to the Office for Protection from Research Risks, HHS.

(b) Departments and agencies will conduct or support research covered by this policy only if the institution has an assurance approved as provided in this section, and only if the institution has certified to the department or agency head that the research has been reviewed and approved by an IRB provided for in the assurance, and will be subject to continuing review by the IRB. Assurances applicable to federally supported or conducted research shall at a minimum include:

(1) A statement of principles governing the institution in the discharge of its responsibilities for protecting the rights and welfare of human subjects of research conducted at or sponsored by the institution, regardless of whether the research is subject to federal regulation. This may include an appropriate existing code, declaration, or statement of ethical principles, or a statement formulated by the institution itself. This requirement does not preempt provisions of this policy applicable to department- or agency-supported or regulated research and need not be applicable to any research exempted or waived under §46.101 (b) or (i).

(2) Designation of one or more IRBs established in accordance with the requirements of this policy, and for which provisions are made for meeting space and sufficient staff to support the IRB's review and recordkeeping duties.

(3) A list of IRB members identified by name; earned degrees; representative capacity; indications of experience such as board certifications, licenses, etc., sufficient to describe each member's chief anticipated contributions to IRB deliberations; and any employment or other relationship between each member and the institution; for example: full-time employee, part-time employee, member of governing panel or board, stockholder, paid or unpaid consultant. Changes in IRB membership shall be reported to the department or agency head, unless in accord with §46.103(a) of this policy, the existence of an HHS-approved assurance is accepted. In this case, change in IRB membership shall be reported to the Office for Protection from Research Risks, HHS.

(4) Written procedures which the IRB will follow (i) for conducting its initial and continuing review of research and for reporting its findings and actions to the investigator and the institution; (ii) for determining which projects require review more often than annually and which projects need verification from sources other than the investigators that no material changes have occurred since previous IRB review; and (iii) for ensuring prompt reporting to the IRB of proposed

changes in a research activity, and for ensuring that such changes in approved research, during the period for which IRB approval has already been given, may not be initiated without IRB review and approval except when necessary to eliminate apparent immediate hazards to the subject.

(5) Written procedures for ensuring prompt reporting to the IRB, appropriate institutional officials, and the department or agency head of (i) any unanticipated problems involving risks to subjects or others or any serious or continuing noncompliance with this policy or the requirements or determinations of the IRB and (ii) any suspension or termination of IRB approval.

(c) The assurance shall be executed by an individual authorized to act for the institution and to assume on behalf of the institution the obligations imposed by this policy and shall be filed in such form and manner as the department or agency head prescribes.

(d) The department or agency head will evaluate all assurances submitted in accordance with this policy through such officers and employees of the department or agency and such experts or consultants engaged for this purpose as the department or agency head determines to be appropriate. The department or agency head's evaluation will take into consideration the adequacy of the proposed IRB in light of the anticipated scope of the institution's research activities and the types of subject populations likely to be involved, the appropriateness of the proposed initial and continuing review procedures in light of the probable risks, and the size and complexity of the institution.

(e) On the basis of this evaluation, the department or agency head may approve or disapprove the assurance, or enter into negotiations to develop an approvable one. The department or agency head may limit the period during which any particular approved assurance or class of approved assurances shall remain effective or otherwise condition or restrict approval.

(f) Certification is required when the research is supported by a federal department or agency and not otherwise exempted or waived under §46.101 (b) or (i). An institution with an approved assurance shall certify that each application or proposal for research covered by the assurance and by §46.103 of this Policy has been reviewed and approved by the IRB. Such certification must be submitted with the application or proposal or by such later date as may be prescribed by the department or agency to which the application or proposal is submitted. Under no condition shall research covered by §46.103 of the Policy be supported prior to receipt of the certification that the research has been reviewed and approved by the IRB. Institutions without an approved assurance covering the research shall certify within 30 days after receipt of a request for such a certification from the department or agency, that the application or proposal has been approved by the IRB. If the certification is not submitted within these time limits, the application or proposal may be returned to the institution.

§46.104-106 [Reserved]

§46.107 IRB membership.

(a) Each IRB shall have at least five members, with varying backgrounds to promote complete and adequate review of research activities commonly conducted by the institution. The IRB shall be sufficiently qualified through the experience and expertise of its members, and the diversity of the members, including consideration of race, gender, and cultural backgrounds and sensitivity to such issues as community attitudes, to promote respect for its advice and counsel in safeguarding the rights and welfare of human subjects. In addition to possessing the professional competence necessary to review specific research activities, the IRB shall be able to ascertain the acceptability of proposed research in terms of institutional commitments and regulations, applicable law, and standards of professional conduct and practice. The IRB shall therefore include persons knowledgeable in these areas. If an IRB regularly reviews research that involves a vulnerable category of subjects, such as children, prisoners, pregnant women, or handicapped or mentally disabled persons, consideration shall be given to the inclusion of one or more individuals who are knowledgeable about and experienced in working with these subjects.

(b) Every nondiscriminatory effort will be made to ensure that no IRB consists entirely of men or entirely of women, including the institution's consideration of qualified persons of both sexes, so long as no selection is made to the IRB on the basis of gender. No IRB may consist entirely of members of one profession.

(c) Each IRB shall include at least one member whose primary concerns are in scientific areas and at least one member whose primary concerns are in nonscientific areas.

(d) Each IRB shall include at least one member who is not otherwise affiliated with the institution and who is not part of the immediate family of a person who is affiliated with the institution.

(e) No IRB may have a member participate in the IRB's initial or continuing review of any project in which the member has a conflicting interest, except to provide information requested by the IRB.

(f) An IRB may, in its discretion, invite individuals with competence in special areas to assist in the review of issues which require expertise beyond or in addition to that available on the IRB. These individuals may not vote with the IRB.

§46.108 IRB functions and operations.

In order to fulfill the requirements of this policy each IRB shall:

(a) Follow written procedures in the same detail as described in §46.103(b)(4) and, to the extent required by, §46.103(b)(5).

(b) Except when an expedited review procedure is used (see §46.110), review proposed research at convened meetings at which a majority of the members of the IRB are present, including at least one member whose primary concerns are in nonscientific areas. In order for the research to be approved, it shall receive the approval of a majority of those members present at the meeting.

§46.109 IRB review of research.

(a) An IRB shall review and have authority to approve, require modifications in (to secure approval), or disapprove all research activities covered by this policy.

(b) An IRB shall require that information given to subjects as part of informed consent is in accordance with §46.116. The IRB may require that information, in addition to that specifically mentioned in §46.116, be given to the subjects when in the IRB's judgment the information would meaningfully add to the protection of the rights and welfare of subjects.

(c) An IRB shall require documentation of informed consent or may waive documentation in accordance with §46.117.

(d) An IRB shall notify investigators and the institution in writing of its decision to approve or disapprove the proposed research activity, or of modifications required to secure IRB approval of the research activity. If the IRB decides to disapprove a research activity, it shall include in its written notification a statement of the reasons for its decision and give the investigator an opportunity to respond in person or in writing.

(e) An IRB shall conduct continuing review of research covered by this policy at intervals appropriate to the degree of risk, but not less than once per year, and shall have authority to observe or have a third party observe the consent process and the research.

§46.110 Expedited review procedures for certain kinds of research involving no more than minimal risk, and for minor changes in approved research.

[The expedited review list referenced here is reproduced in this volume. See "DHHS—Research Activities which may be Reviewed through Expedited Review Procedures," page 71, below.—*The Editors*]

(a) The Secretary, HHS, has established, and published as a Notice in the *Federal Register*, a list of categories of research that may be reviewed by the IRB through an expedited review procedure. The list will be amended, as appropriate after consultation with other departments and agencies, through periodic republication by the Secretary, HHS, in the *Federal Register*. A copy of the list is available from the Office for Protection from Research Risks, National Institutes of Health, HHS, Bethesda, Maryland 20892.

(b) An IRB may use the expedited review procedure to review either or both of the following:

(1) Some or all of the research appearing on the list and found by the reviewer(s) to involve no more than minimal risk,

(2) Minor changes in previously approved research during the period (of one year or less) for which approval is authorized.

Under an expedited review procedure, the review may be carried out by the IRB chairperson or by one or more experienced reviewers designated by the chairperson from among members of the IRB. In reviewing the research, the reviewers may exercise all of the authorities of the IRB except that the reviewers may not disapprove the research. A research activity may be disapproved only after review in accordance with the non-expedited procedure set forth in § 46.108(b).

(c) Each IRB which uses an expedited review procedure shall adopt a method for keeping all members advised of research proposals which have been approved under the procedure.

(d) The department or agency head may restrict, suspend, terminate, or choose not to authorize an institution's or IRB's use of the expedited review procedure.

§46.111 Criteria for IRB approval of research.

(a) In order to approve research covered by this policy the IRB shall determine that all of the following requirements are satisfied:

(1) Risks to subjects are minimized: (i) By using procedures which are consistent with sound research design and which do not unnecessarily expose subjects to risk, and (ii) whenever appropriate, by using procedures already being performed on the subjects for diagnostic or treatment purposes.

(2) Risks to subjects are reasonable in relation to anticipated benefits, if any, to subjects, and the importance of the knowledge that may reasonably be expected to result. In evaluating risks and benefits, the IRB should consider only those risks and benefits that may result from the research (as distinguished from risks and benefits of therapies subjects would receive even if not participating in the research). The IRB should not consider possible long-range effects of applying knowledge gained in the research (for example, the possible effects of the research on public policy) as among those research risks that fall within the purview of its responsibility.

(3) Selection of subjects is equitable. In making this assessment the IRB should take into account the purposes of the research and the setting in which the research will be conducted and should be particularly cognizant of the special problems of research involving vulnerable populations, such as children, prisoners, pregnant women, mentally disabled persons, or economically or educationally disadvantaged persons.

(4) Informed consent will be sought from each prospective subject or the subject's legally authorized representative, in accordance with, and to the extent required by §46.116.

(5) Informed consent will be appropriately documented, in accordance with, and to the extent required by §46.117.

(6) When appropriate, the research plan makes adequate provision for monitoring the data collected to ensure the safety of subjects.

(7) When appropriate, there are adequate provisions to protect the privacy of subjects and to maintain the confidentiality of data.

(b) When some or all of the subjects are likely to be vulnerable to coercion or undue influence, such as children, prisoners, pregnant women, mentally disabled persons, or economically or educationally disadvantaged persons, additional safeguards have been included in the study to protect the rights and welfare of these subjects.

§46.112 Review by institution.

Research covered by this policy that has been approved by an IRB may be subject to further appropriate review and approval or disapproval by officials of the institution. However, those officials may not approve the research if it has not been approved by an IRB.

§46.113 Suspension or termination of IRB approval of research.

An IRB shall have authority to suspend or terminate approval of research that is not being conducted in accordance with the IRB's requirements or that has been associated with unexpected serious harm to subjects. Any suspension or termination of approval shall include a statement of the reasons for the IRB's action and shall be reported promptly to the investigator, appropriate institutional officials, and the department or agency head.

§46.114 Cooperative research.

Cooperative research projects are those projects covered by this policy which involve more than one institution. In the conduct of cooperative research projects, each institution is responsible for safeguarding the rights and welfare of human subjects and for complying with this policy. With the approval of the department or agency head, an institution participating in a cooperative project may enter into a joint review arrangement, rely upon the review of another qualified IRB, or make similar arrangements for avoiding duplication of effort.

§46.115 IRB records.

(a) An institution, or when appropriate an IRB, shall prepare and maintain adequate documentation of IRB activities, including the following:

    (1) Copies of all research proposals reviewed, scientific evaluations, if any, that accompany the proposals, approved sample consent documents, progress reports submitted by investigators, and reports of injuries to subjects.

    (2) Minutes of IRB meetings which shall be in sufficient detail to show attendance at the meetings; actions taken by the IRB; the vote on these actions including the number of members voting for, against, and abstaining; the basis for requiring changes in or disapproving

research; and a written summary of the discussion of controverted issues and their resolution.

(3) Records of continuing review activities.

(4) Copies of all correspondence between the IRB and the investigators.

(5) A list of IRB members in the same detail as described is §46.103(b)(3).

(6) Written procedures for the IRB in the same detail as described in §46.103(b)(4) and §46.103(b)(5).

(7) Statements of significant new findings provided to subjects, as required by §46.116(b)(5).

(b) The records required by this policy shall be retained for at least 3 years, and records relating to research which is conducted shall be retained for at least 3 years after completion of the research. All records shall be accessible for inspection and copying by authorized representatives of the department or agency at reasonable times and in a reasonable manner.

§46.116 General requirements for informed consent.

Except as provided elsewhere in this policy, no investigator may involve a human being as a subject in research covered by this policy unless the investigator has obtained the legally effective informed consent of the subject or the subject's legally authorized representative. An investigator shall seek such consent only under circumstances that provide the prospective subject or the representative sufficient opportunity to consider whether or not to participate and that minimize the possibility of coercion or undue influence. The information that is given to the subject or the representative shall be in language understandable to the subject or the representative. No informed consent, whether oral or written, may include any exculpatory language through which the subject or the representative is made to waive or appear to waive any of the subject's legal rights, or releases or appears to release the investigator, the sponsor, the institution or its agents from liability for negligence.

(a) Basic elements of informed consent. Except as provided in paragraph (c) or (d) of this section, in seeking informed consent the following information shall be provided to each subject:

(1) A statement that the study involves research, an explanation of the purposes of the research and the expected duration of the subject's participation, a description of the procedures to be followed, and

identification of any procedures which are experimental;

(2) A description of any reasonably foreseeable risks or discomforts to the subject;

(3) A description of any benefits to the subject or to others which may reasonably be expected from the research;

(4) A disclosure of appropriate alternative procedures or courses of treatment, if any, that might be advantageous to the subject;

(5) A statement describing the extent, if any, to which confidentiality of records identifying the subject will be maintained;

(6) For research involving more than minimal risk, an explanation as to whether any compensation and an explanation as to whether any medical treatments are available if injury occurs and, if so, what they consist of, or where further information may be obtained;

(7) An explanation of whom to contact for answers to pertinent questions about the research and research subjects' rights, and whom to contact in the event of a research-related injury to the subject; and

(8) A statement that participation is voluntary, refusal to participate will involve no penalty or loss of benefits to which the subject is otherwise entitled, and the subject may discontinue participation at any time without penalty or loss of benefits to which the subject is otherwise entitled.

(b) Additional elements of informed consent. When appropriate, one or more of the following elements of information shall also be provided to each subject:

(1) A statement that the particular treatment or procedure may involve risks to the subject (or to the embryo or fetus, if the subject is or may become pregnant) which are currently unforeseeable;

(2) Anticipated circumstances under which the subject's participation may be terminated by the investigator without regard to the subject's consent;

(3) Any additional costs to the subject that may result from participation in the research;

(4) The consequences of a subject's decision to withdraw from the research and procedures for orderly termination of participation by the subject;

(5) A statement that significant new findings developed during the course of the research which may relate to the subject's willingness to continue participation will be provided to the subject; and

(6) The approximate number of subjects involved in the study.

(c) An IRB may approve a consent procedure which does not include, or which alters, some or all of the elements of informed consent set forth above, or waive the requirement to obtain informed consent provided the IRB finds and documents that:

(1) The research or demonstration project is to be conducted by or subject to the approval of state or local government officials and is designed to study, evaluate, or otherwise examine: (i) Public benefit of service programs; (ii) procedures for obtaining benefits or services under those programs; (iii) possible changes in or alternatives to those programs or procedures; or (iv) possible changes in methods or levels of payment for benefits or services under those programs; and

(2) The research could not practicably be carried out without the waiver or alteration.

(d) An IRB may approve a consent procedure which does not include, or which alters, some or all of the elements of informed consent set forth in this section, or waive the requirements to obtain informed consent provided the IRB finds and documents that:

(1) The research involves no more than minimal risk to the subjects;

(2) The waiver or alteration will not adversely affect the rights and welfare of the subjects;

(3) The research could not practicably be carried out without the waiver or alteration; and

(4) Whenever appropriate, the subjects will be provided with additional pertinent information after participation.

(e) The informed consent requirements in this policy are not intended to preempt any applicable federal, state, or local laws which require additional information to be disclosed in order for informed consent to be legally effective.

(f) Nothing in this policy is intended to limit the authority of a physician to provide emergency medical care, to the extent the physician is permitted to do so under applicable federal, state, or local law.

§46.117 Documentation of informed consent.

(a) Except as provided in paragraph (c) of this section, informed consent shall be documented by the use of a written consent form approved by the IRB and signed by the subject or the subject's legally authorized representative. A copy shall be given to the person signing the form.

(b) Except as provided in paragraph (c) of this section, the consent form may be either of the following:

(1) A written consent document that embodies the elements of informed consent required by §46.116. This form may be read to the subject or the subject's legally authorized representative, but in any event, the investigator shall give either the subject or the representative adequate opportunity to read it before it is signed; or

(2) A short form written consent document stating that the elements of informed consent required by §46.116 have been presented orally to the subject or the subject's legally authorized representative. When this method is used, there shall be a witness to the oral presentation. Also, the IRB shall approve a written summary of what is to be said to the subject or the representative. Only the short form itself is to be signed by the subject or the representative. However, the witness shall sign both the short form and a copy of the summary, and the person actually obtaining consent shall sign a copy of the summary. A copy of the summary shall be given to the subject or the representative, in addition to a copy of the short form.

(c) An IRB may waive the requirement for the investigator to obtain a signed consent form for some or all subjects if it finds either:

(1) That the only record linking the subject and the research would be the consent document and the principal risk would be potential harm resulting from a breach of confidentiality. Each subject will be asked whether the subject wants documentation linking the subject with the research, and the subject's wishes will govern; or

(2) That the research presents no more than minimal risk of harm to subjects and involves no procedures for which written consent is normally required outside of the research context.

In cases in which the documentation requirement is waived, the IRB may require the investigator to provide subjects with a written statement regarding the research.

§46.118 Applications and proposals lacking definite plans for involvement of human subjects.

Certain types of applications for grants, cooperative agreements, or contracts are submitted to departments or agencies with the knowledge that subjects may be involved within the period of support, but definite plans would not normally be set forth in the application or proposal. These include activities such as institutional type grants when selection of specific projects is the institution's responsibility; research training grants in which the activities involving subjects remain to be selected; and projects in which human subjects' involvement will depend upon completion of instruments, prior animal studies, or purification of compounds. These applications need not be reviewed by an IRB before an award may be made. However, except for research exempted or waived under §46.101 (b) or (i), no human subjects may be involved in any project supported by these awards until the project has been reviewed and approved by the IRB, as provided in this policy, and certification submitted, by the institution, to the department or agency.

§46.119 Research undertaken without the intention of involving human subjects.

In the event research is undertaken without the intention of involving human subjects, but it is later proposed to involve human subjects in the research, the research shall first be reviewed and approved by an IRB, as provided in this policy, a certification submitted, by the institution, to the department or agency, and final approval given to the proposed change by the department or agency.

§46.120 Evaluation and disposition of applications and proposals for research to be conducted or supported by a Federal Department or Agency.

(a) The department or agency head will evaluate all applications and proposals involving human subjects submitted to the department or agency through such officers and employees of the department or agency and such experts and consultants as the department or agency head determines to be appropriate. This evaluation will take into consideration the risks to the subjects, the adequacy of protection against these risks, the potential benefits of the research to the subjects and others, and the importance of the knowledge gained or to be gained.

(b) On the basis of this evaluation, the department or agency head may approve or disapprove the application or proposal, or enter into negotiations to develop an approvable one.

§46.121 [Reserved]

§46.122 Use of Federal funds.

Federal funds administered by a department or agency may not be expended for research involving human subjects unless the requirements of this policy have been satisfied.

§46.123 Early termination of research support: Evaluation of applications and proposals.

(a) The department or agency head may require that department or agency support for any project be terminated or suspended in the manner prescribed in applicable program requirements, when the department or agency head finds an institution has materially failed to comply with the terms of this policy.

(b) In making decisions about supporting or approving applications or proposals covered by this policy the department or agency head may take into account, in addition to all other eligibility requirements and program criteria, factors such as whether the applicant has been subject to a termination or suspension under paragraph (a) of this section and whether the applicant or the person or persons who would direct or has have directed the scientific and technical aspects of an activity has have, in the judgment of the department or agency head, materially failed to discharge responsibility for the protection of the rights and welfare of human subjects (whether or not the research was subject to federal regulation).

§46.124 Conditions.

With respect to any research project or any class of research projects the department or agency head may impose additional conditions prior to or at the time of approval when in the judgment of the department or agency head additional conditions are necessary for the protection of human subjects.

NOTES

1. Institutions with HHS-approved assurances on file will abide by provisions of title 45 CFR part 46 subparts A-D. Some of the other Departments and Agencies have incorporated all provisions of title 45 CFR part 46 into their policies and procedures as well. However, the exemptions at 45 CFR 46.101(b) do not apply to research involving prisoners, fetuses, pregnant women, or human in vitro fertilization, subparts B and C. The exemption at 45 CFR 46.101(b)(2), for research involving survey or interview procedures or observation of public behavior, does not apply to research with children, subpart D, except for research involving observations of public behavior when the investigator(s) do not participate in the activities being observed.

DHHS—Research Activities which may be Reviewed through Expedited Review Procedures

Department of Health and Human Services
Protection of Human Subjects

46 Federal Register *8392. 26 January 1981.*
Contact: *Office for Protection from Research Risks, National Institutes of Health, 6100 Executive Blvd., Suite 3B01, Rockville, Md. 20892-7507; Telephone: (301) 496-7005.*

[Revision of this list is under consideration (62 *Federal Register* 60607 —10 November 1997). For further information, contact the Office for Protection from Research Risks, National Institutes of Health, 6100 Executive Blvd., Suite 3B01, Rockville, Md. 20892-7507; Telephone: (301)435-5649 or (301) 496-7005.—THE EDITORS]

SUMMARY

This notice contains a list of research activities which Institutional Review Boards may review through the expedited review procedures set forth in HHS regulations for the protection of human subjects.

SUPPLEMENTARY INFORMATION

[Cross reference to 45 *Code of Federal Regulations* 46 subpart A omitted.—THE EDITORS]

Section 46.110 of the new final regulations provides that: "The Secretary will publish in the *Federal Register* a list of categories of research activities, involving no more than minimal risk, that may be reviewed by the Institutional Review Board, through an expedited review procedure * * * " This notice is published in accordance with §46.110.

Research activities involving no more than minimal risk, *and* in which the only involvement of human subjects will be in one or more of the following categories (carried out through standard methods) may be reviewed by the Institutional Review Board through the expedited review procedure authorized in §46.110 of 45 CFR Part 46.

1. Collection of: hair and nail clippings, in a nondisfiguring manner; deciduous teeth; and permanent teeth if patient care indicates a need for extraction.

2. Collection of excreta and external secretions including sweat, uncannulated saliva, placenta removed at delivery, and amniotic fluid at the time of rupture of the membrane prior to or during labor.

3. Recording of data from subjects 18 years of age or older using noninvasive procedures routinely employed in clinical practice. This includes the use of physical sensors that are applied either to the surface of the body or at a distance and do not involve input of matter or significant amounts of energy into the subject or an invasion of the subject's privacy. It also includes such procedures as weighing, testing sensory acuity, electrocardiography, electroencephalography, thermography, detection of naturally occurring radioactivity, diagnostic echography, and electroretinography. It does not include exposure to electromagnetic radiation outside the visible range (for example, x-rays, microwaves).

4. Collection of blood samples by venipuncture, in amounts not exceeding 450 milliliters in an eight-week period and no more often than two times per week, from subjects 18 years of age or older and who are in good health and not pregnant.

5. Collection of both supra- and subgingival dental plaque and calculus, provided the procedure is not more invasive than routine prophylactic scaling of the teeth and the process is accomplished in accordance with accepted prophylactic techniques.

6. Voice recordings made for research purposes such as investigations of speech defects.

7. Moderate exercise by healthy volunteers.

8. The study of existing data, documents, records, pathological specimens, or diagnostic specimens.

9. Research on individual or group behavior or characteristics of individuals, such as studies of perception, cognition, game theory, or test development, where the investigator does not manipulate subjects' behavior and the research will not involve stress to subjects.

10. Research on drugs or devices for which an investigational new drug exemption or an investigational device exemption is not required.

FDA—Protection of Human Subjects

*21 Code of Federal Regulations 50. Last revised 23 July 1997.
Contact: Office of Health Affairs HFY-20, Food and Drug Administration, 5600 Fishers Lane, Rockville, Md. 20857; Telephone: (301) 827-1685; Fax: (301) 443-0232.*

Subpart A—General Provisions

§50.1 Scope.

(a) This part applies to all clinical investigations regulated by the Food and Drug Administration under sections 505(i), 507(d), and 520(g) of the Federal Food, Drug, and Cosmetic Act, as well as clinical investigations that support applications for research or marketing permits for products regulated by the Food and Drug Administration, including food and color additives, drugs for human use, medical devices for human use, biological products for human use, and electronic products. Additional specific obligations and commitments of, and standards of conduct for, persons who sponsor or monitor clinical investigations involving particular test articles may also be found in other parts (e.g., parts 312 and 812). Compliance with these parts is intended to protect the rights and safety of subjects involved in investigations filed with the Food and Drug Administration pursuant to sections 406, 409, 502, 503, 505, 506, 507, 510, 513-516, 518-520, 721, and 801 of the Federal Food, Drug, and Cosmetic Act and sections 351 and 354-360F of the Public Health Service Act.

(b) References in this part to regulatory sections of the Code of Federal Regulations are to chapter I of title 21, unless otherwise noted.

§50.3 Definitions.

As used in this part:

(a) *Act* means the Federal Food, Drug, and Cosmetic Act, as amended (§§201—902, 52 Stat. 1040 et seq. as amended (21 U.S.C. 321—392)).

(b) *Application for research or marketing permit* includes:
  (1) A color additive petition, described in part 71.
  (2) A food additive petition, described in parts 171 and 571.
  (3) Data and information about a substance submitted as part of the procedures for establishing that the substance is generally recognized as safe for use that results or may reasonably be expected to result, directly or indirectly, in its becoming a component or otherwise affecting the characteristics of any food, described in §§170.30 and 570.30.
  (4) Data and information about a food additive submitted as part of the procedures for food additives permitted to be used on an interim basis pending additional study, described in §180.1.
  (5) Data and information about a substance submitted as part of the procedures for establishing a tolerance for unavoidable contaminants in food and food-packaging materials, described in section 406 of the act.
  (6) An investigational new drug application, described in part 312 of this chapter.
  (7) A new drug application, described in part 314.
  (8) Data and information about the bioavailability or bioequivalence of drugs for human use submitted as part of the procedures for issuing, amending, or repealing a bioequivalence requirement, described in part 320.
  (9) Data and information about an over-the-counter drug for human use submitted as part of the procedures for classifying these drugs as generally recognized as safe and effective and not misbranded, described in part 330.
  (10) Data and information about a prescription drug for human use submitted as part of the procedures for classifying these drugs as generally recognized as safe and effective and not misbranded, described in this chapter.
  (11) Data and information about an antibiotic drug submitted as part of the procedures for issuing, amending, or repealing regulations for these drugs, described in §314.300 of this chapter.
  (12) An application for a biological product license, described in part 601.
  (13) Data and information about a biological product submitted as part of the procedures for determining that licensed biological products are safe and effective and not misbranded, described in part 601.
  (14) Data and information about an in vitro diagnostic product submitted as part of the procedures for establishing, amending, or repealing a standard for these products, described in part 809.

(15) An Application for an Investigational Device Exemption, described in part 812.

(16) Data and information about a medical device submitted as part of the procedures for classifying these devices, described in section 513.

(17) Data and information about a medical device submitted as part of the procedures for establishing, amending, or repealing a standard for these devices, described in section 514.

(18) An application for premarket approval of a medical device, described in section 515.

(19) A product development protocol for a medical device, described in section 515.

(20) Data and information about an electronic product submitted as part of the procedures for establishing, amending, or repealing a standard for these products, described in section 358 of the Public Health Service Act.

(21) Data and information about an electronic product submitted as part of the procedures for obtaining a variance from any electronic product performance standard, as described in §1010.4.

(22) Data and information about an electronic product submitted as part of the procedures for granting, amending, or extending an exemption from a radiation safety performance standard, as described in §1010.5.

(c) *Clinical investigation* means any experiment that involves a test article and one or more human subjects and that either is subject to requirements for prior submission to the Food and Drug Administration under section 505(i), 507(d), or 520(g) of the act, or is not subject to requirements for prior submission to the Food and Drug Administration under these sections of the act, but the results of which are intended to be submitted later to, or held for inspection by, the Food and Drug Administration as part of an application for a research or marketing permit. The term does not include experiments that are subject to the provisions of part 58 of this chapter, regarding nonclinical laboratory studies.

(d) *Investigator* means an individual who actually conducts a clinical investigation, i.e., under whose immediate direction the test article is administered or dispensed to, or used involving, a subject, or, in the event of an investigation conducted by a team of individuals, is the responsible leader of that team.

(e) *Sponsor* means a person who initiates a clinical investigation, but who does not actually conduct the investigation, i.e., the test article is administered or dispensed to or used involving, a subject under the immediate direction of another individual. A person other than an individual (e.g., corporation or agency) that uses one or more of its own employees to conduct a clinical investigation it has initiated is considered to be a sponsor (not a sponsor-investigator), and the employees are considered to be investigators.

(f) *Sponsor-investigator* means an individual who both initiates and actually conducts, alone or with others, a clinical investigation, i.e., under whose immediate direction the test article is administered or dispensed to, or used involving, a subject. The term does not include any person other than an individual, e.g., corporation or agency.

(g) *Human subject* means an individual who is or becomes a participant in research, either as a recipient of the test article or as a control. A subject may be either a healthy human or a patient.

(h) *Institution* means any public or private entity or agency (including Federal, State, and other agencies). The word facility as used in section 520(g) of the act is deemed to be synonymous with the term institution for purposes of this part.

(i) *Institutional review board (IRB)* means any board, committee, or other group formally designated by an institution to review biomedical research involving humans as subjects, to approve the initiation of and conduct periodic review of such research. The term has the same meaning as the phrase institutional review committee as used in section 520(g) of the act.

(j) *Test article* means any drug (including a biological product for human use), medical device for human use, human food additive, color additive, electronic product, or any other article subject to regulation under the act or under sections 351 and 354-360F of the Public Health Service Act (42 U.S.C. 262 and 263b-263n).

(k) *Minimal risk* means that the probability and magnitude of harm or discomfort anticipated in the research are not greater in and of themselves than those ordinarily encountered in daily life or during the performance of routine physical or psychological examinations or tests.

(l) *Legally authorized representative* means an individual or judicial or other body authorized under applicable law to consent on behalf of a prospective subject to the subject's particpation in the procedure(s) involved in the research.

(m) *Family member* means any one of the following legally competent persons: Spouse; parents; children (including adopted children); brothers, sisters, and spouses of brothers and sisters; and any individual related by blood or affinity whose close association with the subject is the equivalent of a family relationship.

Subpart B—Informed Consent of Human Subjects

§50.20 General requirements for informed consent.

Except as provided in §50.23, no investigator may involve a human being as a subject in research covered by these regulations unless the investigator has obtained the legally effective informed consent of the subject or the subject's legally authorized representative. An investigator shall seek such consent only under circumstances that provide the prospective subject or the representative sufficient opportunity to consider whether or not to participate and that minimize the possibility of coercion or undue influence. The information that is given to the subject or the representative shall be in language understandable to the subject or the representative. No informed consent, whether oral or written, may include any exculpatory language through which the subject or the representative is made to waive or appear to waive any of the subject's legal rights, or releases or appears to release the investigator, the sponsor, the institution, or its agents from liability for negligence.

§50.21 Effective date.

The requirements for informed consent set out in this part apply to all human subjects entering a clinical investigation that commences on or after July 27, 1981.

§50.23 Exception from general requirements.

(a) The obtaining of informed consent shall be deemed feasible unless, before use of the test article (except as provided in paragraph (b) of this section), both the investigator and a physician who is not otherwise participating in the clinical investigation certify in writing all of the following:

(1) The human subject is confronted by a life-threatening situation necessitating the use of the test article;

(2) Informed consent cannot be obtained from the subject because of an inability to communicate with, or obtain legally effective consent from, the subject;

(3) Time is not sufficient to obtain consent from the subject's legal representative; and

(4) There is available no alternative method of approved or generally recognized therapy that provides an equal or greater likelihood of saving the life of the subject.

(b) If immediate use of the test article is, in the investigator's opinion, required to preserve the life of the subject, and time is not sufficient to obtain the independent determination required in paragraph (a) of this section in advance of using the test article, the determinations of the clinical investigator shall be made and, within 5 working days after the use of the article, be reviewed and evaluated in writing by a physician who is not participating in the clinical investigation.

(c) The documentation required in paragraph (a) or (b) of this section shall be submitted to the IRB within 5 working days after the use of the test article.

(d)(1) The Commissioner may also determine that obtaining informed consent is not feasible when the Assistant Secretary of Defense (Health Affairs) requests such a determination in connection with the use of an investigational drug (including an antibiotic or biological product) in a specific protocol under an investigational new drug application (IND) sponsored by the Department of Defense (DOD). DOD's request for a determination that obtaining informed consent from military personnel is not feasible must be limited to a specific military operation involving combat or the immediate threat of combat. The request must also include a written justification supporting the conclusions of the physician(s) responsible for the medical care of the military personnel involved and the investigator(s) identified in the IND that a military combat exigency exists because of special military combat (actual or threatened) circumstances in which, in order to facilitate the accomplishment of the military mission, preservation of the health of the individual and the safety of other personnel require that a particular treatment be provided to a specified group of military personnel, without regard to what might be any individual's personal preference for no treatment or for some alternative treatment. The written request must also include a statement that a duly constituted institutional review board has reviewed and approved the use of the investigational drug without informed consent. The Commissioner may find that informed consent is not feasible only when withholding treatment would be contrary to the best interests of military personnel and there is no available satisfactory alternative therapy.

(2) In reaching a determination under paragraph (d)(1) of this section that obtaining informed consent is not feasible and withholding treatment would be contrary to the best interests of military personnel, the Commissioner will review the request submitted under paragraph (d)(1) of this section and take into account all pertinent factors, including, but not limited to:

(i) The extent and strength of the evidence of the safety and effectiveness of the investigational drug for the intended use;

(ii) The context in which the drug will be administered, e.g., whether it is intended for use in a battlefield or hospital setting or whether it will be self-administered or will be administered by a health professional;

(iii) The nature of the disease or condition for which the preventive or therapeutic treatment is intended; and

(iv) The nature of the information to be provided to the recipients of the drug concerning the potential benefits and risks of taking or not taking the drug.

(3) The Commissioner may request a recommendation from appropriate experts before reaching a determination on a request submitted under paragraph (d)(1) of this section.

(4) A determination by the Commissioner that obtaining informed consent is not feasible and withholding treatment would be contrary to the best interests of military personnel will expire at the end of 1 year, unless renewed at DOD's request, or when DOD informs the Commissioner that the specific military operation creating the need for the use of the investigational drug has ended, whichever is earlier. The Commissioner may also revoke this determination based on changed circumstances.

§50.24 Exception from informed consent requirements for emergency research.

(a) The IRB responsible for the review, approval, and continuing review of the clinical investigation described in this section may approve that investigation without requiring that informed consent of all research subjects be obtained if the IRB (with the concurrence of a licensed physician who is a member of or consultant to the IRB and who is not otherwise participating in the clinical investigation) finds and documents each of the following:

(1) The human subjects are in a life-threatening situation, available treatments are unproven or unsatisfactory, and the collection of valid

scientific evidence, which may include evidence obtained through randomized placebo-controlled investigations, is necessary to determine the safety and effectiveness of particular interventions;

(2) Obtaining informed consent is not feasible because:

(i) The subjects will not be able to give their informed consent as a result of their medical condition;

(ii) The intervention under investigation must be administered before consent from the subjects' legally authorized representatives is feasible; and

(iii) There is no reasonable way to identify prospectively the individuals likely to become eligible for participation in the clinical investigation;

(3) Participation in the research holds out the prospect of direct benefit to the subjects because:

(i) Subjects are facing a life-threatening situation that necessitates intervention;

(ii) Appropriate animal and other preclinical studies have been conducted, and the information derived from those studies and related evidence support the potential for the intervention to provide a direct benefit to the individual subjects; and

(iii) Risks associated with the investigation are reasonable in relation to what is known about the medical condition of the potential class of subjects, the risks and benefits of standard therapy, if any, and what is known about the risks and benefits of the proposed intervention or activity;

(4) The clinical investigation could not practicably be carried out without the waiver;

(5) The proposed investigational plan defines the length of the potential therapeutic window based on scientific evidence, and the investigator has committed to attempting to contact a legally authorized representative for each subject within that window of time and, if feasible, to asking the legally authorized representative contacted for consent within that window rather than proceeding without consent. The investigator will summarize efforts made to contact legally authorized representatives and make this information available to the IRB at the time of continuing review;

(6) The IRB has reviewed and approved informed consent procedures and an informed consent document consistent with § 50.25. These procedures and the informed consent document are to be used with subjects or their legally authorized representatives in situations where

use of such procedures and documents is feasible. The IRB has reviewed and approved procedures and information to be used when providing an opportunity for a family member to object to a subject's participation in the clinical investigation consistent with paragraph (a)(7)(v) of this section; and

(7) Additional protections of the rights and welfare of the subjects will be provided, including, at least:

(i) Consultation (including, where appropriate, consultation carried out by the IRB) with representatives of the communities in which the clinical investigation will be conducted and from which the subjects will be drawn;

(ii) Public disclosure to the communities in which the clinical investigation will be conducted and from which the subjects will be drawn, prior to initiation of the clinical investigation, of plans for the investigation and its risks and expected benefits;

(iii) Public disclosure of sufficient information following completion of the clinical investigation to apprise the community and researchers of the study, including the demographic characteristics of the research population, and its results;

(iv) Establishment of an independent data monitoring committee to exercise oversight of the clinical investigation; and

(v) If obtaining informed consent is not feasible and a legally authorized representative is not reasonably available, the investigator has committed, if feasible, to attempting to contact within the therapeutic window the subject's family member who is not a legally authorized representative, and asking whether he or she objects to the subject's participation in the clinical investigation. The investigator will summarize efforts made to contact family members and make this information available to the IRB at the time of continuing review.

(b) The IRB is responsible for ensuring that procedures are in place to inform, at the earliest feasible opportunity, each subject, or if the subject remains incapacitated, a legally authorized representative of the subject, or if such a representative is not reasonably available, a family member, of the subject's inclusion in the clinical investigation, the details of the investigation and other information contained in the informed consent document. The IRB shall also ensure that there is a procedure to inform the subject, or if the subject remains incapacitated, a legally authorized representative of the subject, or if such a representative is not reasonably available, a family member, that he or she may discontinue the subject's participation at any time without penalty or loss of benefits to which the subject is otherwise entitled. If a legally authorized representative or family member is told about the clinical investigation and the subject's condition improves, the subject is also to be informed as soon as feasible. If a subject is entered into a clinical investigation with waived consent and the subject dies before a legally authorized representative or family member can be contacted, information about the clinical investigation is to be provided to the subject's legally authorized representative or family member, if feasible.

(c) The IRB determinations required by paragraph (a) of this section and the documentation required by paragraph (e) of this section are to be retained by the IRB for at least 3 years after completion of the clinical investigation, and the records shall be accessible for inspection and copying by FDA in accordance with §56.115(b) of this chapter.

(d) Protocols involving an exception to the informed consent requirement under this section must be performed under a separate investigational new drug application (IND) or investigational device exemption (IDE) that clearly identifies such protocols as protocols that may include subjects who are unable to consent. The submission of those protocols in a separate IND/IDE is required even if an IND for the same drug product or an IDE for the same device already exists. Applications for investigations under this section may not be submitted as amendments under §§312.30 or 812.35 of this chapter.

(e) If an IRB determines that it cannot approve a clinical investigation because the investigation does not meet the criteria in the exception provided under paragraph (a) of this section or because of other relevant ethical concerns, the IRB must document its findings and provide these findings promptly in writing to the clinical investigator and to the sponsor of the clinical investigation. The sponsor of the clinical investigation must promptly disclose this information to FDA and to the sponsor's clinical investigators who are participating or are asked to participate in this or a substantially equivalent clinical investigation of the sponsor, and to other IRB's that have been, or are, asked to review this or a substantially equivalent investigation by that sponsor.

§50.25 Elements of informed consent.

(a) *Basic elements of informed consent.* In seeking informed consent, the following information shall be provided to each subject:

(1) A statement that the study involves research, an explanation of the purposes of the research and the expected duration of the subject's

participation, a description of the procedures to be followed, and identification of any procedures which are experimental;

(2) A description of any reasonably foreseeable risks or discomforts to the subject;

(3) A description of any benefits to the subject or to others which may reasonably be expected from the research;

(4) A disclosure of appropriate alternative procedures or courses of treatment, if any, that might be advantageous to the subject;

(5) A statement describing the extent, if any, to which confidentiality of records identifying the subject will be maintained and that notes the possibility that the Food and Drug Administration may inspect the records;

(6) For research involving more than minimal risk, an explanation as to whether any compensation and an explanation as to whether any medical treatments are available if injury occurs and, if so, what they consist of, or where further information may be obtained;

(7) An explanation of whom to contact for answers to pertinent questions about the research and research subjects' rights, and whom to contact in the event of a research-related injury to the subject; and

(8) A statement that participation is voluntary, that refusal to participate will involve no penalty or loss of benefits to which the subject is otherwise entitled, and that the subject may discontinue participation at any time without penalty or loss of benefits to which the subject is otherwise entitled.

(b) *Additional elements of informed consent.* When appropriate, one or more of the following elements of information shall also be provided to each subject:

(1) A statement that the particular treatment or procedure may involve risks to the subject (or to the embryo or fetus, if the subject is or may become pregnant) which are currently unforeseeable;

(2) Anticipated circumstances under which the subject's participation may be terminated by the investigator without regard to the subject's consent;

(3) Any additional costs to the subject that may result from participation in the research;

(4) The consequences of a subject's decision to withdraw from the research and procedures for orderly termination of participation by the subject;

(5) A statement that significant new findings developed during the course of the research which may relate to the subject's willingness to continue participation will be provided to the subject; and

(6) The approximate number of subjects involved in the study.

(c) The informed consent requirements in these regulations are not intended to preempt any applicable Federal, State, or local laws which require additional information to be disclosed for informed consent to be legally effective.

(d) Nothing in these regulations is intended to limit the authority of a physician to provide emergency medical care to the extent the physician is permitted to do so under applicable Federal, State, or local law.

§50.27 Documentation of informed consent.

(a) Except as provided in §56.109(c), informed consent shall be documented by the use of a written consent form approved by the IRB and signed and dated by the subject or the subject's legally authorized representative at the time of consent. A copy shall be given to the person signing the form.

(b) Except as provided in §56.109(c), the consent form may be either of the following:

(1) A written consent document that embodies the elements of informed consent required by §50.25. This form may be read to the subject or the subject's legally authorized representative, but, in any event, the investigator shall give either the subject or the representative adequate opportunity to read it before it is signed; or

(2) A *short form* written consent document stating that the elements of informed consent required by §50.25 have been presented orally to the subject or the subject's legally authorized representative. When this method is used, there shall be a witness to the oral presentation. Also, the IRB shall approve a written summary of what is to be said to the subject or the representative. Only the short form itself is to be signed by the subject or the representative. However, the witness shall sign both the short form and a copy of the summary, and the person actually obtaining the consent shall sign a copy of the summary. A copy of the summary shall be given to the subject or the representative in addition to a copy of the short form.

FDA—Institutional Review Boards

21 Code of Federal Regulations 56. Last revised 2 October 1996. Contact: Office of Health Affairs HFY-20, Food and Drug Administration, 5600 Fishers Lane, Rockville, Md. 20857; Telephone: (301) 827-1685; Fax: (301) 443-0232.

Subpart A—General Provisions

§ 56.101 Scope.

(a) This part contains the general standards for the composition, operation, and responsibility of an Institutional Review Board (IRB) that reviews clinical investigations regulated by the Food and Drug Administration under sections 505(i), 507(d), and 520(g) of the act, as well as clinical investigations that support applications for research or marketing permits for products regulated by the Food and Drug Administration, including food and color additives, drugs for human use, medical devices for human use, biological products for human use, and electronic products. Compliance with this part is intended to protect the rights and welfare of human subjects involved in such investigations.

(b) References in this part to regulatory sections of the Code of Federal Regulations are to chapter I of title 21, unless otherwise noted.

§56.102 Definitions.

As used in this part:

(a) *Act* means the Federal Food, Drug, and Cosmetic Act, as amended (§§201-902, 52 Stat. 1040 *et seq.*, as amended (21 U.S.C. 321-392)).

(b) *Application for research* or *marketing permit* includes:

(1) A color additive petition, described in part 71;

(2) Data and information regarding a substance submitted as part of the procedures for establishing that a substance is generally recognized as safe for a use which results or may reasonably be expected to result, directly or indirectly, in its becoming a component or otherwise affecting the characteristics of any food, described in §170.35;

(3) A food additive petition, described in part 171;

(4) Data and information regarding a food additive submitted as part of the procedures regarding food additives permitted to be used on an interim basis pending additional study, described in §180.1;

(5) Data and information regarding a substance submitted as part of the procedures for establishing a tolerance for unavoidable contaminants in food and food-packaging materials, described in section 406 of the act;

(6) An investigational new drug application, described in part 312 of this chapter;

(7) A new drug application, described in part 314;

(8) Data and information regarding the bioavailability or bioequivalence of drugs for human use submitted as part of the procedures for issuing, amending, or repealing a bioequivalence requirement, described in part 320;

(9) Data and information regarding an over-the-counter drug for human use submitted as part of the procedures for classifying such drugs as generally recognized as safe and effective and not misbranded, described in part 330;

(10) Data and information regarding an antibiotic drug submitted as part of the procedures for issuing, amending, or repealing regulations for such drugs, described in §314.300 of this chapter;

(11) An application for a biological product license, described in part 601;

(12) Data and information regarding a biological product submitted as part of the procedures for determining that licensed biological products are safe and effective and not misbranded, as described in part 601;

(13) An *Application for an Investigational Device Exemption*, described in parts 812 and 813;

(14) Data and information regarding a medical device for human use submitted as part of the procedures for classifying such devices, described in part 860;

(15) Data and information regarding a medical device for human use submitted as part of the procedures for establishing, amending, or repealing a standard for such device, described in part 861;

(16) An application for premarket approval of a medical device for human use, described in section 515 of the act;

(17) A product development protocol for a medical device for human use, described in section 515 of the act;

(18) Data and information regarding an electronic product submitted as part of the procedures for establishing, amending, or

repealing a standard for such products, described in section 358 of the Public Health Service Act;

(19) Data and information regarding an electronic product submitted as part of the procedures for obtaining a variance from any electronic product performance standard, as described in §1010.4;

(20) Data and information regarding an electronic product submitted as part of the procedures for granting, amending, or extending an exemption from a radiation safety performance standard, as described in §1010.5; and

(21) Data and information regarding an electronic product submitted as part of the procedures for obtaining an exemption from notification of a radiation safety defect or failure of compliance with a radiation safety performance standard, described in subpart D of part 1003.

(c) *Clinical investigation* means any experiment that involves a test article and one or more human subjects, and that either must meet the requirements for prior submission to the Food and Drug Administration under section 505(i), 507(d), or 520(g) of the act, or need not meet the requirements for prior submission to the Food and Drug Administration under these sections of the act, but the results of which are intended to be later submitted to, or held for inspection by, the Food and Drug Administration as part of an application for a research or marketing permit. The term does not include experiments that must meet the provisions of part 58, regarding nonclinical laboratory studies. The terms research, clinical research, clinical study, study, and clinical investigation are deemed to be synonymous for purposes of this part.

(d) *Emergency use* means the use of a test article on a human subject in a life-threatening situation in which no standard acceptable treatment is available, and in which there is not sufficient time to obtain IRB approval.

(e) *Human subject* means an individual who is or becomes a participant in research, either as a recipient of the test article or as a control. A subject may be either a healthy individual or a patient.

(f) *Institution* means any public or private entity or agency (including Federal, State, and other agencies). The term facility as used in section 520(g) of the act is deemed to be synonymous with the term institution for purposes of this part.

(g) *Institutional Review Board (IRB)* means any board, committee, or other group formally designated by an institution to review, to approve the initiation of, and to conduct periodic review of, biomedical research involving human subjects. The primary purpose of such review is to assure the protection of the rights and welfare of the human subjects. The term has the same meaning as the phrase institutional review committee as used in section 520(g) of the act.

(h) *Investigator* means an individual who actually conducts a clinical investigation (i.e., under whose immediate direction the test article is administered or dispensed to, or used involving, a subject) or, in the event of an investigation conducted by a team of individuals, is the responsible leader of that team.

(i) *Minimal risk* means that the probability and magnitude of harm or discomfort anticipated in the research are not greater in and of themselves than those ordinarily encountered in daily life or during the performance of routine physical or psychological examinations or tests.

(j) *Sponsor* means a person or other entity that initiates a clinical investigation, but that does not actually conduct the investigation, i.e., the test article is administered or dispensed to, or used involving, a subject under the immediate direction of another individual. A person other than an individual (e.g., a corporation or agency) that uses one or more of its own employees to conduct an investigation that it has initiated is considered to be a sponsor (not a sponsor-investigator), and the employees are considered to be investigators.

(k) *Sponsor-investigator* means an individual who both initiates and actually conducts, alone or with others, a clinical investigation, i.e., under whose immediate direction the test article is administered or dispensed to, or used involving, a subject. The term does not include any person other than an individual, e.g., it does not include a corporation or agency. The obligations of a sponsor-investigator under this part include both those of a sponsor and those of an investigator.

(l) *Test article* means any drug for human use, biological product for human use, medical device for human use, human food additive, color additive, electronic product, or any other article subject to regulation under the act or under sections 351 or 354-360F of the Public Health Service Act.

(m) *IRB approval* means the determination of the IRB that the clinical investigation has been reviewed and may be conducted at an institution within the constraints set forth by the IRB and by other institutional and Federal requirements.

§56.103 Circumstances in which IRB review is required.

(a) Except as provided in §56.104 and 56.105, any clinical investigation which must meet the requirements for prior submission (as required in parts 312, 812, and 813) to the Food and Drug Administration shall not be initiated unless that investigation has been reviewed and approved by, and remains subject to continuing review by, an IRB meeting the requirements of this part.

(b) Except as provided in §§56.104 and 56.105, the Food and Drug Administration may decide not to consider in support of an application for a research or marketing permit any data or information that has been derived from a clinical investigation that has not been approved by, and that was not subject to initial and continuing review by, an IRB meeting the requirements of this part. The determination that a clinical investigation may not be considered in support of an application for a research or marketing permit does not, however, relieve the applicant for such a permit of any obligation under any other applicable regulations to submit the results of the investigation to the Food and Drug Administration.

(c) Compliance with these regulations will in no way render inapplicable pertinent Federal, State, or local laws or regulations.

§56.104 Exemptions from IRB requirement.

The following categories of clinical investigations are exempt from the requirements of this part for IRB review:

(a) Any investigation which commenced before July 27, 1981 and was subject to requirements for IRB review under FDA regulations before that date, provided that the investigation remains subject to review of an IRB which meets the FDA requirements in effect before July 27, 1981.

(b) Any investigation commenced before July 27, 1981 and was not otherwise subject to requirements for IRB review under Food and Drug Administration regulations before that date.

(c) Emergency use of a test article, provided that such emergency use is reported to the IRB within 5 working days. Any subsequent use of the test article at the institution is subject to IRB review.

(d) Taste and food quality evaluations and consumer acceptance studies, if wholesome foods without additives are consumed or if a food is consumed that contains a food ingredient at or below the level and for a use found to be safe, or agricultural, chemical, or environmental contaminant at or below the level found to be safe, by the Food and Drug Administration or approved by the Environmental Protection Agency or the Food Safety and Inspection Service of the U.S. Department of Agriculture.

§56.105 Waiver of IRB requirement.

On the application of a sponsor or sponsor-investigator, the Food and Drug Administration may waive any of the requirements contained in these regulations, including the requirements for IRB review, for specific research activities or for classes of research activities, otherwise covered by these regulations.

Subpart B—Organization and Personnel

§56.107 IRB membership.

(a) Each IRB shall have at least five members, with varying backgrounds to promote complete and adequate review of research activities commonly conducted by the institution. The IRB shall be sufficiently qualified through the experience and expertise of its members, and the diversity of the members, including consideration of race, gender, cultural backgrounds, and sensitivity to such issues as community attitudes, to promote respect for its advice and counsel in safeguarding the rights and welfare of human subjects. In addition to possessing the professional competence necessary to review the specific research activities, the IRB shall be able to ascertain the acceptability of proposed research in terms of institutional commitments and regulations, applicable law, and standards or professional conduct and practice. The IRB shall therefore include persons knowledgeable in these areas. If an IRB regularly reviews research that involves a vulnerable category of subjects, such as children, prisoners, pregnant women, or handicapped or mentally disabled persons, consideration shall be given to the inclusion of one or more individuals who are knowledgeable about and experienced in working with those subjects.

(b) Every nondiscriminatory effort will be made to ensure that no IRB consists entirely of men or entirely of women, including the institution's consideration of qualified persons of both sexes, so long as no selection is made to the IRB on the basis of gender. No IRB may consist entirely of members of one profession.

(c) Each IRB shall include at least one member whose primary concerns are in the scientific area and at least one member whose primary concerns are in the nonscientific areas.

(d) Each IRB shall include at least one member who is not otherwise affiliated with the institution and who is not part of the immediate family of a person who is affiliated with the institution.

(e) No IRB may have a member participate in the IRB's initial or continuing review of any project in which the member has a conflicting interest, except to provide information requested by the IRB.

(f) An IRB may, in its discretion, invite individuals with competence in special areas to assist in the review of complex issues which require expertise beyond or in addition to that available on the IRB. These individuals may not vote with the IRB.

Subpart C—IRB Functions and Operations

§56.108 IRB functions and operations.

In order to fulfill the requirements of these regulations, each IRB shall:

(a) Follow written procedures: (1) For conducting its initial and continuing review of research and for reporting its findings and actions to the investigator and the institution; (2) for determining which projects require review more often than annually and which projects need verification from sources other than the investigator that no material changes have occurred since previous IRB review; (3) for ensuring prompt reporting to the IRB of changes in research activity; and (4) for ensuring that changes in approved research, during the period for which IRB approval has already been given, may not be initiated without IRB review and approval except where necessary to eliminate apparent immediate hazards to the human subjects.

(b) Follow written procedures for ensuring prompt reporting to the IRB, appropriate institutional officials, and the Food and Drug Administration of: (1) Any unanticipated problems involving risks to human subjects or others; (2) any instance of serious or continuing noncompliance with these regulations or the requirements or determinations of the IRB; or (3) any suspension or termination of IRB approval.

(c) Except when an expedited review procedure is used (see § 56.110), review proposed research at convened meetings at which a majority of the members of the IRB are present, including at least one member whose primary concerns are in nonscientific areas. In order for the research to be approved, it shall receive the approval of a majority of those members present at the meeting.

§56.109 IRB review of research.

(a) An IRB shall review and have authority to approve, require modifications in (to secure approval), or disapprove all research activities covered by these regulations.

(b) An IRB shall require that information given to subjects as part of informed consent is in accordance with §50.25. The IRB may require that information, in addition to that specifically mentioned in §50.25, be given to the subjects when in the IRB's judgment the information would meaningfully add to the protection of the rights and welfare of subjects.

(c) An IRB shall require documentation of informed consent in accordance with §50.27 of this chapter, except as follows:

(1) The IRB may, for some or all subjects, waive the requirement that the subject, or the subject's legally authorized representative, sign a written consent form if it finds that the research presents no more than minimal risk of harm to subjects and involves no procedures for which written consent is normally required outside the research context; or

(2) The IRB may, for some or all subjects, find that the requirements in §50.24 of this chapter for an exception from informed consent for emergency research are met.

(d) In cases where the documentation requirement is waived under paragraph (c)(1) of this section, the IRB may require the investigator to provide subjects with a written statement regarding the research.

(e) An IRB shall notify investigators and the institution in writing of its decision to approve or disapprove the proposed research activity, or of modifications required to secure IRB approval of the research activity. If the IRB decides to disapprove a research activity, it shall include in its written notification a statement of the reasons for its decision and give the investigator an opportunity to respond in person or in writing. For investigations involving an exception to informed consent under §50.24 of this chapter, an IRB shall promptly notify in writing the investigator and the sponsor of the research when an IRB determines that it cannot approve the research because it does not meet the criteria in the exception provided under §50.24(a) of this chapter or because of other relevant ethical concerns. The written notification shall include a statement of the reasons for the IRB's determination.

(f) An IRB shall conduct continuing review of research covered by these regulations at intervals appropriate to the degree of risk, but not less than once per year, and shall have authority to observe or have a third party observe the consent process and the research.

(g) An IRB shall provide in writing to the sponsor of research involving an exception to informed consent under §50.24 of this chapter a copy of information that has been publicly disclosed under §50.24(a)(7)(ii) and (a)(7)(iii) of this chapter. The IRB shall provide this information to the sponsor promptly so that the sponsor is aware that such disclosure has occurred. Upon receipt, the sponsor shall provide copies of the information disclosed to FDA.

§56.110 Expedited review procedures for certain kinds of research involving no more than minimal risk, and for minor changes in approved research.

[The expedited review list referenced here is reproduced in this volume. See "FDA—Clinical Investigations which may be Reviewed through Expedited Review Procedures Set Forth in FDA Regulations," page 100, below.—*The Editors*]

(a) The Food and Drug Administration has established, and published in the FEDERAL REGISTER, a list of categories of research that may be reviewed by the IRB through an expedited review procedure. The list will be amended, as appropriate, through periodic republication in the FEDERAL REGISTER.

(b) An IRB may use the expedited review procedure to review either or both of the following: (1) Some or all of the research appearing on the list and found by the reviewer(s) to involve no more than minimal risk; and (2) minor changes in previously approved research during the period (of 1 year or less) for which approval is authorized. Under an expedited review procedure, the review may be carried out by the IRB chairperson or by one or more experienced reviewers designated by the IRB chairperson from among the members of the IRB. In reviewing the research, the reviewers may exercise all of the authorities of the IRB except that the reviewers may not disapprove the research. A research activity may be disapproved only after review in accordance with the nonexpedited review procedure set forth in §56.108(c).

(c) Each IRB which uses an expedited review procedure shall adopt a method for keeping all members advised of research proposals which have been approved under the procedure.

(d) The Food and Drug Administration may restrict, suspend, or terminate an institution's or IRB's use of the expedited review procedure when necessary to protect the rights or welfare of subjects.

§56.111 Criteria for IRB approval of research.

(a) determine that all of the following requirements are satisfied:

(1) Risks to subjects are minimized: (i) By using procedures which are consistent with sound research design and which do not unnecessarily expose subjects to risk, and (ii) whenever appropriate, by using procedures already being performed on the subjects for diagnostic or treatment purposes;

(2) Risks to subjects are reasonable in relation to anticipated benefits, if any, to subjects, and the importance of the knowledge that may be expected to result. In evaluating risks and benefits, the IRB should consider only those risks and benefits that may result from the research (as distinguished from risks and benefits of therapies that subjects would receive even if not participating in the research). The IRB should not consider possible long-range effects of applying knowledge gained in the research (for example, the possible effects of the research on public policy) as among those research risks that fall within the purview of its responsibility;

(3) Selection of subjects is equitable. In making this assessment the IRB should take into account the purposes of the research and the setting in which the research will be conducted and should be particularly cognizant of the special problems of research involving vulnerable populations, such as children, prisoners, pregnant women, handicapped, or mentally disabled persons, or economically or educationally disadvantaged persons;

(4) Informed consent will be sought from each prospective subject or the subject's legally authorized representative, in accordance with and to the extent required by part 50;

(5) Informed consent will be appropriately documented, in accordance with and to the extent required by §50.27;

(6) Where appropriate, the research plan makes adequate provision for monitoring the data collected to ensure the safety of subjects; and

(7) Where appropriate, there are adequate provisions to protect the privacy of subjects and to maintain the confidentiality of data.

(b) When some or all of the subjects, such as children, prisoners, pregnant women, handicapped, or mentally disabled persons, or economically or educationally disadvantaged persons, are likely to be vulnerable to coercion or undue influence additional safeguards have been included in the study to protect the rights and welfare of these subjects.

§56.112 Review by institution.

Research covered by these regulations that has been approved by an IRB may be subject to further appropriate review and approval or disapproval by officials of the institution. However, those officials may not approve the research if it has not been approved by an IRB.

§56.113 Suspension or termination of IRB approval of research.

An IRB shall have authority to suspend or terminate approval of research that is not being conducted in accordance with the IRB's requirements or that has been associated with unexpected serious harm to subjects. Any suspension or termination of approval shall include a statement of the reasons for the IRB's action and shall be reported promptly to the investigator, appropriate institutional officials, and the Food and Drug Administration.

§56.114 Cooperative research.

In complying with these regulations, institutions involved in multi-institutional studies may use joint review, reliance upon the review of another qualified IRB, or similar arrangements aimed at avoidance of duplication of effort.

Subpart D—Records and Reports

§56.115 IRB records.

(a) An institution, or where appropriate an IRB, shall prepare and maintain adequate documentation of IRB activities, including the following:

(1) Copies of all research proposals reviewed, scientific evaluations, if any, that accompany the proposals, approved sample consent documents, progress reports submitted by investigators, and reports of injuries to subjects.

(2) Minutes of IRB meetings which shall be in sufficient detail to show attendance at the meetings; actions taken by the IRB; the vote on these actions including the number of members voting for, against, and abstaining; the basis for requiring changes in or disapproving research;

and a written summary of the discussion of controverted issues and their resolution.

(3) Records of continuing review activities.

(4) Copies of all correspondence between the IRB and the investigators.

(5) A list of IRB members identified by name; earned degrees; representative capacity; indications of experience such as board certifications, licenses, etc., sufficient to describe each member's chief anticipated contributions to IRB deliberations; and any employment or other relationship between each member and the institution; for example: full-time employee, part-time employee, a member of governing panel or board, stockholder, paid or unpaid consultant.

(6) Written procedures for the IRB as required by §56.108 (a) and (b).

(7) Statements of significant new findings provided to subjects, as required by §50.25.

(b) The records required by this regulation shall be retained for at least 3 years after completion of the research, and the records shall be accessible for inspection and copying by authorized representatives of the Food and Drug Administration at reasonable times and in a reasonable manner.

(c) The Food and Drug Administration may refuse to consider a clinical investigation in support of an application for a research or marketing permit if the institution or the IRB that reviewed the investigation refuses to allow an inspection under this section.

Subpart E—Administrative Actions for Noncompliance

§56.120 Lesser administrative actions.

(a) If apparent noncompliance with these regulations in the operation of an IRB is observed by an FDA investigator during an inspection, the inspector will present an oral or written summary of observations to an appropriate representative of the IRB. The Food and Drug Administration may subsequently send a letter describing the noncompliance to the IRB and to the parent institution. The agency will require that the IRB or the parent institution respond to this letter within a time period specified by FDA and describe the corrective actions that will be taken by the IRB, the institution, or both to achieve compliance with these regulations.

(b) On the basis of the IRB's or the institution's response, FDA may schedule a reinspection to confirm the adequacy of corrective actions. In addition, until the IRB or the parent institution takes appropriate corrective action, the agency may:

(1) Withhold approval of new studies subject to the requirements of this part that are conducted at the institution or reviewed by the IRB;

(2) Direct that no new subjects be added to ongoing studies subject to this part;

(3) Terminate ongoing studies subject to this part when doing so would not endanger the subjects; or

(4) When the apparent noncompliance creates a significant threat to the rights and welfare of human subjects, notify relevant State and Federal regulatory agencies and other parties with a direct interest in the agency's action of the deficiencies in the operation of the IRB.

(c) The parent institution is presumed to be responsible for the operation of an IRB, and the Food and Drug Administration will ordinarily direct any administrative action under this subpart against the institution. However, depending on the evidence of responsibility for deficiencies, determined during the investigation, the Food and Drug Administration may restrict its administrative actions to the IRB or to a component of the parent institution determined to be responsible for formal designation of the IRB.

§56.121 Disqualification of an IRB or an institution.

(a) Whenever the IRB or the institution has failed to take adequate steps to correct the noncompliance stated in the letter sent by the agency under §56.120(a), and the Commissioner of Food and Drugs determines that this noncompliance may justify the disqualification of the IRB or of the parent institution, the Commissioner will institute proceedings in accordance with the requirements for a regulatory hearing set forth in part 16.

(b) The Commissioner may disqualify an IRB or the parent institution if the Commissioner determines that:

(1) The IRB has refused or repeatedly failed to comply with any of the regulations set forth in this part; and

(2) The noncompliance adversely affects the rights or welfare of the human subjects in a clinical investigation.

(c) If the Commissioner determines that disqualification is appropriate, the Commissioner will issue an order that explains the basis for the determination and that prescribes any actions to be taken with regard to ongoing clinical research conducted under the review of the IRB. The Food and Drug Administration will send notice of the disqualification to the IRB and the parent institution. Other parties with a direct interest, such as sponsors and clinical investigators, may also be sent a notice of the disqualification. In addition, the agency may elect to publish a notice of its action in the FEDERAL REGISTER.

(d) The Food and Drug Administration will not approve an application for a research permit for a clinical investigation that is to be under the review of a disqualified IRB or that is to be conducted at a disqualified institution, and it may refuse to consider in support of a marketing permit the data from a clinical investigation that was reviewed by a disqualified IRB as conducted at a disqualified institution, unless the IRB or the parent institution is reinstated as provided in §56.123.

§56.122 Public disclosure of information regarding revocation.

A determination that the Food and Drug Administration has disqualified an institution and the administrative record regarding that determination are disclosable to the public under part 20.

§56.123 Reinstatement of an IRB or an institution.

An IRB or an institution may be reinstated if the Commissioner determines, upon an evaluation of a written submission from the IRB or institution that explains the corrective action that the institution or IRB plans to take, that the IRB or institution has provided adequate assurance that it will operate in compliance with the standards set forth in this part. Notification of reinstatement shall be provided to all persons notified under §56.121(c).

§56.124 Actions alternative or additional to disqualification.

Disqualification of an IRB or of an institution is independent of, and neither in lieu of nor a precondition to, other proceedings or actions authorized by the act. The Food and Drug Administration may, at any time, through the Department of Justice institute any appropriate judicial proceedings (civil or criminal) and any other appropriate regulatory action, in addition to or in lieu of, and before, at the time of, or after, disqualification. The agency may also refer pertinent matters to another Federal, State, or local government agency for any action that that agency determines to be appropriate.

FDA—Clinical Investigations which may be Reviewed through Expedited Review Procedures Set Forth in FDA Regulations

46 Federal Register *8980. 27 January 1981.*
Contact: *Office of Health Affairs (HFY-20), Food and Drug Administration, 5600 Fishers Lane, Rockville, Md. 20857;* Telephone: *(301) 827-1685.*

[Revision of this list is under consideration (62 *Fed. Reg.* 60604--10 November 1997). For further information, contact the Office of Health Affairs (HFY-20), Food and Drug Administration, 5600 Fishers Lane, Rockville, Md. 20857; Telephone: (301) 827-1685.—THE EDITORS]

SUMMARY

This notice contains a list of research activities which institutional review boards may review through the expedited review procedures set forth in FDA regulations for the protection of human research subjects.

SUPPLEMENTARY INFORMATION

[Cross reference to 21 *Code of Federal Regulations* 56.110 deleted.—THE EDITORS]

Notice is published in accordance with §56.110.

The agency concludes that research activities with human subjects involving no more than minimal risk and involving one or more of the following categories (carried out through standard methods), may be reviewed by an IRB through the expedited review procedure authorized in §56.110.

(1) Collection of hair and nail clippings in a non-disfiguring manner; of deciduous teeth; and of permanent teeth if patient care indicates a need for extraction.

(2) Collection of excreta and external secretions including sweat and uncannulated saliva; of placenta at delivery; and of amniotic fluid at the time of rupture of the membrane before or during labor.

(3) Recording of data from subjects who are 18 years of age or older using noninvasive procedures routinely employed in clinical practice. This category includes the use of physical sensors that are applied either to the surface of the body or at a distance and do not involve input of matter or significant amounts of energy into the subject or an invasion of the subject's privacy. It also includes such procedures as weighting, electrocardiography, electroencephalography, thermography, detection of naturally occurring radioactivity, diagnostic echography, and electroretinography. This category does not include exposure to electromagnetic radiation outside the visible range (for example, x-rays or microwaves).

(4) Collection of blood samples by venipuncture, in amounts not exceeding 450 milliliters in an eight-week period and no more often than two times per week, from subjects who are 18 years of age or older and who are in good health and not pregnant.

(5) Collection of both supra- and subgingival dental plaque and calculus, provided the procedure is not more invasive than routine prophylactic scaling of the teeth, and the process is accomplished in accordance with accepted prophylactic techniques.

(6) Voice recordings made for research purposes such as investigations of speech defects.

(7) Moderate exercise by healthy volunteers.

(8) The study of existing data, documents, records, pathological specimens, or diagnostic specimens.

(9) Research on drugs or devices for which an investigational new drug exemption or an investigational device exemption is not required.

This list will be amended as appropriate and a current list will be published periodically to the *Federal Register*.

FDA—Financial Disclosure by Clinical Investigators

21 Code of Federal Regulations 54. Last revised 2 February 1998; effective 2 February 1999.
Contact: Office of External Affairs, Food and Drug Administration (HF-60), 5600 Fishers Lane, Rockville, Md. 20857; Telephone: (301) 827-3440; Fax: (301) 594-0113.

§54.1 Purpose.

(a) The Food and Drug Administration (FDA) evaluates clinical studies submitted in marketing applications, required by law, for new human drugs and biological products and marketing applications and reclassification petitions for medical devices.

(b) The agency reviews data generated in these clinical studies to determine whether the applications are approvable under the statutory requirements. FDA may consider clinical studies inadequate and the data inadequate if, among other things, appropriate steps have not been taken in the design, conduct, reporting, and analysis of the studies to minimize bias. One potential source of bias in clinical studies is a financial interest of the clinical investigator in the outcome of the study because of the way payment is arranged (e.g., a royalty) or because the investigator has a proprietary interest in the product (e.g., a patent) or because the investigator has an equity interest in the sponsor of the covered study. This section and conforming regulations require an applicant whose submission relies in part on clinical data to disclose certain financial arrangements between sponsor(s) of the covered studies and the clinical investigators and certain interests of the clinical investigators in the product under study or in the sponsor of the covered studies. FDA will use this information, in conjunction with information about the design and purpose of the study, as well as information obtained through on-site inspections, in the agency's assessment of the reliability of the data.

§54.2 Definitions.

For the purposes of this part:

(a) *Compensation affected by the outcome of clinical studies* means compensation that could be higher for a favorable outcome than for an unfavorable outcome, such as compensation that is explicitly greater for a favorable result or compensation to the investigator in the form of an equity interest in the sponsor of a covered study or in the form of compensation tied to sales of the product, such as a royalty interest.

(b) *Significant equity interest in the sponsor of a covered study* means any ownership interest, stock options, or other financial interest whose value cannot be readily determined through reference to public prices (generally, interests in a nonpublicly traded corporation), or any equity interest in a publicly traded corporation that exceeds $50,000 during the time the clinical investigator is carrying out the study and for 1 year following completion of the study.

(c) *Proprietary interest in the tested product* means property or other financial interest in the product including, but not limited to, a patent, trademark, copyright or licensing agreement.

(d) *Clinical investigator* means any listed or identified investigator or subinvestigator who is directly involved in the treatment or evaluation of research subjects. The term also includes the spouse and each dependent child of the investigator.

(e) *Covered clinical study* means any study of a drug or device in humans submitted in a marketing application or reclassification petition subject to this part that the applicant or FDA relies on to establish that the product is effective (including studies that show equivalence to an effective product) or that make a significant contribution to the demonstration of safety. An applicant may consult with FDA as to which clinical studies constitute "covered clinical studies" for purposes of complying with financial disclosure requirements.

(f) *Significant payments of other sorts* means payments made by the sponsor of a covered study to the investigator or the institution to support activities of the investigator that have a monetary value of more than $25,000, exclusive of the costs of conducting the clinical study or other clinical studies, (e.g., a grant to fund ongoing research, compensation in the form of equipment or retainers for ongoing consultation or honoraria) during the time the clinical investigator is carrying out the study and for 1 year following the completion of the study.

(g) *Applicant* means the party who submits a marketing application to FDA for approval of a drug, device, or biologic product. The applicant is responsible for submitting the appropriate certification and disclosure statements required in this part.

(h) *Sponsor of the covered clinical study* means the party supporting a particular study at the time it was carried out.

§54.3 Scope.

The requirements in this part apply to any applicant who submits a marketing application for a human drug, biological product, or device and who submits covered clinical studies. The applicant is responsible for making the appropriate certification or disclosure statement where the applicant either contracted with one or more clinical investigators to conduct the studies or submitted studies conducted by others not under contract to the applicant.

§54.4 Certification and disclosure requirements.

For purposes of this part, an applicant must submit a list of all clinical investigators who conducted covered clinical studies to determine whether the applicant's product meets FDA's marketing requirements, identifying those clinical investigators who are full-time or part-time employees of the sponsor of each covered study. The applicant must also completely and accurately disclose or certify information concerning the financial interests of a clinical investigator who is not a full-time or part-time employee of the sponsor for each covered clinical study. Clinical investigators subject to investigational new drug or investigational device exemption regulations must provide the sponsor of the study with sufficient accurate information needed to allow subsequent disclosure or certification. The applicant is required to submit for each clinical investigator who participates in a covered study, either a certification that none of the financial arrangements described in §54.2 exist, or disclose the nature of those arrangements to the agency. Where the applicant acts with due diligence to obtain the information required in this section but is unable to do so, the applicant shall certify that despite the applicant's due diligence in attempting to obtain the information, the applicant was unable to obtain the information and shall include the reason.

(a) The applicant (of an application submitted under sections 505, 506, 507, 519(k), 513, or 515 of the Federal Food, Drug, and Cosmetic

Act, or section 351 of the Public Health Service Act) that relies in whole or in part on clinical studies shall submit, for each clinical investigator who participated in a covered clinical study, either a certification described in paragraph (a)(1) of this section or a disclosure statement described in paragraph (a)(3) of this section.

(1) Certification: The applicant covered by this section shall submit for all clinical investigators (as defined in §54.2(d)), to whom the certification applies, a completed Form FDA 3454 attesting to the absence of financial interests and arrangements described in paragraph (a)(3) of this section. The form shall be dated and signed by the chief financial officer or other responsible corporate official or representative.

(2) If the certification covers less than all covered clinical data in the application, the applicant shall include in the certification a list of the studies covered by this certification.

(3) Disclosure Statement: For any clinical investigator defined in §54.2(d) for whom the applicant does not submit the certification described in paragraph (a)(1) of this section, the applicant shall submit a completed Form FDA 3455 disclosing completely and accurately the following:

(i) Any financial arrangement entered into between the sponsor of the covered study and the clinical investigator involved in the conduct of a covered clinical trial, whereby the value of the compensation to the clinical investigator for conducting the study could be influenced by the outcome of the study;

(ii) Any significant payments of other sorts from the sponsor of the covered study, such as a grant to fund ongoing research, compensation in the form of equipment, retainer for ongoing consultation, or honoraria;

(iii) Any proprietary interest in the tested product held by any clinical investigator involved in a study;

(iv) Any significant equity interest in the sponsor of the covered study held by any clinical investigator involved in any clinical study; and

(v) Any steps taken to minimize the potential for bias resulting from any of the disclosed arrangements, interests, or payments.

(b) The clinical investigator shall provide to the sponsor of the covered study sufficient accurate financial information to allow the sponsor to submit complete and accurate certification or disclosure statements as required in paragraph (a) of this section. The investigator shall promptly update this information if any relevant changes occur in the course of the investigation or for 1 year following completion of the study.

(c) Refusal to file application. FDA may refuse to file any marketing application described in paragraph (a) of this section that does not contain the information required by this section or a certification by the applicant that the applicant has acted with due diligence to obtain the information but was unable to do so and stating the reason.

§54.5 Agency evaluation of financial interests.

(a) *Evaluation of disclosure statement*. FDA will evaluate the information disclosed under §54.4(a)(2) about each covered clinical study in an application to determine the impact of any disclosed financial interests on the reliability of the study. FDA may consider both the size and nature of a disclosed financial interest (including the potential increase in the value of the interest if the product is approved) and steps that have been taken to minimize the potential for bias.

(b) *Effect of study design*. In assessing the potential of an investigator's financial interests to bias a study, FDA will take into account the design and purpose of the study. Study designs that utilize such approaches as multiple investigators (most of whom do not have a disclosable interest), blinding, objective endpoints, or measurement of endpoints by someone other than the investigator may adequately protect against any bias created by a disclosable financial interest.

(c) *Agency actions to ensure reliability of data*. If FDA determines that the financial interests of any clinical investigator raise a serious question about the integrity of the data, FDA will take any action it deems necessary to ensure the reliability of the data including:

(1) Initiating agency audits of the data derived from the clinical investigator in question;

(2) Requesting that the applicant submit further analyses of data, e.g., to evaluate the effect of the clinical investigator's data on overall study outcome;

(3) Requesting that the applicant conduct additional independent studies to confirm the results of the questioned study; and

(4) Refusing to treat the covered clinical study as providing data that can be the basis for an agency action.

§54.6 Recordkeeping and record retention.

(a) *Financial records of clinical investigators to be retained*. An applicant who has submitted a marketing application containing covered clinical studies shall keep on file certain information pertaining to the financial interests of clinical investigators who conducted studies on which the application relies and who are not full or part-time employees of the applicant, as follows:

(1) Complete records showing any financial interest or arrangement as described in §54.4(a)(3)(i) paid to such clinical investigators by the sponsor of the covered study.

(2) Complete records showing significant payments of other sorts, as described in §54.4(a)(3)(ii), made by the sponsor of the covered clinical study to the clinical investigator.

(3) Complete records showing any financial interests held by clinical investigators as set forth in §§54.4(a)(3)(iii) and (a)(3)(iv).

(b) *Requirements for maintenance of clinical investigators' financial records.*

(1) For any application submitted for a covered product, an applicant shall retain records as described in paragraph (a) of this section for 2 years after the date of approval of the application.

(2) The person maintaining these records shall, upon request from any properly authorized officer or employee of FDA, at reasonable times, permit such officer or employee to have access to and copy and verify these records.

FDA—Reporting of Demographic Subgroups*

* *Actual title: FDA—Investigational New Drug Applications and New Drug Applications*
63 Federal Register 6854. 1998. To be codified at 21 CFR § 312.33, § 314.50. Effective 10 August 1998.
Contact: Center for Drug Evaluation and Research (HFD-1), Food and Drug Administration, Woodmont Bldg. #2, 1451 Rockville Pike, Rockville, Md. 20852; Telephone: (301) 594-5400; Fax: (301) 594-6197.

[Policy is excerpted, as indicated in the text.—THE EDITORS]

SUMMARY: The Food and Drug Administration (FDA) is amending its regulations pertaining to new drug applications (NDA's) to clearly define in the NDA format and content regulations the requirement to present effectiveness and safety data for important demographic subgroups, specifically gender, age, and racial subgroups. FDA also is amending its regulations pertaining to investigational new drug applications (IND's) to require sponsors to tabulate in their annual reports the numbers of subjects enrolled to date in clinical studies for drug and biological products according to age group, gender, and race. This action is intended to alert sponsors as early as possible to potential demographic deficiencies in enrollment that could lead to avoidable deficiencies later in the NDA submission. This rule does not address the requirements for the conduct of clinical studies and does not require sponsors to conduct additional studies or collect additional data. It also does not require the inclusion of a particular number of individuals from specific subgroups in any study or overall. The rule refers only to the presentation of data already collected.

[Introductory information has been omitted.—THE EDITORS]

SUPPLEMENTARY INFORMATION:

I. Background.

In the Federal Register of September 8, 1995 (60 FR 46794), FDA proposed to amend its NDA regulations at §314.50(d)(5) (21 CFR 314.50(d)(5)) to require sponsors of NDA's to include in their applications analyses of effectiveness and safety data for important demographic subgroups, specifically gender, age, and racial subgroups and, as appropriate, other subgroups of the population of patients being treated, such as patients with renal failure or patients with different severity levels of the disease. This action codifies expectations that FDA has described in previous guidance. FDA also proposed to amend its IND regulations at §312.33(a)(2) (21 CFR 312.33(a)(2)) to require IND sponsors to characterize in their annual reports the numbers of subjects enrolled in a clinical study for a drug or biological product according to age group, gender, and race.

FDA's regulations on NDA content and format require the clinical data section of the NDA to include, among other things, an integrated summary of the data demonstrating substantial evidence of effectiveness for the claimed indications. Evidence also is required to support the dosage and administration section of the labeling, including support for the dosage and dose interval recommended, and modifications for specific subgroups (e.g., pediatrics, geriatrics, patients with renal failure) * * * [and] an integrated summary of all available information about the safety of the drug product * * *. However, as discussed in section I of this document, a review of various agency studies and examinations of NDA data bases has revealed that in many cases (about half) data collected and submitted as part of an NDA still are not being analyzed consistently to look for differences in response to drugs among various population subgroups.

This final rule reflects the growing recognition within the agency and the health community that: (1) Different subgroups of the population may respond differently to a specific drug product and (2) although the effort should be made to look for differences in effectiveness and adverse reactions among such subgroups that effort is not being made consistently.

Since the early 1980's, FDA has been concerned about possible differences in response to drugs among subsets of the overall population, such as age, gender, or racial subsets. The agency has addressed in various ways the question of how to obtain information that would permit individualization of therapy. Evaluation of potential differences among demographic subsets requires that individuals from these subsets be included in studies and that analyses to seek differences in response be carried out. During the past decade, FDA has encouraged demographic subgroup analyses in various guidance documents and other regulatory actions. FDA also has examined the extent of participation of patient subgroups in drug development programs.

In 1983 and again in 1989, FDA examined the relative numbers of individuals in NDA databases from two important demographic subgroups, women and the elderly (58 FR 39406 at 39412, July 22, 1993). The agency found that, in general, the proportions of women and men included in the clinical trials were similar to the respective proportions of women and men who had the diseases for which the drugs were being studied, taking into account the age range of the population studied. The agency also found that, in general, the elderly were reasonably well represented in clinical trials.

In a study of drugs approved during the period 1988 through 1991, conducted by the General Accounting Office (GAO) entitled "FDA Needs to Ensure More Study of Gender Differences in Prescription Drug Testing," GAO/HRD-93-17, women were found to typically represent a majority of patients in NDA data bases of drugs used to treat conditions more common, or more commonly treated, in women, and a minority, generally a sizable one, in tests of drugs for conditions that occur predominantly in males in the age range usually included in the clinical trials. Analysis also showed that, even when enough women are included in testing, trial data often are not analyzed to determine if women's responses to a drug differed from those of men. The study also showed that the participation of women took place primarily during the later phases of drug development.

FDA's first formal encouragement to analyze population subsets appeared in the 1985 version of §314.50, in which paragraph (d)(5)(v) (integrated summary of effectiveness) called for evidence to support modifications of dosage for specific subgroups, e.g., pediatrics, geriatrics, patients with renal failure. In 1988, the agency developed the "Guideline for the Format and Content of the Clinical and Statistical Sections of New Drug Applications" to explain aspects of the 1985 revision of §314.50. In that guidance, FDA discussed the importance of analyzing data from population subsets within NDA data bases to look for differences in effectiveness and adverse reactions to drugs. The guidance addressed the importance of subgroup analyses of both safety and effectiveness and of analyses in subgroups other than those mentioned in the regulations.

In 1989, after several years of public discussion, the agency addressed the need to develop information on the elderly in a guideline entitled "Guideline for the Study of Drugs Likely to be Used in the Elderly." The guideline provides guidance regarding the inclusion of elderly patients in clinical trials and the assessment of clinical and pharmacokinetic differences between older and younger patients. In addition, the agency issued a final rule in the Federal Register of August 27, 1997 (62 FR 45313), entitled "Specific Requirements on Content and Format of Labeling for Human Prescription Drugs; Addition of Geriatric Use' Subsection in the Labeling," which, among other things, requires the inclusion of a subsection on geriatric use in the labeling of drugs.

In the **Federal Register** of July 22, 1993 (58 FR 39406), FDA published a guideline entitled "Guideline for the Study and Evaluation of Gender Differences in the Clinical Evaluation of Drugs." The guideline provides guidance on FDA's expectations regarding including both men and women in drug development, the need to analyze clinical data by gender, the assessment of potential pharmacokinetic differences between genders, and the conduct of specific additional studies in women, where indicated. The 1993 guideline also describes how concerns about the adequacy of data on the effects of drugs in women have arisen within the context of an increasing awareness of the need to individualize treatment in the face of the wide variety of demographic, disease-related, and individual patient-related factors that can lead to different responses in subsets of the population. Optimal use of drugs requires identification of these factors so that appropriate adjustments in dose, concomitant therapy, or monitoring can be made.

In 1993, FDA also published guidance on the agency's use of the refusal-to-file (RTF) option. The guidance states that the agency generally can exercise its RTF authority under 21 CFR 314.101(d)(3) if there is "inadequate evaluation for safety and/or effectiveness of the population intended to use the drug, including pertinent subsets, such as gender, age, and racial subsets * * *."

Despite repeated agency encouragement in both regulations and guidance, FDA and GAO have found that the analysis of effectiveness and safety data in relevant population subgroups, including age, gender, and racial subgroups, is not being carried out consistently. This rule makes the need for these subgroup analyses completely clear.

II. Highlights of the Final Rule.

This final rule revises current IND annual report regulations at §312.33(a)(2) to require that the number of subjects entered to date into a clinical study for drug or biological products be tabulated by age group, gender, and race. This action is intended to alert sponsors and the FDA as early as possible to potential demographic deficiencies in enrollment that could lead to avoidable deficiencies in the NDA submission.

The current wording of NDA content and format regulations at §314.50(d)(5) does not fully reflect the need to present in the NDA the safety and effectiveness data by subgroup. It also omits specific mention of some important subgroups, including those of gender and race. Therefore, this final rule also revises NDA content and format regulations at §314.50(d)(5) to require that effectiveness and safety data be presented for demographic subgroups including age group, gender, and race and, when appropriate, other subgroups of the population of patients treated, such as patients with renal failure, or patients with different severity levels of the disease.

In response to comments received on the proposed rule, the agency is making minor changes to the wording to clarify the intent of the rule. In §312.33(a)(2), "characterized" has been changed to "tabulated" to make clear that the numbers of the subjects enrolled to date in clinical studies need only be counted and listed in tabular form in annual reports according to age group, gender, and race. No analysis of data is being required for annual reports. Some comments asked for clarification of the phrase, "as appropriate" in §314.50(d)(5)(v) and (d)(5)(vi). When data suggest a different response to a drug product in a subgroup other than age group, gender, or race, it is appropriate to present the data for such a subgroup in the NDA. Examples of such subgroups include subjects who seem to respond differently because of a concomitant disease, renal failure, or different severity level of the disease. The agency is changing the phrase "as appropriate" to "when appropriate." The phrase "and shall identify any modifications of dose or dose interval needed for specific subgroups" has been added to the end of the second sentence in §314.50(d)(5)(v) to restore wording that was removed in the proposal. The agency believes that the reinsertion of this wording makes the intent of the rule clearer than the proposed wording.

FDA believes this final rule will help focus drug sponsors' attention throughout the drug development process on the enrollment in clinical drug trials of subjects representing the various subgroups of the population expected to use the drug being tested once it is approved and marketed. Although enrollment generally is broad and reflects the population with the disease, this is not always the case. The rule also will help sponsors better evaluate in their NDA's the safety and efficacy profiles of drugs for various subgroups. Because this rule clarifies agency expectations about the analysis of data that should be included in the NDA to evaluate possible differences in response among gender, age, and racial subgroups, an RTF action based on failure to carry out such critical analyses will be less likely.

[Sections III through VI have been omitted.—THE EDITORS]

Therefore, under the Federal Food, Drug, and Cosmetic Act, the Public Health Service Act, and under authority delegated to the Commissioner of Food and Drugs, 21 CFR parts 312 and 314 are amended as follows:

PART 312—INVESTIGATIONAL NEW DRUG APPLICATION

1. The authority citation for 21 CFR part 312 continues to read as follows:

Authority: 21 U.S.C. 321, 331, 351, 352, 353, 355, 356, 357, 371; 42 U.S.C. 262.

2. Section 312.33 is amended by revising paragraph (a)(2) to read as follows:

Sec. 312.33 Annual reports

* * * * *

(a) * * *

(2) The total number of subjects initially planned for inclusion in the study; the number entered into the study to date, tabulated by age group, gender, and race; the number whose participation in the study was completed as planned; and the number who dropped out of the study for any reason.

* * * * *

PART 314—APPLICATIONS FOR FDA APPROVAL TO MARKET A NEW DRUG OR AN ANTIBIOTIC DRUG

3. The authority citation for 21 CFR part 314 continues to read as follows:

Authority: 21 U.S.C. 321, 331, 351, 352, 353, 355, 356, 357, 371, 374, 379e.

4. Section 314.50 is amended by revising the second sentence and adding two new sentences after the second sentence in paragraph (d)(5)(v), and by adding two new sentences after the first sentence in paragraph (d)(5)(vi)(a) to read as follows:

§314.50—Content and format of an application

* * * * *
   (d) * * *
     (5) * * *
       (v) * * * Evidence is also required to support the dosage and administration section of the labeling, including support for the dosage and dose interval recommended. The effectiveness data shall be presented by gender, age, and racial subgroups and shall identify any modifications of dose or dose interval needed for specific subgroups. Effectiveness data from other subgroups of the population of patients treated, when appropriate, such as patients with renal failure or patients with different levels of severity of the disease, also shall be presented.
       (vi) * * *
  (a) * * * The safety data shall be presented by gender, age, and racial subgroups. When appropriate, safety data from other subgroups of the population of patients treated also shall be presented, such as for patients with renal failure or patients with different levels of severity of the disease. * * *

* * * * *

[Filing information has been omitted.—*The Editors*]

NIH—Guidelines on the Inclusion of Women and Minorities as Subjects in Clinical Research

59 Federal Register 14508. 28 March 1994.
Contact: Office of Research on Women's Health, National Institutes of Health, Building 1, Room 201, 9000 Rockville Pike, Bethesda, Md. 20892; Telephone: (301) 402-1770; Fax: (301) 402-1798.

I. Introduction

This document sets forth guidelines on the inclusion of women and members of minority groups and their subpopulations in clinical research, including clinical trials, supported by the National Institutes of Health (NIH). For the purposes of this document, clinical research is defined as NIH-supported biomedical and behavioral research involving human subjects. These guidelines, implemented in accordance with section 492B of the Public Health Service Act, added by the NIH Revitalization Act of 1993, Public Law. (Pub.L.) 103-43, supersede and strengthen the previous policies, NIH/ADAMHA Policy Concerning the Inclusion of Women in Study Populations, and ADAMHA/NIH Policy Concerning the Inclusion of Minorities in Study Populations, published in the NIH GUIDE FOR GRANTS AND CONTRACTS, 1990.

The 1993 guidelines continue the 1990 guidelines with three major additions. The new policy requires that, in addition to the continuing inclusion of women and members of minority groups in all NIH-supported biomedical and behavioral research involving human subjects, the NIH must:

• Ensure that women and members of minorities and their subpopulations are included in all human subject research;
• For Phase III clinical trials, ensure that women and minorities and their subpopulations must be included such that valid analyses of differences in intervention effect can be accomplished;

- Not allow cost as an acceptable reason for excluding these groups; and,
- Initiate programs and support for outreach efforts to recruit these groups into clinical studies.

Since a primary aim of research is to provide scientific evidence leading to a change in health policy or a standard of care, it is imperative to determine whether the intervention or therapy being studied affects women or men or members of minority groups and their subpopulations differently. To this end, the guidelines published here are intended to ensure that all future NIH-supported biomedical and behavioral research involving human subjects will be carried out in a manner sufficient to elicit information about individuals of both genders and the diverse racial and ethnic groups and, in the case of clinical trials, to examine differential effects on such groups. Increased attention, therefore, must be given to gender, race, and ethnicity in earlier stages of research to allow for informed decisions at the Phase III clinical trial stage.

These guidelines reaffirm NIH's commitment to the fundamental principles of inclusion of women and racial and ethnic minority groups and their subpopulations in research. This policy should result in a variety of new research opportunities to address significant gaps in knowledge about health problems that affect women and racial/ethnic minorities and their subpopulations.

The NIH recognizes that issues will arise with the implementation of these guidelines and thus welcomes comments. During the first year of implementation, NIH will review the comments, and consider modifications, within the scope of the statute, to the guidelines.

II. Background

The NIH Revitalization Act of 1993, PL 103-43, signed by President Clinton on June 10, 1993, directs the NIH to establish guidelines for inclusion of women and minorities in clinical research. This guidance shall include guidelines regarding—

(A) the circumstances under which the inclusion of women and minorities as subjects in projects of clinical research is inappropriate * * *;

(B) the manner in which clinical trials are required to be designed and carried out * * *; and

(C) the operation of outreach programs * * * 492B(d)(1)

The statute states that

> In conducting or supporting clinical research for the purposes of this title, the Director of NIH shall * * * ensure that—
> A. women are included as subjects in each project of such research; and
> B. members of minority groups are included in such research. 492B(a)(1)

The statute further defines "clinical research" to include "clinical trials" and states that

> In the case of any clinical trial in which women or members of minority groups will be included as subjects, the Director of NIH shall ensure that the trial is designed and carried out in a manner sufficient to provide for valid analysis of whether the variables being studied in the trial affect women or members of minority groups, as the case may be, differently than other subjects in the trial. 492B(C)

Specifically addressing the issue of minority groups, the statute states that

> The term "minority group" includes subpopulations of minority groups. The Director of NIH shall, through the guidelines established * * * defines the terms "minority group" and "subpopulation" for the purposes of the preceding sentence. 492B(g)(2)

The statute speaks specifically to outreach and states that

> The Director of NIH, in consultation with the Director of the Office of Research of Women's Health and the Director of the Office of Research on Minority Health, shall conduct or support outreach programs for the recruitment of women and members of minority groups as subjects in the projects of clinical research. 492B(a)(2)

The statute includes a specific provision pertaining to the cost of clinical research and, in particular clinical trials.

(A) (i) In the case of a clinical trial, the guidelines shall provide that the costs of such inclusion in the trial is (sic) not a permissible consideration in determining whether such inclusion is inappropriate. 492B(d)(2)
(ii) In the case of other projects of clinical research, the guidelines shall provide that the costs of such inclusion in the project is (sic) not a permissible consideration in determining whether such inclusion is inappropriate unless the data regarding women or members of minority groups, respectively, that would be obtained in such project (in the event that such inclusion were required) have been or are being obtained through other means that provide data of comparable quality. 492B(d)(2)

Exclusions to the requirement for inclusion of women and minorities are stated in the statute, as follows:

The requirements established regarding women and members of minority groups shall not apply to the project of clinical research if the inclusion, as subjects in the project, of women and members of minority groups, respectively

(1) Is inappropriate with respect to the health of the subjects;
(2) Is inappropriate with respect to the purpose of the research; or
(3) Is inappropriate under such other circumstances as the Director of NIH may designate. 492B(b)
(B) In the case of a clinical trial, the guidelines may provide that such inclusion in the trial is not required if there is substantial scientific data demonstrating that there is no significant difference between
(i) The effects that the variables to be studied in the trial have on women or members of minority groups, respectively; and
(ii) The effects that variables have on the individuals who would serve as subjects in the trial in the event that such inclusion were not required. 492B(d)(2)

III. Policy

A. Research Involving Human Subjects

It is the policy of NIH that women and members of minority groups and their subpopulations must be included in all NIH-supported biomedical and behavioral research projects involving human subjects, unless a clear and compelling rationale and justification establishes to the satisfaction of the relevant Institute/Center Director that inclusion is inappropriate with respect to the health of the subjects or the purpose of the research. Exclusion under other circumstances may be made by the Director, NIH, upon the recommendation of a Institute/Center Director based on a compelling rationale and justification. Cost is not an acceptable reason for exclusion except when the study would duplicate data from other sources. Women of childbearing potential should not be routinely excluded from participation in clinical research. All NIH-supported biomedical and behavioral research involving human subjects is defined as clinical research. This policy applies to research subjects of all ages.

The inclusion of women and members of minority groups and their subpopulations must be addressed in developing a research design appropriate to the scientific objectives of the study. The research plan should describe the composition of the proposed study population in terms of gender and racial/ethnic group, and provide a rationale for selection of such subjects. Such a plan should contain a description of the proposed outreach programs for recruiting women and minorities as participants.

B. Clinical Trials

Under the statute, when a Phase III clinical trial (see Definitions, Section V-A) is proposed, evidence must be reviewed to show whether or not clinically important gender or race/ethnicity differences in the intervention effect are to be expected. This evidence may include, but is not limited to, data derived from prior animal studies, clinical observations, metabolic studies, genetic studies, pharmacology studies, and observational, natural history, epidemiology and other relevant studies.

As such, investigators must consider the following when planning a Phase III clinical trial for NIH support.

- If the data from prior studies strongly indicate the existence of significant differences of clinical or public health importance in intervention effect among subgroups (gender and/or racial/ethnic subgroups), the primary question(s) to be addressed by the proposed Phase III trial and the design of that trial must specifically accommodate this. For example, if men and women are thought to respond differently to an intervention, then the Phase III trial must be designed to answer two separate primary questions, one for men and the other for women, with adequate sample size for each.
- If the data from prior studies strongly support no significant differences of clinical or public health importance in intervention effect between subgroups, then gender or race/ethnicity will not be required as subject selection criteria. However, the inclusion of gender or racial/ethnic subgroups is still strongly encouraged.
- If the data from prior studies neither support strongly nor negate strongly the existence of significant differences of clinical or public health importance in intervention effect between subgroups, then the Phase III trial will be required to include sufficient and appropriate entry of gender and racial/ethnic subgroups, so that valid analysis of the intervention effect in subgroups can be performed. However, the trial will not be required to provide high statistical power for each subgroup.

Cost is not an acceptable reason for exclusion of women and minorities from clinical trials.

C. Funding

NIH funding components will not award any grant, cooperative agreement or contract or support any intramural project to be conducted or funded in Fiscal Year 1995 and thereafter which does not comply with this policy. For research awards that are covered by this policy, awardees will report annually on enrollment of women and men, and on the race and ethnicity of research participants.

IV. Implementation

A. Date of Implementation

This policy applies to all applications/proposals and intramural projects to be submitted on and after June 1, 1994 (the date of full implementation) seeking Fiscal Year 1995 support. Projects funded prior to June 10, 1993, must still comply with the 1990 policy and report annually on enrollment of subjects using gender and racial/ethnic categories as required in the Application for Continuation of a Public Health Service Grant (PHS Form 2590), in contracts and in intramural projects.

B. Transition Policy

NIH-supported biomedical and behavioral research projects involving human subjects, with the exception of Phase III clinical trial projects as discussed below, that are awarded between June 10, 1993, the date of enactment, and September 30, 1994, the end of Fiscal Year 1994, shall be subject to the requirements of the 1990 policy and the annual reporting requirements on enrollment using gender and racial/ethnic categories.

For all Phase III clinical trial projects proposed between June 10, 1993 and June 1, 1994, and those awarded between June 10, 1993 and September 30, 1994, Institute/Center staff will examine the applications/proposals, pending awards, awards and intramural projects to determine if the study was developed in a manner consistent with the new guidelines. If it is deemed inconsistent, NIH staff will contact investigators to discuss approaches to accommodate the new policy. Administrative actions may be needed to accommodate or revise the pending trials. Institutes/Centers may need to consider initiating a complementary activity to address any gender or minority representation concerns.

The NIH Director will determine whether the Phase III clinical trial being considered during this transition is in compliance with this policy, whether acceptable modifications have been made, or whether the Institute/Center will initiate a complementary activity that addresses the gender or minority representation concerns. Pending awards will not be funded without this determination.

Solicitations issued by the NIH planned for release after the date of publication of the guidelines in the *Federal Register* will include the new requirements.

C. Roles and Responsibilities

While this policy applies to all applicants for NIH-supported biomedical and behavioral research involving human subjects, certain individuals and groups have special roles and responsibilities with regard to the adoption and implementation of these guidelines.

The NIH staff will provide educational opportunities for the extramural and intramural community concerning this policy; monitor its implementation during the development, review, award and conduct of research; and manage the NIH research portfolio to address the policy.

1. Principal Investigators

Principal investigators should assess the theoretical and/or scientific linkages between gender, race/ethnicity, and their topic of study. Following this assessment, the principal investigator and the applicant institution will address the policy in each application and proposal, providing the required information on inclusion of women and minorities and their subpopulations in research projects, and any required justifications for exceptions to the policy. Depending on the purpose of the study, NIH recognizes that a single study may not include all minority groups.

2. Institutional Review Boards (IRBs)

As the IRBs implement the guidelines, described herein, for the inclusion of women and minorities and their subpopulations, they must also implement the regulations for the protection of human subjects as described in title 45 CFR part 46, "Protection of Human Subjects." They should take into account the Food and Drug Administration's "Guidelines for the Study and Evaluation of Gender Differences in the Clinical Evaluation of Drugs," Vol. 58 *Federal Register* 39406.

3. Peer Review Groups

In conducting peer review for scientific and technical merit, appropriately constituted initial review groups (including study sections), technical evaluation groups, and intramural review panels will be instructed, as follows:

- To evaluate the proposed plan for the inclusion of minorities and both genders for appropriate representation or to evaluate the proposed justification when representation is limited or absent,
- To evaluate the proposed exclusion of minorities and women on the basis that a requirement for inclusion is inappropriate with respect to the health of the subjects,
- To evaluate the proposed exclusion of minorities and women on the basis that a requirement for inclusion is inappropriate with respect to the purpose of the research,

- To determine whether the design of clinical trials is adequate to measure differences when warranted,
- To evaluate the plans for recruitment/outreach for study, participants, and
- To include these criteria as part of the scientific assessment and assigned score.

4. NIH Advisory Councils

In addition to its current responsibilities for review of projects where the peer review groups have raised questions about the appropriate inclusion of women and minorities, the Advisory Council/Board of each Institute/Center shall prepare biennial reports, for inclusion in the overall NIH Director's biennial report, describing the manner in which the Institute/Center has complied with the provisions of the statute.

5. Institute/Center Directors

Institute/Center Directors and their staff shall determine whether: (a) The research involving human subjects, (b) the Phase III clinical trials, and (c) the exclusions meet the requirements of the statute and these guidelines.

6. NIH Director

The NIH Director may approve, on a case-by-case basis, the exclusion of projects, as recommended by the Institute/Center Director, that may be inappropriate to include within the requirements of these guidelines on the basis of circumstances other than the health of the subjects, the purpose of the research, or costs.

7. Recruitment Outreach by Extramural and Intramural Investigators

Investigators and their staff(s) are urged to develop appropriate and culturally sensitive outreach programs and activities commensurate with the goals of the study. The objective should be to actively recruit the most diverse study population consistent with the purposes of the research project. Indeed, the purpose should be to establish a relationship between the investigator(s) and staff(s) and populations and community(ies) of interest such that mutual benefit is derived for participants in the study. Investigator(s) and staff(s) should take precautionary measures to ensure that ethical concerns are clearly noted, such that there is minimal possibility of coercion or undue influence in the incentives or rewards offered in recruiting into or retaining participants in studies. It is also the responsibility of the IRBs to address these ethical concerns.

Furthermore, while the statute focuses on recruitment outreach, NIH staff underscore the need to appropriately retain participants in clinical studies, and thus, the outreach programs and activities should address both recruitment and retention.

To assist investigators and potential study participants, NIH staff have prepared a notebook, "NIH Outreach Notebook On the Inclusion of Women and Minorities in Biomedical and Behavioral Research." The notebook addresses both recruitment and retention of women and minorities in clinical studies, provides relevant references and case studies, and discusses ethical issues. It is not intended as a definitive text on this subject, but should assist investigators in their consideration of an appropriate plan for recruiting and retaining participants in clinical studies. The notebook is expected to be available early in 1994.

8. Educational Outreach by NIH to Inform the Professional Community

NIH staff will present the new guidelines to investigators, IRB members, peer review groups, and Advisory Councils in a variety of public educational forums.

9. Applicability to Foreign Research Involving Human Subjects

For foreign awards, the NIH policy on inclusion of women in research conducted outside the U.S. is the same as that for research conducted in the U.S.

However, with regard to the population of the foreign country, the definition of the minority groups may be different than in the U.S. If there is scientific rationale for examining subpopulation group differences within the foreign population, investigators should consider designing their studies to accommodate these differences.

V. Definitions

Throughout the section of the statute pertaining to the inclusion of women and minorities, terms are used which require definition for the purpose of implementing these guidelines. These terms, drawn directly from the statute, are defined below.

A. Clinical Trial

For the purpose of these guidelines, a "clinical trial" is a broadly based prospective Phase III clinical investigation, usually involving several hundred or more human subjects, for the purpose of evaluating an experimental intervention in comparison with a standard or control intervention or comparing two or more existing treatments. Often the aim of such investigation is to provide evidence leading to a scientific basis for consideration of a change in health policy or standard of care. The definition includes pharmacologic, non-pharmacologic, and behavioral interventions given for disease prevention, prophylaxis, diagnosis, or therapy. Community trials and other population-based intervention trials are also included.

B. Research Involving Human Subjects

All NIH-supported biomedical and behavioral research involving human subjects is defined as clinical research under this policy. Under this policy, the definition of human subjects in title 45 CFR part 46, the Department of Health and Human Services regulations for the protection of human subjects applies: "Human subject means a living individual about whom an investigator (whether professional or student) conducting research obtains: (1) Data through intervention or interaction with the individual, or (2) identifiable private information." These regulations specifically address the protection of human subjects from research risks. It should be noted that there are research areas (Exemptions 1-6) that are exempt from these regulations. However, under these guidelines, NIH-supported biomedical and behavioral research projects involving human subjects which are exempt from the human subjects regulations should still address the inclusion of women and minorities in their study design. Therefore, all biomedical and behavioral research projects involving human subjects will be evaluated for compliance with this policy.

C. Valid Analysis

The term "valid analysis" means an unbiased assessment. Such an assessment will, on average, yield the correct estimate of the difference in outcomes between two groups of subjects. Valid analysis can and should be conducted for both small and large studies. A valid analysis does not need to have a high statistical power for detecting a stated effect. The principal requirements for ensuring a valid analysis of the question of

interest are:
- Allocation of study participants of both genders and from different racial/ethnic groups to the intervention and control groups by an unbiased process such as randomization,
- Unbiased evaluation of the outcome(s) of study participants, and
- Use of unbiased statistical analyses and proper methods of inference to estimate and compare the intervention effects among the gender and racial/ethnic groups.

D. Significant Difference

For purposes of this policy, a "significant difference" is a difference that is of clinical or public health importance, based on substantial scientific data. This definition differs from the commonly used "statistically significant difference," which refers to the event that, for a given set of data, the statistical test for a difference between the effects in two groups achieves statistical significance. Statistical significance depends upon the amount of information in the data set. With a very large amount of information, one could find a statistically significant, but clinically small difference that is of very little clinical importance. Conversely, with less information one could find a large difference of potential importance that is not statistically significant.

E. Racial and Ethnic Categories

1. Minority Groups

A minority group is a readily identifiable subset of the U.S. population which is distinguished by either racial, ethnic, and/or cultural heritage.

The Office of Management and Budget (OMB) Directive No. 15 defines the minimum standard of basic racial and ethnic categories, which are used below. NIH has chosen to continue the use of these definitions because they allow comparisons to many national data bases, especially national health data bases. Therefore, the racial and ethnic categories described below should be used as basic guidance, cognizant of the distinction based on cultural heritage.

American Indian or Alaskan Native: A person having origins in any of the original peoples of North America, and who maintains cultural identification through tribal affiliation or community recognition.

Asian or Pacific Islander: A person having origins in any of the original peoples of the Far East, Southeast Asia, the Indian subcontinent, or the

Pacific Islands. This area includes, for example, China, India, Japan, Korea, the Philippine Islands and Samoa.

Black, not of Hispanic Origin: A person having origins in any of the black racial groups of Africa.

Hispanic: A person of Mexican, Puerto Rican, Cuban, Central or South American or other Spanish culture or origin, regardless of race.

2. Majority Group

White, not of Hispanic Origin: A person having origins in any of the original peoples of Europe, North Africa, or the Middle East.

NIH recognizes the diversity of the U.S. population and that changing demographics are reflected in the changing racial and ethnic composition of the population. The terms "minority groups" and "minority subpopulations" are meant to be inclusive, rather than exclusive, of differing racial and ethnic categories.

3. Subpopulations

Each minority group contains subpopulations which are delimited by geographic origins, national origins and/or cultural differences. It is recognized that there are different ways of defining and reporting racial and ethnic subpopulation data. The subpopulation to which an individual is assigned depends on self-reporting of specific racial and ethnic origin. Attention to subpopulations also applies to individuals of mixed racial and/or ethnic parentage. Researchers should be cognizant of the possibility that these racial/ethnic combinations may have biomedical and/or cultural implications related to the scientific question under study.

F. Outreach Strategies

These are outreach efforts by investigators and their staff(s) to appropriately recruit and retain populations of interest into research studies. Such efforts should represent a thoughtful and culturally sensitive plan of outreach and generally include involvement of other individuals and organizations relevant to the populations and communities of interest, e.g., family, religious organizations, community leaders and informal gatekeepers, and public and private institutions and organizations. The objective is to establish appropriate lines of communication and cooperation to build mutual trust and cooperation such that both the study and the participants benefit from such collaboration.

G. Research Portfolio

Each Institute and Center at the NIH has its own research portfolio, i.e., its "holdings" in research grants, cooperative agreements, contracts and intramural studies. The Institute or Center evaluates the research awards in its portfolio to identify those areas where there are knowledge gaps or which need special attention to advance the science involved. NIH may consider funding projects to achieve a research portfolio reflecting diverse study populations. With the implementation of this new policy, there will be a need to ensure that sufficient resources are provided within a program to allow for data to be developed for a smooth transition from basic research to Phase III clinical trials that meet the policy requirements.

VI. Discussion-Issues in Scientific Plans and Study Designs

A. Issues in Research Involving Human Subjects

The biomedical and behavioral research process can be viewed as a stepwise process progressing from discovery of new knowledge through research in the laboratory, research involving animals, research involving human subjects, validation of interventions through clinical trials, and broad application to improve the health of the public.

All NIH-supported biomedical and behavioral research involving human subjects is defined broadly in this guidance as clinical research. This is broader than the definition provided in the 1990 NIH Guidance and in many program announcements, requests for applications, and requests for proposals since 1990.

The definition was broadened because of the need to obtain data about minorities and both genders early in the research process when hypotheses are being formulated, baseline data are being collected, and various measurement instruments and intervention strategies are being developed. Broad inclusion at these early stages of research provides valuable information for designing broadly based clinical trials, which are a subset of studies under the broad category of research studies.

The policy on inclusion of minorities and both genders applies to all NIH-supported biomedical and behavioral research involving human subjects so that the maximum information may be obtained to understand the implications of the research findings on the gender or minority group.

Investigators should consider the types of information concerning gender and minority groups which will be required when designing future Phase III clinical trials, and try to obtain it in their earlier stages of research involving human subjects. NIH recognizes that the understanding of health problems and conditions of different U.S. populations may require attention to socioeconomic differences involving occupation, education, and income gradients.

B. Issues in Clinical Trials

The statute requires appropriate representation of subjects of different gender and race/ethnicity in clinical trials so as to provide the opportunity for detecting major qualitative differences (if they exist) among gender and racial/ethnic subgroups and to identify more subtle differences that might, if warranted, be explored in further specifically targeted studies. Other interpretations may not serve as well the health needs of women, minorities, and all other constituencies.

Preparatory to any Phase III clinical trial, certain data are typically obtained. Such data are necessary for the design of an appropriate Phase III trial and include observational clinical study data, basic laboratory (i.e. *in vitro* and animal) data, and clinical, physiologic, pharmacokinetic, or biochemical data from Phase I and Phase II studies. Genetic studies, behavioral studies, and observational, natural history, and epidemiological studies may also contribute data.

It is essential that data be reviewed from prior studies on a diverse population, that is, in subjects of both genders and from different racial/ethnic groups. These data must be examined to determine if there are significant differences of clinical or public health importance observed between the subgroups.

While data from prior studies relating to possible differences among intervention effects in different subgroups must be reviewed, evidence of this nature is likely to be less convincing than that deriving from the subgroup analyses that can be performed in usual-sized Phase III trials. This is because the evidence from preliminary studies is likely to be of a more indirect nature (e.g. based on surrogate endpoints), deriving from uncontrolled studies (e.g. non-randomized Phase II trials), and based on smaller numbers of subjects than in Phase III secondary analyses. For this reason, it is likely that data from preliminary studies will, in the majority of cases, neither clearly reveal significant differences of clinical or public health importance between subgroups of patients, nor strongly negate them.

In these cases, Phase III trials should still have appropriate gender and racial/ethnic representation, but they would not need to have the large sample sizes necessary to provide a high statistical power for detecting differences in intervention effects among subgroups. Nevertheless, analyses of subgroup effects must be conducted and comparisons between the subgroups must be made. Depending on the results of these analyses, the results of other relevant research, and the results of meta-analyses of clinical trials, one might initiate subsequent trials to examine more fully these subgroup differences.

C. Issues Concerning Appropriate Gender Representation

The "population at risk" may refer to only one gender where the disease, disorders, or conditions are gender specific. In all other cases, there should be approximately equal numbers of both sexes in studies of populations or sub-populations at risk, unless different proportions are appropriate because of the known prevalence, incidence, morbidity, mortality rates, or expected intervention effect.

D. Issues Concerning Appropriate Representation of Minority Groups and Subpopulations in All Research Involving Human Subjects Including Phase III Clinical Trials

While the inclusion of minority subpopulations in research is a complex and challenging issue, it nonetheless provides the opportunity for researchers to collect data on subpopulations where knowledge gaps exist. Researchers must consider the inclusion of subpopulations in all stages of research design. In meeting this objective, they should be aware of concurrent research that addresses specific subpopulations, and consider potential collaborations which may result in complementary subpopulation data.

At the present time, there are gaps in baseline and other types of data necessary for research involving certain minority groups and/or subpopulations of minority groups. In these areas, it would be appropriate for researchers to obtain such data, including baseline data, by studying a single minority group.

It would also be appropriate for researchers to test survey instruments, recruitment procedures, and other methodologies used in the majority or other population(s) with the objective of assessing their feasibility, applicability, and cultural competence/relevance to a particular minority group or subpopulation. This testing may provide data on the validity of the methodologies across groups. Likewise, if an intervention has been tried in the majority population and not in certain minority groups, it would be appropriate to assess the intervention effect on a single minority group and compare the effect to that obtained in the majority population. These types of studies will advance scientific research and assist in closing knowledge gaps.

A complex issue arises over how broad or narrow the division into different subgroups should be, given the purpose of the research. Division into many racial/ethnic subgroups is tempting in view of the cultural and biological differences that exist among these groups and the possibility that some of these differences may in fact impact in some way upon the scientific question. Alternatively, from a practical perspective, a limit has to be placed on the number of such subgroups that can realistically be studied in detail for each intervention that is researched. The investigator should clearly address the rationale for inclusion or exclusion of subgroups in terms of the purpose of the research. Emphasis should be placed upon inclusion of subpopulations in which the disease manifests itself or the intervention operates in an appreciable different way. Investigators should report the subpopulations included in the study.

An important issue is the appropriate representation of minority groups in research, especially in geographical locations which may have limited numbers of racial/ethnic population groups available for study. The investigator must address this issue in terms of the purpose of the research, and other factors, such as the size of the study, relevant characteristics of the disease, disorder or condition, and the feasibility of making a collaboration or consortium or other arrangements to include minority groups. A justification is required if there is limited representation. Peer reviewers and NIH staff will consider the justification in their evaluations of the project.

NIH interprets the statute in a manner that leads to feasible and real improvements in the representativeness of different racial/ethnic groups in research and places emphasis on research in those subpopulations that are disproportionately affected by certain diseases or disorders.

CDC/ATSDR—Policy on the Inclusion of Women and Racial and Ethnic Minorities in Externally Awarded Research

60 Federal Register *47947*. *15 September 1995*.
Contact: *Centers for Disease Control and Prevention, 1600 Clifton Road N.E., Atlanta, Ga. 30333; Telephone: (404) 639-3311.*

I. Introduction

The Centers for Disease Control and Prevention (CDC) is committed to protecting the health of all people regardless of their sex, race, ethnicity, national origin, religion, sexual orientation, socioeconomic status, or other characteristics. To the extent that participation in research offers direct benefits to the participants, underrepresentation of certain population subgroups denies them the opportunity to benefit. Moreover, for purposes of generalizing study results, investigators must include the widest possible range of population groups.

A growing body of evidence indicates that the health conditions and needs of women are different from those of men. Some health conditions are unique to women and others are more prevalent in women. For some illnesses, there are marked distinctions, not only in onset and progression of disease, but also in the preventive, treatment and educational approaches necessary to combat them in women. Furthermore, initial entry into the health care system may be different for some subgroups of women, such as low-income and uninsured women. Lesbians may also enter the health care system differently because they may be less likely to access prevention services, like cancer screening, because they may not utilize family planning services. The Public Health Service Task Force on Women's Health Issues published a report in 1987 stating that it is becoming more important to note the environmental, economic, social, and demographic characteristics that influence a woman's health status. The Task Force focused on the direct and indirect effects these factors could have on the status of a woman's health and noted that when a woman is "outside the normal range of societal expectations,'" that is, she is of a racial, ethnic or cultural minority or if she is physically or mentally disabled, her health status is potentially at greater risk. These basic observations are not always recognized or reflected in study protocols and proposals.

The disparity in health outcomes between majority and some racial and ethnic minority groups is now well documented. Although some minority populations, e.g., some Asian groups, have better overall health status than non-Hispanic whites, many racial and ethnic minority populations have dramatically shorter life expectancy, higher morbidity rates and inadequate access to quality health care. The Secretary for the Department of Health and Human Services' Task Force on Black and Minority Health issued a report in 1985 noting the underrepresentation of racial and ethnic minorities in research. This underrepresentation has resulted in significant gaps in knowledge about the health of racial and ethnic minority populations and their responses to interventions.

II. Definitions

A. Human Subjects

Under this policy, the definition of human subjects in title 45 CFR part 46, the Department of Health and Human Services regulations for the protection of human subjects, applies: "Human subject means a living individual about whom an investigator conducting research obtains (1) data through intervention or interaction with the individual or (2) identifiable private information."

B. Research

Under this policy, the definition of research in title 45 CFR part 46, the Department of Health and Human Services regulations for the protection of human subjects, applies: "Research means a systematic investigation, including research development, testing and evaluation, designed to develop or contribute to generalizable knowledge." All proposed research involving human subjects and conducted using CDC funding will be evaluated for compliance with this policy, including those projects that are exempt from Institutional Review Board (IRB) review (as specified in title 45 CFR part 46). However, nothing in this policy is intended to require IRB review of protocols which otherwise would be exempt. This policy applies to all CDC externally awarded research regardless of the mechanism of financial support (e.g., grant, cooperative agreement, contract, purchase order, etc.). This policy does not apply to those projects in which the investigator has no control over the composition of the study population (e.g., cohort studies in which the population has been previously selected, or research to follow-up outbreak investigations).

C. Racial and Ethnic Categories.

1. Minority Groups.

This policy shall comply with the Office of Management and Budget (OMB) Directive No. 15, and any subsequent revisions to the Directive. OMB Directive No. 15 defines the minimum standard of basic racial and ethnic categories. Despite limitations (as outlined in the Public Health Reports "Papers from the CDC/ATSDR Workshop on the Use of Race and Ethnicity in Public Health Surveillance"), these categories are useful because they allow comparisons among many national data bases, especially Bureau of the Census and national health data bases. Therefore, the racial and ethnic categories described below should be used as basic minimum guidance, cognizant of their limitations.

American Indian or Alaskan Native: A person having origins in any of the original peoples of North America, and who maintains cultural identification through tribal affiliation or community recognition

Asian or Pacific Islander: A person having origins in any of the original peoples of Far East, Southeast Asia, the Indian subcontinent, or the Pacific Islands. This area includes, for example, China, India, Japan, Korea, the Philippine Islands, and Samoa

Black, not of Hispanic Origin: A person having origins in any of the black racial groups of Africa

Hispanic: A person of Mexican, Puerto Rican, Cuban, Central or South American or other Spanish culture or origin, regardless of race.

2. Majority Group.

White, not of Hispanic Origin: A person having origins in any of the original peoples of Europe, North Africa, or the Middle East.

While investigators should focus primary attention on the above categories, CDC recognizes the diversity of the population. For example, Blacks describe themselves in several different ways, including African-

American, Caribbean (Haitian, Jamaican, West Indian, Trinidadian), etc. Native Hawaiians have expressed the desire to be considered a separate racial/ethnic category exclusive of the current Asian/Pacific Islander designation. Therefore, investigators are encouraged to investigate national or geographic origin or other cultural factors (e.g., customs, beliefs, religious practices) in studies of race and ethnicity, and their relationship to health problems. Furthermore, since race, ethnicity, and cultural heritage may serve as markers for other important characteristics or conditions associated with a health problem or outcome, investigators should actively seek to identify these other characteristics or conditions.

III. Policy

Research Involving Human Subjects
Applicant institutions must ensure that women and racial and ethnic minority populations are appropriately represented in their proposals for research.

Women and members of racial and ethnic minority groups should be adequately represented in all CDC-supported studies involving human subjects, unless a clear and compelling rationale and justification establishes to the satisfaction of CDC that inclusion is inappropriate or clearly not feasible. Although this policy does not apply to studies when the investigator cannot control the race, ethnicity, and sex of subjects, women and racial and ethnic minority populations must not be routinely and/or arbitrarily excluded from such investigations.

In addition, women of childbearing potential should also not be routinely and/or arbitrarily excluded from participation even though there are ethical/risk issues to consider for inclusion and exclusion. Information on adverse differences in outcome or risk profiles for pregnant women may be reason for exclusion. Therefore, pregnancy status may need to be determined prior to enrollment for some studies and, if necessary, during an intervention to safeguard the participants' health.

IV. Guidance for Applicant Institution Investigators and Decision Makers in Complying with this Policy

A. General

In determining whether special efforts should be made to set specific enrollment goals for women and members of racial and ethnic minority groups, or whether to design special studies to specifically address health problems in such populations, principal investigators should consider the following points:

- Is the disease or condition under study unique to, or is it relatively rare in men, women or one or more racial and/or ethnic minority populations?
- What are the characteristics of the population to which the protocol results will be applied? Does it include both men and women? Does it include specific racial and ethnic minority populations?
- Are there scientific reasons to anticipate significant differences between men and women and among racial and ethnic minority populations with regard to the hypothesis under investigation?
- Are there study design or recruitment limitations in the protocol that could result, unnecessarily, in underrepresentation of one sex or certain racial and ethnic minority populations?
- Could such underrepresentation cause an adverse impact on the generalizability and application of results?
- Is the underrepresentation correctable?
- Does racial and ethnic characterization of study subjects serve a bona fide purpose or might it serve only to stigmatize a group?

Inclusion of women and/or racial and ethnic minority groups in research can be addressed either by including all appropriate groups in one single study or by conducting multiple studies. In general, protocols and proposals for support of studies involving human subjects should employ a design with sex and/or minority representation appropriate to the scientific objectives. It is not an automatic requirement that the study design provide sufficient statistical power to answer the questions posed for men and women and racial and ethnic groups separately; however, whenever there are scientific reasons to anticipate differences between men and women and/or racial and ethnic groups, with regard to the hypothesis under investigation, investigators should include an evaluation of these sex and minority group differences in the study proposal. If adequate inclusion of one sex and/or minority group is impossible or inappropriate with respect to the purpose of the proposed study, or if in the only study population available, there is a disproportionate representation of one sex or minority/majority group, the rationale for the study population must be well explained and justified. The cost of inclusion of women and/or racial and ethnic minority groups shall not be a permissible consideration for exclusion from a given study unless data regarding women and/or racial and ethnic minority groups have been or will be obtained through other means that provide data of comparable quality. Acceptable reasons for exclusion are as follows:

(1) Inclusion is inappropriate with respect to the health of the subjects;
(2) Inclusion is inappropriate with respect to the purpose of the study;
(3) Substantial scientific evidence indicates there is no significant difference between the effects that the variables to be studied have on women and/or racial and ethnic minority groups;
(4) Substantial scientific data already exist on the effects that variables have on the excluded population; and
(5) Inclusion is inappropriate under other circumstances as determined by CDC.

In each protocol or proposal, the composition and rationale for inclusion of the proposed study population must be described in terms of sex and racial and ethnic group. Sex and racial and ethnic characteristics, conditions, and other relevant issues should be addressed in developing a study design and sample size appropriate for the scientific objectives of the investigation. The proposal should contain a description of proposed outreach programs, if necessary, for recruiting women and racial and ethnic minorities as participants. Investigators must facilitate the informed consent process by promoting open and free communication with the study participants. Investigators must seek to understand cultural and linguistic variables inherent in the population to be enrolled, and procedures must be established to ensure appropriate translation of the consent document whenever necessary.

B. Studies of Public Health Interventions

Investigators must consider the following when planning an intervention trial or a clinical trial:

• If the data from prior studies strongly indicate the existence of significant differences of clinical or public health importance in intervention effect between the sexes or among racial and ethnic populations, the primary question(s) to be addressed by the scientific investigation and the design of that study must specifically accommodate the difference(s). For example, if men, women, and racial and ethnic minority groups are thought to respond differently to an intervention, then the study should be designed to answer separate primary questions that apply to men, women, and/or specific racial and ethnic groups with adequate sample size for each.

• If the data from prior studies strongly support no significant differences of clinical or public health importance in intervention effect between subgroups, then sex and race and ethnicity are not required as subject selection criteria; however, the inclusion of sex and racial and ethnic subgroups is still strongly encouraged.

- If the data from prior studies neither support nor negate the existence of significant differences of clinical or public health importance in intervention effect, then the study should include sufficient and appropriate male and female and racial and ethnic minority populations so that valid analysis of the intervention effect in each subgroup can be performed.

- If women of childbearing potential are to be included and if there is reason to suspect that adverse events may occur in pregnant women, pregnancy status should be determined prior to enrollment.

V. Implementation

A. Date of Implementation

This policy applies for all CDC externally awarded research projects submitted in response to CDC Program Announcements (Requests for Assistance) and solicitations (Requests for Proposals) announced on or after October 1, 1995.

B. Roles and Responsibilities

Certain individuals and groups have special roles and responsibilities with regard to the implementation of these guidelines.

1. Applicant Institution Investigators

Applicant institution investigators should assess the theoretical and/or scientific linkages between sex, race and ethnicity and their topic of study. Following this assessment, the applicant institution investigator will address the policy in each protocol, application and proposal, providing the required information on inclusion of women and minorities, and any required justifications for exclusions of any groups.

2. CDC Technical/Peer Review Groups

In conducting technical/peer review of contract, grant, or cooperative agreement applications for scientific and technical merit, CDC Center/Institute/Office (C/I/O) Directors will ensure that CDC technical/peer review groups, to the extent possible, include women and racial and ethnic minorities, and will do the following:*

- Evaluate the proposed plan for the inclusion of both sexes and racial and ethnic minority populations for appropriate representation.
- Evaluate the appropriateness of the proposed justification when representation is limited or absent.
- Determine whether the design of the study is adequate to measure differences when warranted.
- Evaluate the plans for recruitment and outreach for study participants including whether the process of establishing partnerships with community(ies) and recognition of mutual benefits will be documented.
- Include these criteria as part of the technical assessment and assign a score.

3. CDC Center/Institute/Office Directors

CDC C/I/O Directors are responsible for ensuring that CDC externally awarded research involving human subjects meets the requirements of these guidelines. CDC C/I/O Directors will also inform externally awarded investigators concerning this policy and monitor its implementation during the development, review, award, and conduct of research.

4. CDC Institutional Review Boards (IRBs)

CDC IRBs are expected to consider whether CDC investigators have adequately addressed the inclusion of women and racial and ethnic minorities, in research protocols that require CDC IRB approval, as an additional criterion for IRB approval.

C. External Award Consideration

CDC project officers shall design their Requests for Contracts and Requests for Assistance in compliance with this policy. CDC C/I/O Directors shall ensure this policy is fully considered and implemented prior to the release of the Request for Contract and Request for Assistance

---

* C/I/O Directors may waive this requirement if it is clearly inappropriate or clearly not feasible.

to the CDC Procurement and Grants Office. CDC funding components will not award any grant, cooperative agreement, or contract for external research projects announced on or after October 1, 1995, and thereafter which does not comply with this policy.

D. Recruitment Outreach by Externally Awarded Investigators

Externally awarded investigators and their staff(s) are urged to develop appropriate and culturally sensitive outreach programs and activities commensurate with the goals of the research. The purpose should be to establish a relationship between the investigator(s), populations, and community(ies) of interest so that mutual benefit is achieved by all groups participating in the study. Investigators should document the process for establishing a partnership with the community(ies) and the mutual benefits of the study and ensure that any factors (e.g., educational level, nonproficiency in English, low socioeconomic status) are accounted for and handled appropriately. In addition, investigator(s) and staff should ensure that ethical concerns are clearly noted and enforced, such that there is minimal possibility of coercion or undue influence in the incentives or rewards offered in recruiting into or retaining participants in scientific studies.

E. Dissemination of Research Results

Externally awarded investigators are urged to make special efforts to disseminate relevant research results to the communities who participated in the studies and to the affected populations, especially racial and ethnic minority populations that may have cultural, language, and socioeconomic barriers to the easy receipt of such information.

VI. Evaluation

CDC Inclusion Review Committee Responsibility and Members

A CDC Inclusion Review Committee (IRC) with representatives from the CDC Office of the Associate Director for Science, the CDC Office of the Associate Director for Minority Health, and the CDC Office of the Associate Director for Women's Health will review any questions, issues, or comments pertaining to this policy and recommend necessary changes or modifications to the Director, CDC. This committee will meet regularly to review compliance with this policy and evaluate the impact of this policy on research activities at CDC. The CDC IRC may periodically conduct random audits of research protocols to assess compliance with this policy.

NIH—Guidelines on the Inclusion of Women and Minorities as Subjects in Clinical Research

59 Federal Register *14508. 28 March 1994.*
Contact: *Office of Research on Women's Health, National Institutes of Health, Building 1, Room 201, 9000 Rockville Pike, Bethesda, Md. 20892; Telephone: (301) 402-1770; Fax: (301) 402-1798.*

See "NIH—Guidelines on the Inclusion of Women and Minorities as Subjects in Clinical Research," page 115, above.

CDC/ATSDR—Policy on the Inclusion of Women and Racial and Ethnic Minorities in Externally Awarded Research

60 Federal Register 47947. 15 September 1995.
Contact: Centers for Disease Control and Prevention, 1600 Clifton Road N.E., Atlanta, Ga. 30333; Telephone: (404) 639-3311.

See "CDC/ATSDR—Policy on the Inclusion of Women and Racial and Ethnic Minorities in Externally Awarded Research," page 132, above.

FDA—Guideline for the Study and Evaluation of Gender Differences in the Clinical Evaluation of Drugs

58 Federal Register 39409. 22 July 1993.
Contact: CDER Executive Secretariat Staff (HFD-6), Food and Drug Administration, 5600 Fishers Lane, Rockville, Md. 20857; Telephone: (301) 594-6470; Fax: (301) 594-5493.

[Introductory material omitted.—THE EDITORS]

The new guideline replaces that portion of the 1977 guideline that dealt with women of childbearing potential. The text of the new guideline on gender differences follows:

Guideline for the Study and Evaluation of Gender Differences in the Clinical Evaluation of Drugs

Introduction

The Food and Drug Administration (FDA) advises that this guideline represents its current position on the clinical evaluation of drugs in humans. This guideline does not bind the agency, and it does not create or confer any rights, privileges, or benefits for or on any person.

The principles of inclusion of women in product development programs and analysis of subgroup differences outlined in this guideline also apply to the clinical development of biological products and medical devices.

A. Abstract

In general, drugs should be studied prior to approval in subjects representing the full range of patients likely to receive the drug once it is marketed. Although in most cases, drugs behave qualitatively similarly in demographic (age, gender, race) and other (concomitant illness, concomitant drugs) subsets of the population, there are many quantitative differences, for example, in dose-response, maximum size of effect, or in the risk of an adverse effect. Recognition of these differences can allow safer and more effective use of drugs. Rarely, there may be qualitative differences as well. It is very difficult to evaluate subsets of the overall population as thoroughly as the entire population, but sponsors are expected to include a full range of patients in their studies, carry out appropriate analyses to evaluate potential subset differences in the patients they have studied, study possible pharmacokinetic differences in patient subsets, and carry out targeted studies to look for subset pharmacodynamic differences that are especially probable, are suggested by existing data, or that would be particularly important if present. Study protocols are also expected to provide appropriate precautions against exposure of fetuses to potentially dangerous agents. Where animal data suggest possible effects on fertility, such as decreased sperm production, special studies in humans may be needed to evaluate this potential toxicity.

B. Underlying Observations

The following general observations and conclusions underlie the recommendations set forth in this guideline:

1. Variations in response to drugs, including gender-related differences, can arise from pharmacokinetic differences (that is, differences in the way a drug is absorbed, excreted, metabolized, or distributed) or pharmacodynamic differences (i.e., differences in the pharmacologic or clinical response to a given concentration of the drug in blood or other tissue).

2. Gender-related variations in drug effects may arise from a variety of sources. Some of these are specifically associated with gender, e.g., effects of endogenous and exogenous hormones. Gender-related differences could also arise, however, not because of gender itself, but because the frequency of a particular characteristic (for example, small size, concomitant hepatic disease or concomitant drug treatment, or habits such as smoking or alcohol use) is different in one gender, even if the

characteristic could occur in either gender. Proper management of patients of both genders thus requires that physicians know all the factors that can influence the pharmacokinetics of a drug. An approach is needed that will identify, better than is done at present, all such factors. Understanding how various factors may influence pharmacokinetics will greatly enhance our ability to treat people of both genders appropriately.

3. For a number of practical and theoretical reasons, the evaluation of possible gender-related differences in response should focus initially on the evaluation of potential pharmacokinetic differences. Such differences are known to occur and have, at least to date, been documented much more commonly than documented pharmacodynamic differences. Moreover, pharmacokinetic differences are relatively easy to discover. Once reliable assays are developed for a drug and its metabolites (such assays are now almost always available early in the development of the drug), techniques exist for readily assessing gender-related or other subgroup-related pharmacokinetic differences.

Formal pharmacokinetic studies are one means of answering questions about specific subgroups. Another approach is use of a screening procedure, a "pharmacokinetic screen" (see "Guideline for the Study of Drugs Likely To Be Used in the Elderly"). [This document is reproduced in this volume. See "FDA—Guideline for the Study of Drugs Likely to be Used in the Elderly," page 176 below.—*THE EDITORS*] Carried out in phase 2 and 3 study populations, the pharmacokinetic screen can greatly increase the ability to detect pharmacokinetic differences in subpopulations and individuals, even when these differences are not anticipated. By obtaining a small number of blood concentration determinations in most or all phase 2 and 3 patients, it is possible to detect markedly atypical pharmacokinetic behavior in individuals, such as that seen in slow metabolizers of debrisoquin, and pharmacokinetic differences in population subsets, such as patient populations of different gender, age, or race, or patients with particular underlying diseases or concomitant therapy. The screen may also detect interactions of two factors, e.g., gender and age. The relative ease with which pharmacokinetic differences among population subsets can be assessed contrasts with the difficulty of developing precise relationships of most clinical responses to drug dose or to the drug concentration in blood, which usually would be necessary when attempting to observe pharmacodynamic differences between two subgroups.

A final reason to emphasize pharmacokinetic evaluation is that it must be carried out to allow relevant assessment of pharmacodynamic differences or relationships. Assessing pharmacodynamic differences between groups or establishing blood concentration-response relationships is possible only when groups are reasonably well matched for blood concentrations. Enough pharmacokinetic data must therefore be available to permit the investigator to administer doses that will produce comparable blood concentrations in the subsets to be compared or, alternatively, to compare subsets that have been titrated to similar blood concentrations.

4. The number of documented gender-related pharmacodynamic differences of clinical consequence is at this time small, and conducting formal pharmacodynamic/effectiveness studies to detect them may be difficult, depending on the clinical endpoint. Such studies are therefore not routinely necessary. The by-gender analyses of clinical trials that include both men and women, however, which are specified in the 1988 guideline entitled "Guideline for the Format and Content of the Clinical and Statistical Sections of New Drug Applications" are not difficult to carry out. Particularly if these analyses are accompanied by blood concentration data for each patient, they can detect important pharmacodynamic/effectiveness differences related to gender.

C. Inclusion of Both Genders in Clinical Studies

The patients included in clinical studies should, in general, reflect the population that will receive the drug when it is marketed. For most drugs, therefore, representatives of both genders should be included in clinical trials in numbers adequate to allow detection of clinically significant gender-related differences in drug response. Although it may be reasonable to exclude certain patients at early stages because of characteristics that might make evaluation of therapy more difficult (e.g., patients on concomitant therapy), such exclusions should usually be abandoned as soon as possible in later development so that possible drug-drug and drug-disease interactions can be detected. Thus, for example, there is ordinarily no good reason to exclude women using oral contraceptives or estrogen replacement from trials. Rather, they should be included and differences in responses between them and patients not on such therapy examined. Pharmacokinetic interaction studies (or screening approaches) to look at the interactions resulting from concomitant treatment are also useful.

Ordinarily, patients of both genders should be included in the same trials. This permits direct comparisons of genders within the studies. In some cases, however, it may be appropriate to conduct studies in a single gender, e.g., to evaluate the effects of phases of the menstrual cycle on drug response.

Although clinical or pharmacokinetic data collected during phase 3 may provide evidence of gender-related differences, these data may become available too late to affect the design and dose-selection of the pivotal controlled trials. Inclusion of women in the earliest phases of clinical development, particularly in early pharmacokinetic studies, is, therefore, encouraged so that information on gender differences may be used to refine the design of later trials. Note that the strict limitation on the participation of women of childbearing potential in phase 1 and early phase 2 trials that was imposed by the 1977 guideline entitled, "General Considerations for the Clinical Evaluation of Drugs," has been eliminated.

There is no regulatory or scientific basis for routine exclusion of women from bioequivalence trials. For certain drugs, however, it is possible that changes during the menstrual cycle may lead to increases in intra-subject variability. Such variability could be related to hormonally-mediated differences in metabolism or changes in fluid balance. Sponsors of bioequivalence trials are encouraged to examine available information on the pharmacokinetics and metabolism of the test drugs and related drugs to determine whether there is a basis for concern about variability in pharmacokinetics during the menstrual cycle. Where the available information does raise such concern, measures could be taken to reduce or adjust for variability, e.g., administration of each drug at the same phase of the menstrual cycle, or inclusion of larger numbers of subjects. Sponsors are encouraged to collect data that will contribute to the understanding of the relationship between hormonal variations and pharmacokinetics.

D. Analysis of Effectiveness and Adverse Effects by Gender

FDA's guideline on the clinical and statistical sections of NDA's calls for analyses of effectiveness, adverse effects, dose-response, and, if available, blood concentration-response, to look for the influence of: (1) Demographic features, such as age, gender, and race; and (2) other patient characteristics, such as body size (body weight, lean body mass, fat mass), renal, cardiac, and hepatic status, the presence of concomitant illness, and concomitant use of drugs, including ethanol and nicotine. Analyses to detect the influence of gender should be carried out both for individual studies and in the overall integrated analyses of effectiveness and safety. Such analyses of subsets with particular characteristics can be expected to detect only relatively large gender-related differences, but in general, small differences are not likely to be clinically important. The results of these analyses may suggest the need for more formal dose-response or blood concentration-response studies in men or women or in other patient subsets. Depending on the magnitude of the findings, or their potential importance (e.g., they would be more important for drugs with low therapeutic indices), these additional studies might be carried out before or after marketing.

E. Defining the Pharmacokinetics of the Drug in Both Genders

The factors most commonly having a major influence on pharmacokinetics are renal function, for drugs excreted by the kidney, and hepatic function, for drugs that are metabolized or excreted by the liver; these should be assessed directly as part of the ordinary development of drugs. The pharmacokinetic effects of other subgroup characteristics such as gender can be assessed either by a pharmacokinetic screening approach, described in the 1989 guideline entitled, "Guideline for the Study of Drugs Likely to Be Used in the Elderly," or by formal pharmacokinetic studies in specific gender or age groups.

Using either a specific pharmacokinetic study or a pharmacokinetic screen, the pharmacokinetics of a drug should be defined for both genders. In general, it is prudent to at least carry out pilot studies to look for major pharmacokinetic differences before conducting definitive controlled trials, so that differences that might lead to the need for different dosing regimens can be detected. Such studies are particularly important for drugs with low therapeutic indices, where the smaller average size of women alone might be sufficient to require modified dosing, and for drugs with nonlinear kinetics, where the somewhat higher milligram per kilogram dose caused by a woman's smaller size could lead to much larger differences in blood concentrations of drug. Gender may interact with other factors, such as age. The potential for such interactions should be explored.

Three pharmacokinetic issues related specifically to women that should be considered during drug development are: (1) The influence of menstrual status on the drug's pharmacokinetics, including both comparisons of premenopausal and postmenopausal patients and examination of within-cycle changes; (2) the influence of concomitant supplementary estrogen treatment or systemic contraceptives (oral contraceptives, long-acting progesterone) on the drug's pharmacokinetics;

and (3) the influence of the drug on the pharmacokinetics of oral contraceptives. Which of these influences should be studied in a given case would depend on the drug's excretion, metabolism, and other pharmacokinetic properties, and on the steepness of the dose-response curve.

Hormonal status during the menstrual cycle may affect plasma volume and the volume of distribution (and thus clearance) of drugs. The activity of certain cytochrome P450 enzymes may be influenced by estrogen levels and, in addition, microsomal oxidation by these enzymes may decline in the elderly more in men than women. Oral contraceptives can cause decreased clearance of drugs (e.g., imipramine, diazepam, chlordiazepoxide, phenytoin, caffeine, and cyclosporine), apparently by inhibiting hepatic metabolism. They can also increase clearance by inducing drug metabolism (e.g., of acetaminophen, salicylic acid, morphine, lorazepam, temazepam, oxazepam, and clofibrate). Certain anticonvulsants (carbamazepine, phenytoin) and antibiotics (rifampin) can reduce the effectiveness of oral contraceptives. Many of the potential interactions of gender and gender-related characteristics (e.g., use of oral contraceptives) can be evaluated with the pharmacokinetic screen. In some cases, specific studies will be needed.

F. Gender-Specific Pharmacodynamic Studies

Because documented demographic differences in pharmacodynamics appear to be relatively uncommon, it is not necessary to carry out separate pharmacodynamic/effectiveness studies in each gender routinely. Evidence of such differences should be sought, however, in the data from clinical trials by carrying out the by-gender analyses suggested in the guideline on the clinical and statistical sections of NDA's. These analyses of controlled trials involving both genders are probably more likely to detect differences than studies carried out entirely in one gender. Experience has shown that gender differences can be detected with such approaches.

If the by-gender analyses suggest gender-related differences, or if such differences would be particularly important, e.g., because of a low therapeutic index, additional formal studies to seek such differences between the blood level-response curves of men and women should be conducted. Even in the absence of a particular concern based on the by-gender analyses, if there is a readily measured pharmacodynamic endpoint, such as blood pressure or rate of ventricular premature beats, and if there are good dose-response data for the overall population, it should be feasible to develop dose response data from population subsets (e.g., both genders) in the critical clinical trials.

G. Precautions in Clinical Trials Including Women of Childbearing Potential

Appropriate precautions should be taken in clinical studies to guard against inadvertent exposure of fetuses to potentially toxic agents and to inform subjects and patients of potential risk and the need for precautions. In all cases, the informed consent document and investigator's brochure should include all available information regarding the potential risk of fetal toxicity. If animal reproductive toxicity studies are complete, the results should be presented, with some explanation of their significance in humans. If these studies have not been completed, other pertinent information should be provided, such as a general assessment of fetal toxicity in drugs with related structures or pharmacologic effects. If no relevant information is available, the informed consent should explicitly note the potential for fetal risk.

In general, it is expected that reproductive toxicity studies will be completed before there is large-scale exposure of women of childbearing potential, i.e., usually by the end of phase 2 and before any expanded access program is implemented.

Except in the case of trials intended for the study of drug effects during pregnancy, clinical protocols should also include measures that will minimize the possibility of fetal exposure to the investigational drug. These would ordinarily include providing for the use of a reliable method of contraception (or abstinence) for the duration of drug exposure (which may exceed the length of the study), use of pregnancy testing (beta HCG) to detect unsuspected pregnancy prior to initiation of study treatment, and timing of studies (easier with studies of short duration) to coincide with, or immediately follow, menstruation. Female subjects should be referred to a study physician or other counselor knowledgeable in the selection and use of contraceptive approaches.

H. Potential Effects on Fertility

Where abnormalities of reproductive organs or their function (spermatogenesis or ovulation) have been observed in experimental animals, the decision to include patients of reproductive age in a clinical study should be based on a careful risk-benefit evaluation, taking into account the nature of the abnormalities, the dosage needed to induce them, the consistency of findings in different species, the severity of the illness being treated, the potential importance of the drug, the availability of alternative treatment, and the duration of therapy. Where patients of reproductive potential are included in studies of drugs showing reproductive toxicity in animals, the clinical studies should include appropriate monitoring and/or laboratory studies to allow detection of these effects. Long-term follow-up will usually be needed to evaluate the effects of such drugs in humans.

DHHS—Additional Protections Pertaining to Research, Development, and Related Activities Involving Fetuses, Pregnant Women, and Human In Vitro Fertilization

45 Code of Federal Regulations 46, Subpart B. Last revised 1 June 1994. Contact: Office for Protection from Research Risks, 6100 Executive Blvd., Suite 3B01, MSC-7507, Rockville, Md. 20892-7507; Telephone: (301) 402-5913.

[Revision of this policy is under consideration. See 63 *Federal Register* 27793—20 May 1998.—THE EDITORS]

§46.201 Applicability.

(a) The regulations in this subpart are applicable to all Department of Health and Human Services grants and contracts supporting research, development, and related activities involving: (1) The fetus; (2) pregnant women; and (3) human *in vitro* fertilization.

(b) Nothing in this subpart shall be construed as indicating that compliance with the procedures set forth herein will in any way render inapplicable pertinent State or local laws bearing upon activities covered by this subpart.

(c) The requirements of this subpart are in addition to those imposed under the other subparts of this part.

§46.202 Purpose.

It is the purpose of this subpart to provide additional safeguards in reviewing activities to which this subpart is applicable to assure that they conform to appropriate ethical standards and relate to important societal needs.

§46.203 Definitions.

As used in this subpart:

(a) *Secretary* means the Secretary of Health and Human Services and any other officer or employee of the Department of Health and Human Services to whom authority has been delegated.

(b) *Pregnancy* encompasses the period of time from confirmation of implantation (through any of the presumptive signs of pregnancy, such as missed menses, or by a medically acceptable pregnancy test), until expulsion or extraction of the fetus.

(c) *Fetus* means the product of conception from the time of implantation (as evidenced by any of the presumptive signs of pregnancy, such as missed menses, or a medically acceptable pregnancy test), until a determination is made, following expulsion or extraction of the fetus, that it is viable.

(d) *Viable* as it pertains to the fetus means being able, after either spontaneous or induced delivery, to survive (given the benefit of available medical therapy) to the point of independently maintaining heart beat and respiration. The Secretary may from time to time, taking into account medical advances, publish in the Federal Register guidelines to assist in determining whether a fetus is viable for purposes of this subpart. If a fetus is viable after delivery, it is a premature infant.

(e) *Nonviable fetus* means a fetus *ex utero* which, although living, is not viable.

(f) *Dead fetus* means a fetus *ex utero* which exhibits neither heartbeat, spontaneous respiratory activity, spontaneous movement of voluntary muscles, nor pulsation of the umbilical cord (if still attached).

(g) *In vitro fertilization* means any fertilization of human ova which occurs outside the body of a female, either through admixture of donor human sperm and ova or by any other means.

§ 46.204 Ethical Advisory Boards.

[As of the date of this volume's publication, there are no constituted Ethical Advisory Boards.—*THE EDITORS*]

(a) One or more Ethical Advisory Boards shall be established by the Secretary. Members of these board(s) shall be so selected that the board(s) will be competent to deal with medical, legal, social, ethical, and related issues and may include, for example, research scientists, physicians, psychologists, sociologists, educators, lawyers, and ethicists, as well as representatives of the general public. No board member may be a regular, full-time employee of the Department of Health and Human Services.

(b) At the request of the Secretary, the Ethical Advisory Board shall render advice consistent with the policies and requirements of this part as to ethical issues, involving activities covered by this subpart, raised by individual applications or proposals. In addition, upon request by the Secretary, the Board shall render advice as to classes of applications or proposals and general policies, guidelines, and procedures.

(c) A Board may establish, with the approval of the Secretary, classes of applications or proposals which: (1) Must be submitted to the Board; or (2) need not be submitted to the Board. Where the Board so establishes a class of applications or proposals which must be submitted, no application or proposal within the class may be funded by the Department or any component thereof until the application or proposal has been reviewed by the Board and the Board has rendered advice as to its acceptability from an ethical standpoint.

§46.205 Additional duties of the Institutional Review Boards in connection with activities involving fetuses, pregnant women, or human in vitro fertilization.

(a) In addition to the responsibilities prescribed for Institutional Review Boards under Subpart A of this part, the applicant's or offeror's Board shall, with respect to activities covered by this subpart, carry out the following additional duties:

(1) Determine that all aspects of the activity meet the requirements of this subpart;

(2) Determine that adequate consideration has been given to the manner in which potential subjects will be selected, and adequate provision has been made by the applicant or offeror for monitoring the actual informed consent process (e.g., through such mechanisms, when appropriate, as participation by the Institutional Review Board or subject advocates in: (i) Overseeing the actual process by which individual consents required by this subpart are secured either by approving induction of each individual into the activity or verifying, perhaps through sampling, that approved procedures for induction of individuals into the activity are being followed; and (ii) monitoring the progress of the activity

and intervening as necessary through such steps as visits to the activity site and continuing evaluation to determine if any unanticipated risks have arisen); and

(3) Carry out such other responsibilities as may be assigned by the Secretary.

(b) No award may be issued until the applicant or offeror has certified to the Secretary that the Institutional Review Board has made the determinations required under paragraph (a) of this section and the Secretary has approved these determinations, as provided in Sec. 46.120 of Subpart A of this part.

(c) Applicants or offerors seeking support for activities covered by this subpart must provide for the designation of an Institutional Review Board, subject to approval by the Secretary, where no such Board has been established under Subpart A of this part.

§46.206 General limitations.

(a) No activity to which this subpart is applicable may be undertaken unless:

(1) Appropriate studies on animals and nonpregnant individuals have been completed;

(2) Except where the purpose of the activity is to meet the health needs of the mother or the particular fetus, the risk to the fetus is minimal and, in all cases, is the least possible risk for achieving the objectives of the activity;

(3) Individuals engaged in the activity will have no part in: (i) Any decisions as to the timing, method, and procedures used to terminate the pregnancy; and (ii) determining the viability of the fetus at the termination of the pregnancy; and

(4) No procedural changes which may cause greater than minimal risk to the fetus or the pregnant woman will be introduced into the procedure for terminating the pregnancy solely in the interest of the activity.

(b) No inducements, monetary or otherwise, may be offered to terminate pregnancy for purposes of the activity.

§46.207 Activities directed toward pregnant women as subjects.

(a) No pregnant woman may be involved as a subject in an activity covered by this subpart unless: (1) The purpose of the activity is to meet the health needs of the mother and the fetus will be placed at risk only to the minimum extent necessary to meet such needs; or (2) the risk to the fetus is minimal.

(b) An activity permitted under paragraph (a) of this section may be conducted only if the mother and father are legally competent and have given their informed consent after having been fully informed regarding possible impact on the fetus, except that the father's informed consent need not be secured if: (1) The purpose of the activity is to meet the health needs of the mother; (2) his identity or whereabouts cannot reasonably be ascertained; (3) he is not reasonably available; or (4) the pregnancy resulted from rape.

§46.208 Activities directed toward fetuses in utero as subjects.

(a) No fetus in utero may be involved as a subject in any activity covered by this subpart unless: (1) The purpose of the activity is to meet the health needs of the particular fetus and the fetus will be placed at risk only to the minimum extent necessary to meet such needs; or (2) the risk to the fetus imposed by the research is minimal and the purpose of the activity is the development of important biomedical knowledge which cannot be obtained by other means.

(b) An activity permitted under paragraph (a) of this section may be conducted only if the mother and father are legally competent and have given their informed consent, except that the father's consent need not be secured if: (1) His identity or whereabouts cannot reasonably be ascertained; (2) he is not reasonably available; or (3) the pregnancy resulted from rape.

§46.209 Activities directed toward fetuses ex utero, including nonviable fetuses, as subjects.

(a) Until it has been ascertained whether or not a fetus ex utero is viable, a fetus ex utero may not be involved as a subject in an activity covered by this subpart unless:

(1) There will be no added risk to the fetus resulting from the activity, and the purpose of the activity is the development of important biomedical knowledge which cannot be obtained by other means; or

(2) The purpose of the activity is to enhance the possibility of survival of the particular fetus to the point of viability.

(b) No nonviable fetus may be involved as a subject in an activity covered by this subpart unless:

(1) Vital functions of the fetus will not be artificially maintained;

(2) Experimental activities which of themselves would terminate the heartbeat or respiration of the fetus will not be employed; and

(3) The purpose of the activity is the development of important biomedical knowledge which cannot be obtained by other means.

(c) In the event the fetus ex utero is found to be viable, it may be included as a subject in the activity only to the extent permitted by and in accordance with the requirements of other subparts of this part.

(d) An activity permitted under paragraph (a) or (b) of this section may be conducted only if the mother and father are legally competent and have given their informed consent, except that the father's informed consent need not be secured if: (1) His identity or whereabouts cannot reasonably be ascertained; (2) he is not reasonably available; or (3) the pregnancy resulted from rape.

§46.210 Activities involving the dead fetus, fetal material, or the placenta.

Activities involving the dead fetus, mascerated fetal material, or cells, tissue, or organs excised from a dead fetus shall be conducted only in accordance with any applicable State or local laws regarding such activities.

§46.211 Modification or waiver of specific requirements.

Upon the request of an applicant or offeror (with the approval of its Institutional Review Board), the Secretary may modify or waive specific requirements of this subpart, with the approval of the Ethical Advisory Board after such opportunity for public comment as the Ethical Advisory Board considers appropriate in the particular instance. In making such decisions, the Secretary will consider whether the risks to the subject are so outweighed by the sum of the benefit to the subject and the importance of the knowledge to be gained as to warrant such modification or waiver and that such benefits cannot be gained except through a modification or waiver. Any such modifications or waivers will be published as notices in the FEDERAL REGISTER.

Ban on Federal Funding for Embryo and Related Research*

* Actual title: Public Law 105-78, § 513
Excerpted from Public Law 105-78, Section 513. 1997.
Contact: For additional information, we suggest contacting the Office for Protection from Research Risks, 6100 Executive Blvd., Suite 3B01, MSC-7507, Rockville, Md. 20892-7507; Telephone: (301) 402-5913.

An Act

Making appropriations for the Departments of Labor, Health and Human Services, and Education, and related agencies for the fiscal year ending September 30, 1998, and for other purposes.

Be it enacted by the Senate and House of Representatives of the United States of America in Congress assembled, That the following sums are appropriated, out of any money in the Treasury not otherwise appropriated, for the Departments of Labor, Health and Human Services, and Education, and related agencies for the fiscal year ending September 30, 1998, and for other purposes, namely:

[Extensive text not pertaining to the ban omitted.—THE EDITORS]

Sec. 513.
(a) None of the funds made available in this Act may be used for—
    (1) the creation of a human embryo or embryos for research purposes; or
    (2) research in which a human embryo or embryos are destroyed, discarded, or knowingly subjected to risk of injury or death greater than that allowed for research on fetuses in utero under 45 CFR 46.208(a)(2)

and section 498(b) of the Public Health Service Act (42 U.S.C. 289g(b)).

(b) For purposes of this section, the term "human embryo or embryos" includes any organism, not protected as a human subject under 45 CFR 46 as of the date of the enactment of this Act, that is derived by fertilization, parthenogenesis, cloning, or any other means from one or more human gametes or human diploid cells.

DHHS—Additional Protections Pertaining to Research, Development, and Related Activities Involving Fetuses, Pregnant Women, and Human In Vitro Fertilization

45 Code of Federal Regulations 46, subpart B. Last revised 1 June 1994. Contact: Office for Protection from Research Risks, 6100 Executive Blvd., Suite 3B01, MSC-7507, Rockville, Md. 20892-7507; Telephone: (301) 402-5913.

See "DHHS—Additional Protections Pertaining to Research, Development, and Related Activities Involving Fetuses, Pregnant Women, and Human In Vitro Fertilization," page 153, above.

DHHS—Additional DHHS Protections for Children Involved as Subjects in Research

45 Code of Federal Regulations 46, Subpart D. Last revised 28 June 28 1991.
Contact: Office for Protection from Research Risks, National Institutes of Health, Suite 3B01, 6100 Executive Blvd., Rockville, Md. 20892-7507; Telephone: (301) 496-7005.

§46.401 To what do these regulations apply?

(a) This subpart applies to all research involving children as subjects, conducted or supported by the Department of Health and Human Services.

(1) This includes research conducted by Department employees, except that each head of an Operating Division of the Department may adopt such nonsubstantive, procedural modifications as may be appropriate from an administrative standpoint.

(2) It also includes research conducted or supported by the Department of Health and Human Services outside the United States, but in appropriate circumstances, the Secretary may, under paragraph (e) of §46.101 of Subpart A, waive the applicability of some or all of the requirements of these regulations for research of this type.

(b) Exemptions at §46.101(b)(1) and (b)(3) through (b)(6) are applicable to this subpart. The exemption at §46.101(b)(2) regarding educational tests is also applicable to this subpart. However, the exemption at §46.101(b)(2) for research involving survey or interview procedures or observations of public behavior does not apply to research covered by this subpart, except for research involving observation of public behavior when the investigator(s) do not participate in the activities being observed.

(c) The exceptions, additions, and provisions for waiver as they appear in paragraphs (c) through (i) of §46.101 of Subpart A are applicable to this subpart.

§46.402 Definitions.

The definitions in §46.102 of Subpart A shall be applicable to this subpart as well. In addition, as used in this subpart:

(a) *Children* are persons who have not attained the legal age for consent to treatments or procedures involved in the research, under the applicable law of the jurisdiction in which the research will be conducted.

(b) *Assent* means a child's affirmative agreement to participate in research. Mere failure to object should not, absent affirmative agreement, be construed as assent.

(c) *Permission* means the agreement of parent(s) or guardian to the participation of their child or ward in research.

(d) *Parent* means a child's biological or adoptive parent.

(e) *Guardian* means an individual who is authorized under applicable State or local law to consent on behalf of a child to general medical care.

§46.403 IRB duties.

In addition to other responsibilities assigned to IRBs under this part, each IRB shall review research covered by this subpart and approve only research which satisfies the conditions of all applicable sections of this subpart.

§46.404 Research not involving greater than minimal risk.

HHS will conduct or fund research in which the IRB finds that no greater than minimal risk to children is presented, only if the IRB finds that adequate provisions are made for soliciting the assent of the children and the permission of their parents or guardians, as set forth in §46.408.

§46.405 Research involving greater than minimal risk but presenting the prospect of direct benefit to the individual subjects.

HHS will conduct or fund research in which the IRB finds that more than minimal risk to children is presented by an intervention or procedure that holds out the prospect of direct benefit for the individual subject, or by a monitoring procedure that is likely to contribute to the subject's well-being, only if the IRB finds that:

(a) The risk is justified by the anticipated benefit to the subjects;

(b) The relation of the anticipated benefit to the risk is at least as favorable to the subjects as that presented by available alternative approaches; and

(c) Adequate provisions are made for soliciting the assent of the children and permission of their parents or guardians, as set forth in §46.408.

§46.406 Research involving greater than minimal risk and no prospect of direct benefit to individual subjects, but likely to yield generalizable knowledge about the subject's disorder or condition.

HHS will conduct or fund research in which the IRB finds that more than minimal risk to children is presented by an intervention or procedure that does not hold out the prospect of direct benefit for the individual subject, or by a monitoring procedure which is not likely to contribute to the well-being of the subject, only if the IRB finds that:

(a) The risk represents a minor increase over minimal risk;

(b) The intervention or procedure presents experiences to subjects that are reasonably commensurate with those inherent in their actual or expected medical, dental, psychological, social, or educational situations;

(c) The intervention or procedure is likely to yield generalizable knowledge about the subjects' disorder or condition which is of vital importance for the understanding or amelioration of the subjects' disorder or condition; and

(d) Adequate provisions are made for soliciting assent of the children and permission of their parents or guardians, as set forth in § 46.408.

§46.407 Research not otherwise approvable which presents an opportunity to understand, prevent, or alleviate a serious problem affecting the health or welfare of children.

HHS will conduct or fund research that the IRB does not believe meets the requirements of §46.404, §46.405, or §46.406 only if:

(a) The IRB finds that the research presents a reasonable opportunity to further the understanding, prevention, or alleviation of a serious problem affecting the health or welfare of children; and

(b) The Secretary, after consultation with a panel of experts in pertinent disciplines (for example: science, medicine, education, ethics, law) and following opportunity for public review and comment, has determined either:

(1) That the research in fact satisfies the conditions of §46.404, §46.405, or §46.406, as applicable; or

(2) The following:

(i) The research presents a reasonable opportunity to further the understanding, prevention, or alleviation of a serious problem affecting the health or welfare of children;

(ii) The research will be conducted in accordance with sound ethical principles;

(iii) Adequate provisions are made for soliciting the assent of children and the permission of their parents or guardians, as set forth in §46.408.

§46.408 Requirements for permission by parents or guardians and for assent by children.

(a) In addition to the determinations required under other applicable sections of this subpart, the IRB shall determine that adequate provisions are made for soliciting the assent of the children, when in the judgment of the IRB the children are capable of providing assent. In determining whether children are capable of assenting, the IRB shall take into account the ages, maturity, and psychological state of the children involved. This judgment may be made for all children to be involved in research under a particular protocol, or for each child, as the IRB deems appropriate. If the IRB determines that the capability of some or all of the children is so limited that they cannot reasonably be consulted or that the intervention or procedure involved in the research holds out a prospect of direct benefit that is important to the health or well-being of the children and is available only in the context of the research, the assent of the children is not a necessary condition for proceeding with the research. Even where the IRB determines that the subjects are capable of assenting, the IRB may still waive the assent requirement under circumstances in which consent may be waived in accord with §46.116 of Subpart A.

(b) In addition to the determinations required under other applicable sections of this subpart, the IRB shall determine, in accordance with and to the extent that consent is required by §46.116 of Subpart A, that adequate provisions are made for soliciting the permission of each child's parents or guardian. Where parental permission is to be obtained, the IRB may find that the permission of one parent is sufficient for research to be conducted under §46.404 or §46.405. Where research is covered by §§46.406 and 46.407 and permission is to be obtained from parents, both parents must give their permission unless one parent is deceased, unknown, incompetent, or not reasonably available, or when only one parent has legal responsibility for the care and custody of the child.

(c) In addition to the provisions for waiver contained in §46.116 of Subpart A, if the IRB determines that a research protocol is designed for conditions or for a subject population for which parental or guardian permission is not a reasonable requirement to protect the subjects (for example, neglected or abused children), it may waive the consent requirements in Subpart A of this part and paragraph (b) of this section, provided an appropriate mechanism for protecting the children who will participate as subjects in the research is substituted, and provided further that the waiver is not inconsistent with Federal, state or local law. The choice of an appropriate mechanism would depend upon the nature and purpose of the activities described in the protocol, the risk and anticipated benefit to the research subjects, and their age, maturity, status, and condition.

(d) Permission by parents or guardians shall be documented in accordance with and to the extent required by §46.117 of Subpart A.

(e) When the IRB determines that assent is required, it shall also determine whether and how assent must be documented.

§46.409 Wards.

(a) Children who are wards of the state or any other agency, institution, or entity can be included in research approved under §46.406 or §46.407 only if such research is:

(1) Related to their status as wards; or

(2) Conducted in schools, camps, hospitals, institutions, or similar settings in which the majority of children involved as subjects are not wards.

(b) If the research is approved under paragraph (a) of this section, the IRB shall require appointment of an advocate for each child who is a ward, in addition to any other individual acting on behalf of the child as guardian or in loco parentis. One individual may serve as advocate for more than one child. The advocate shall be an individual who has the background and experience to act in, and agrees to act in, the best interests of the child for the duration of the child's participation in the research and who is not associated in any way (except in the role as advocate or member of the IRB) with the research, the investigator(s), or the guardian organization.

NIH—Policy and Guidelines on the Inclusion of Children as Participants in Research Involving Human Subjects

NIH Guide for Grants and Contracts, *volume 27. 6 March 1998.*
Contact: *Office for Protection from Research Risks, National Institutes of Health, 6100 Executive Blvd., Suite 3B01, Rockville, Md. 20892-7507;* Telephone: (301) 496-7005.

I. Introduction

This document sets forth the policy and guidelines on the inclusion of children in research involving human subjects that is supported or conducted by the National Institutes of Health (NIH). The goal of this policy is to increase the participation of children in research so that adequate data will be developed to support the treatment modalities for disorders and conditions that affect adults and may also affect children. For the purposes of this NIH policy, studies involving human subjects include categories of research that would otherwise be exempted from the DHHS Policy for Protection of Human Research Subjects. These categories of research are exempted from the DHHS policy because they pose minimal risk to the participants, and not because the studies should not include children. Examples of such research include surveys, evaluation of educational interventions, and studies of existing data or specimens that should include children as participants. Nevertheless, the inclusion of children as participants in research must be in compliance with all applicable subparts of 45 CFR 46 as well as with other pertinent federal laws and regulations whether or not the research is otherwise exempted from 45 CFR 46.

II. Background

The policy was developed because medical treatments applied to children are often based upon testing done only in adults, and scientifically evaluated treatments are less available to children due to barriers to their inclusion in research studies. These concerns were specifically articulated in Congressional directives to the NIH as reflected in language from the FY 1996 House and Senate Appropriations Committee reports as follows:

HOUSE

The Committee is concerned that inadequate attention and resources are devoted to pediatric research conducted and supported by the National Institutes of Health. Most research on the cause, treatment and cure of diseases which affect children rely primarily on adults as subjects in clinical trials. Consequently, treatment options which may be effective for adults can have an adverse impact on the outcome of children as well as on their future growth and development. The Committee strongly encourages the NIH to strengthen its portfolio of basic, behavioral and clinical research conducted and supported by all of its relevant Institutes, to establish priorities for pediatric research, and to ensure the adequacy of translational research from the laboratory to the clinical setting. The Committee encourages the NIH to establish guidelines to include children in clinical research trials conducted and supported by NIH. The Committee expects NIH to develop performance indicators to measure specific progress on the above, demonstrated by the development of new programs or strengthening of existing programs and to report to the Committee prior to the 1997 appropriations hearings (H.R. Report No. 209, 104th Congress, 1st session, 80-81, 1995).

SENATE

Pediatric research—The Committee recognizes the substantial benefits that biomedical research offers to the health and well-being of our Nation's children. Savings from productive innovations in health care, derived from scientific investigations of the highest quality, can be significant in terms of dollars and quality of life for children. The opportunities for advancements in the prevention and treatment of diseases which affect children or begin in childhood have never been greater. The Committee intends to work with the Office of the Director as it explores ways to take advantage of such opportunities and strengthen the NIH's capacity to support and encourage extramural pediatric research. Of particular interest is the establishment of guidelines to include children in clinical research trials conducted and supported by the NIH (S. Report No. 145, 104th Congress, 1st session, 112, 1995).

In June 1996, the National Institute of Child Health and Human Development (NICHD) and the American Academy of Pediatrics convened a workshop to address the inclusion of children as participants in research. After reviewing reports, background papers, and a study of a sample of NIH-sponsored clinical research abstracts that suggested that 10-20% inappropriately excluded children, the conveners concluded that there is a need to enhance the inclusion of children in clinical research. This conclusion is based upon scientific information, demonstrated human need, and considerations of justice for children in receiving adequately evaluated treatments. The need reaches across a broad spectrum of clinical research, including studies on pharmaceutical and therapeutic agents, behavioral, developmental and life cycle issues including childhood antecedents of adult disease, and prevention and health services research.

The American Academy of Pediatrics has reported that only a small fraction of all drugs and biological products marketed in the U.S. have had clinical trials performed in pediatric patients and a majority of marketed drugs are not labeled for use in pediatric patients. Many drugs used in the treatment of both common childhood illnesses and more serious conditions carry little information in the labels about use in pediatric patients. In order to address these inadequacies, the Food and Drug Administration (FDA) has published (http://www.fda.gov) a proposed regulation calling for changes in the testing of prescription drugs to ensure that manufacturers specifically examine the drugs effects on children if the medications are to have clinically significant use in children.

In January 1997, the NIH announced (NIH Guide for Grants and Contracts, volume 26, Number 3, January 31, 1997) plans to develop a policy for the inclusion of children in NIH-supported human subject research. This publication fulfills the goal of the announced plan.

III. Policy

It is the policy of NIH that children (i.e., individuals under the age of 21) must be included in all human subjects research, conducted or supported by the NIH, unless there are scientific and ethical reasons not to include them. This policy applies to all NIH conducted or supported research involving human subjects, including research that is otherwise "exempt" in accord with Sections 101(b) and 401(b) of 45 CFR 46—Federal Policy for the Protection of Human Subjects. The inclusion of children as subjects in research must be in compliance with all applicable subparts of 45 CFR 46 as well as with other pertinent federal laws and regulations. Therefore, proposals for research involving human subjects must include a description of plans for including children. If children will be excluded from the research, the application or proposal must present an acceptable justification for the exclusion.

In the research plan, the investigator should create a section titled "Participation of Children." This section should provide either a description of the plans to include children and a rationale for selecting or excluding a specific age range of child, or an explanation of the reason(s) for excluding children as participants in the research. When children are included, the plan must also include a description of the expertise of the investigative team for dealing with children at the ages included, of the appropriateness of the available facilities to accommodate the children, and the inclusion of a sufficient number of children to contribute to a meaningful analysis relative to the purpose of the study. Scientific review groups at the NIH will assess each application as being "acceptable" or "unacceptable" in regard to the age-appropriate inclusion or exclusion of children in the research project, in addition to evaluating the plans for conducting the research in accord with these provisions.

Justifications for Exclusions

It is expected that children will be included in all research involving human subjects unless one or more of the following exclusionary circumstances can be fully justified:

1. The research topic to be studied is irrelevant to children.
2. There are laws or regulations barring the inclusion of children in the research. For example, the regulations for protection of human subjects allow consenting adults to accept a higher level of risk than are permitted for children.
3. The knowledge being sought in the research is already available for children or will be obtained from another ongoing study, and an additional study will be redundant. Documentation of other studies justifying the exclusions should be provided. NIH program staff can be contacted for guidance on this issue if the information is not readily available.

4. A separate, age-specific study in children is warranted and preferable. Examples include:

a. The relative rarity of the condition in children, as compared to adults (in that extraordinary effort would be needed to include children, although in rare diseases or disorders where the applicant has made a particular effort to assemble an adult population, the same effort would be expected to assemble a similar child population with the rare condition);

b. The number of children is limited because the majority are already accessed by a nationwide pediatric disease research network, so that requiring inclusion of children in the proposed adult study would be both difficult and unnecessary (in that the topic was already being addressed in children by the network) as well as potentially counterproductive (in that fewer children could be available for the network study if other studies were required to recruit and include them);

c. Issues of study design preclude direct applicability of hypotheses and/or interventions to both adults and children (including different cognitive, developmental, or disease stages or different age-related metabolic processes). While this situation may represent a justification for excluding children in some instances, consideration should be given to taking these differences into account in the study design and expanding the hypotheses tested or the interventions to allow children to be included rather than excluding them.

5. Insufficient data are available in adults to judge potential risk in children (in which case one of the research objectives could be to obtain sufficient adult data to make this judgment). While children usually should not be the initial group to be involved in research studies, in some instances, the nature and seriousness of the illness may warrant their participation earlier based on careful risk and benefit analysis.

6. Study designs aimed at collecting additional data on pre-enrolled adult study participants (e.g., longitudinal follow-up studies that did not include data on children).

7. Other special cases justified by the investigator and found acceptable to the review group and the Institute Director.

IV. Implementation

A. Date of Implementation

This policy applies to all initial applications (Type 1)/proposals and intramural projects submitted for receipt dates after October 1, 1998.

B. Roles and Responsibilities

This policy applies to all NIH-conducted or -supported research involving human subjects. Certain individuals and groups have special roles and responsibilities with regard to the adoption and implementation of these guidelines.

1. Principal Investigators: Principal investigators should assess the scientific rationale for inclusion of children in the context of the topic of the study. Questions that should be considered in developing a study involving human subjects may include, but are not limited to, the following: When is the exclusion of children appropriate? Under what circumstances is it appropriate? At what ages is it appropriate? The principal investigator should address the policy in the application, providing the required information on participation of children in research projects, and required justifications for any exceptions allowed under the policy in the research plan under a section titled "Participation of Children."

2. Institutional Review Boards (IRBs): The IRB addresses the appropriateness of the population studied in terms of the aims of the research and ethical standards. IRBs have the responsibility to examine ethical issues, including equitable selection of research participants in accordance with Federal Regulations (45 CFR 46) The participation of children in research, including children of both genders and children from minority groups, is important to assure that they receive a share of the benefits of research. IRBs have special review requirements (45 CFR 46, Subpart D, Sec. 401-409) to protect the well-being of children who participate in research. IRBs may approve research involving children only if the special provisions are met.

3. Scientific Review Groups: In conducting peer review of applications/proposals for scientific and technical merit, appropriately constituted scientific review groups, technical evaluation groups, and intramural review panels will evaluate the proposed plan for inclusion or exclusion of children as acceptable or unacceptable. Therefore, these groups must include appropriate expertise in research involving children to make the evaluation.

4. Institute/Center Obligations: Following scientific review and Council review, Institute/Center Directors and their staff shall determine whether: (a) the research involves human subjects; and (b) the inclusion or exclusion of children meets the requirements of the policy. Program

staff should assess exceptions to this policy in view of the IC research portfolio.

5. Educational Outreach by NIH to Inform the Professional Community: NIH staff will present these guidelines to investigators, IRB members, peer review groups, and Advisory Councils in a variety of public forums.

6. Applicability to Foreign Research Involving Human Subjects: The policy of inclusion of children in NIH-conducted or supported research activities in foreign countries (including collaborative activities) is the same as that for research conducted in the U.S.

V. Definitions

For the purpose of implementing these guidelines, the following definitions apply.

A. Child

For purposes of this policy, a child is an individual under the age of 21 years. This policy and definition do not affect the human subject protection regulations for research on children (45 CFR 46) and their provisions for assent, permission, and consent, which remain unchanged.

It should be noted that the definition of child described above will pertain notwithstanding the FDA definition of a child as an individual from infancy to 16 years of age, and varying definitions employed by some states. Generally, State laws define what constitutes a "child," and such definitions dictate whether or not a person can legally consent to participate in a research study. However, State laws vary, and many do not address when a child can consent to participate in research. Federal Regulations (45 CFR 46, subpart D, Sec. 401-409) address DHHS protections for children who participate in research, and rely on State definitions of "child" for consent purposes. Consequently, the children included in this policy (persons under the age of 21) may differ in the age at which their own consent is required and sufficient to participate in research under State law. For example, some states consider a person age 18 to be an adult and therefore one who can provide consent without parental permission.

Additionally, IRBs have special review requirements to protect the well-being of children who participate in research. These requirements relate to risk, benefit, parental/guardian consent, and assent by children, and to research involving children who are wards of the State or of another institution. The local IRB approves research that satisfies the conditions set forth in the regulations.

B. Human Subjects

The definition of a human subject appears in Title 45 part 46 of the Department of Health and Human Services Regulations for the Protection of Human Subjects and is as follows: "Human subject means a living individual about whom an investigator (whether professional or student) conducting research obtains: (1) Data through intervention or interaction with the individual, or (2) identifiable private information."

VI. Decision Tree for Participation of Children in Research

The inclusion of children in research is a complex and challenging issue. Nonetheless, it also presents the opportunity for researchers to address the concern that treatment modalities used to treat children for many diseases and disorders are based on research conducted with adults. The linked "decision tree" is intended to facilitate the determination of policy implementation by principal investigators and reviewers with regard to the inclusion of children in research involving human subjects.

VII. Additional Requirements for Research that Includes Children

The following chart summarizes the additional requirements under the DHHS Regulations 45 CFR 46, Subpart D based on the risks and benefits to children who participate in research:

Types of Research	Requirements
No greater than minimal risk	Assent of child and permission of at least one parent
Greater than minimal risk AND prospect of direct benefit	Assent of child and permission of at least one parent
Anticipated benefit justifies the risk, AND
Anticipated benefit is at least as favorable as that of alternative approaches.

Types of Research	Requirements
Greater than minimal risk and no prospect of direct benefit	Assent of child and permission of both parents Only a minor increase over minimal risk Likely to yield generalizable knowledge about the child's disorder or condition that is of vital importance for the understanding or amelioration of the disorder or condition, AND The intervention or procedure presents experiences to the child that are reasonably commensurate with those in the child's actual or expected medical, dental, psychological, social, or educational situations
Any other research	Assent of child and permission of both parents IRB finds that the research presents a reasonable opportunity to further the understanding, prevention, or alleviation of a serious problem affecting the health or welfare of children, AND The Secretary approves, after consultation with a panel of experts in pertinent disciplines (e.g., science, medicine, education, ethics, law) and following publication and public comment

[A list of contacts has been omitted.—THE EDITORS]

FDA—Guideline for the Study of Drugs Likely to be Used in the Elderly

Guidance for Industry, *FDA Center for Drug Evaluation and Research.* November 1989.
Contact: Food and Drug Administration, Center for Drug Evaluation and Research, Office of Drug Evaluation I (HFD-100), 5600 Fishers Lane, Rockville, Md. 20857; Telephone: (301) 443-4330.

[On 12 August 1994, the FDA published a guideline titled "Studies in Support of Special Populations: Geriatrics." The guideline was prepared by a working group of the International Conference on Harmonisation of Technical Requirements for Registrations of Pharmaceuticals for Human Use (ICH). According to the notice announcing the new guideline, "it addresses harmonization in relation to clinical testing programs for drugs intended for use in medicines for the geriatric population, which is expected to increase significantly in the near future in Europe, Japan, and the United States. . . . The recommendations of this guideline do not materially differ from the recommendations of [the 1989 guideline]. Although the ICH harmonized guideline provides much useful information for sponsors submitting applications. . . , the 1989 document contains background and additional commentary not present in the harmonized guideline. For this reason, FDA intends to provide both the ICH harmonized guideline and the 1989 document when information is requested on the study of new drugs in a geriatric population."
The 1994 guideline is available at 59 *Federal Register* 39398—2 August 1994.—THE EDITORS]

FOREWORD

The following guideline provides detailed advice on the study of new drugs in older patients. The guideline is intended to encourage routine and thorough evaluation of the effects of drugs in elderly populations so that physicians will have sufficient information to use drugs properly in their older patients. It is hoped that the guideline will serve as a stimulus to the development of this information, encouraging those sponsors who have not yet started to address the issue at all to begin, and suggesting additional steps to sponsors who are already assessing the effects of their drugs in the elderly.

This guideline presents acceptable current approaches to the study of drugs in the elderly. The guideline contains both generalities and specifics and was developed from experience with available drugs. It is anticipated that with passage of time this guideline will require revision.

The recommendations in this guideline should not be interpreted as mandatory requirements for allowing continuation of clinical trials with an investigational drug or for obtaining approval of a new drug for marketing. This guideline, in part, contains recommendations for clinical studies that are recognized as desirable approaches to be used in the development of more and better information than is currently available on the use of drugs in the elderly.

I. INTRODUCTION

A. Other Pertinent Guidelines:

"General Considerations for the Clinical Evaluation of Drugs" is an important companion document and should be reviewed prior to reading this guideline. It contains suggestions that are applicable to the evaluation of most classes of drugs in all age groups. That guideline now states that "drugs should be studied in all age groups, including the geriatric, for which they will have significant utility." This guideline expands on this general theme and provides detailed advice on the evaluation of a new drug in elderly patients. It is intended to assure that treating physicians will have the information needed to use drugs properly in the elderly.

In addition, the "Guideline for the Format and Content of the Clinical and Statistical Sections of an Application," which now recommends analysis of safety and effectiveness data to determine the influence of demographic factors such as age and sex, can be used to anticipate what information will need to be collected and presented.

B. Underlying Observations:

The following general observations and conclusions underlie the recommendations set forth in this guideline:

1. Age-related differences in response to drugs can arise from pharmacokinetic differences (that is, differences in the way a drug is absorbed, excreted, metabolized, or distributed) or pharmacodynamic differences (i.e., differences in the response to a given blood, or other tissue, concentration of the drug).
2. Age itself is not the only characteristic of the elderly that could affect pharmacokinetic or pharmacodynamic responses to drugs. Most differences seemingly related to age are probably not related to age itself but to conditions that, although common in the elderly, can occur in patients of all ages, such as diminished renal or cardiac function, concomitant illness, and concomitant treatment, especially concomitant drug treatment. An approach is therefore needed that will detect, better than is done at present, the major patient characteristics that influence response to therapy. Understanding their influence will greatly enhance our ability to treat older patients with appropriate doses.
3. For a number of practical and theoretical reasons, the evaluation of possible differences in response between younger and older people should focus on the evaluation of potential pharmacokinetic differences. Such differences are known to occur and are much more frequent than documented pharmacodynamic differences. Most problems with drugs in the elderly identified to date have resulted from pharmacokinetic differences related to age itself or to age-associated conditions such as renal impairment, congestive heart failure, or multiple drug therapy.

Moreover, pharmacokinetic differences are relatively easy to discover. Once a reliable assay for a drug and its metabolites is developed (and an assay is now almost always available early in development), techniques exist for readily assessing age-related or other influence-related effects. Aside from the recognized ability of formal pharmacokinetic studies to answer questions about specific subgroups, a screening procedure, a "pharmacokinetic screen," carried out in Phase 3 populations, has the potential for greatly increasing our ability to detect pharmacokinetic differences in sub-populations and individuals, even when these were not anticipated. That is, by obtaining a small number of blood level determinations in each of many Phase 3 patients, it is possible to detect markedly atypical pharmacokinetic behavior in individuals, such as that seen in slow metabolizers of encainide, and also more subtle pharmacokinetic differences in population subsets, such as patient populations of different age, sex, race, or with particular underlying diseases or concomitant therapy.

The relative ease with which pharmacokinetic differences among population subsets can be assessed must be contrasted with the difficulty of developing precise relationships of most clinical responses to drug-dose or the drug blood level, a necessary step in attempting to compare two subgroups. New drug applications received by the Food and Drug Administration often do not have excellent dose response or blood level response information for effectiveness or adverse effects. This situation is improving, however, and when there is a readily measured pharmacodynamic endpoint, such as blood pressure or rate of ventricular premature beats (VPB's), it is reasonable to expect dose response data from a variety of different populations, particularly when differences could have an important impact on the safety or effectiveness of the drug. However, where the endpoint is not immediately assessable in small populations (e.g., in treating depression or anxiety), good dose response information is difficult to get at all, much less for a subset of the overall population, such as the elderly. It is possible, of course, to examine the clinical data for effectiveness or adverse effects differences between subgroups. Observed differences could reflect pharmacokinetic differences or pharmacodynamic differences such as unusual susceptibility to the pharmacologic effect of the drug.

A final reason to emphasize pharmacokinetic evaluation is that it must be carried out first to allow intelligent assessment of pharmacodynamic differences or relationships. Assessing pharmacodynamic differences between groups or establishing blood level-response relationships is possible only when groups are reasonably well matched for blood concentrations. Enough pharmacokinetic data must therefore be available to permit the investigator to administer doses that will produce comparable blood concentrations in the subsets to be compared or, alternatively, to compare subsets that have been titrated to similar blood concentrations.

4. The number of documented age-related pharmacodynamic differences is at this time so small, and the ability to conduct pharmacodynamic studies to detect them in many situations so uncertain, that additional formal studies to seek such differences between the blood level/response curves of younger and older patients are warranted only if differences are suspected for some reason, such as clinical trial results,

or appear particularly important (e.g., because of a low therapeutic index). The observations made during clinical trials that include both younger and older patients, if properly analyzed and particularly if accompanied by blood level data for each patient, should allow detection of important pharmacodynamic differences related to age or other influences.

II. DETERMINATION THAT A DRUG IS LIKELY TO HAVE SIGNIFICANT USE IN THE ELDERLY

In many cases it is obvious that a drug will be widely used in the elderly because the diseases that it is intended to treat are characteristically diseases of aging, e.g., coronary artery disease, senile dementia, or peripheral vascular disease. In other cases it is not entirely clear what the age of the ultimate population will be. A sponsor should determine, through estimates of the disease prevalence by age or through examination of the age distribution for other drugs of a similar type (using the National Disease and Therapeutic Index, for example), whether a drug is likely to have significant use in the elderly.

III. INCLUSION OF ELDERLY PATIENTS IN CLINICAL STUDIES

The patients included in clinical studies should, in general reflect the population that will receive the drug when it is marketed. Therefore, for drugs likely to be used in the elderly, older patients should be included in clinical trials in reasonable numbers. Although it is appropriate and necessary to exclude patients on the basis of functional characteristics that make it impossible for them to be safely, ethically, and usefully included (e.g., patients who are too infirm to participate, too medically complicated to permit interpretation of results, too likely to suffer serious intercurrent illness, or unable to provide meaningful informed consent), exclusions should not be arbitrary. Moreover, exclusions deemed prudent in early studies need not necessarily be maintained in Phase 3. There is no good basis for the exclusion of patients on the basis of advanced age alone, or because of the presence of any concomitant illness or medication, unless there is reason to believe that the concomitant illness or medication will endanger the patient or lead to confusion in interpreting the results of the study. Attempts should therefore be made to include patients over 75 years of age and those with concomitant illness and treatments, if they are stable and willing to participate. Ordinarily, elderly patients should be included in the same trials as younger patients. This permits direct comparisons with younger, but otherwise similar, patients in the same studies. In some cases, however, especially for drugs targeted to older patients or where age-related differences or problems are anticipated, trials might be carried out specifically in the elderly. These could include special monitoring procedures, e.g., of cognitive function. An alternative to a separate trial would be a study that includes both young and old patients in the same clinical environment but is stratified by age to allow special care or monitoring of the older patients.

IV. ANALYSIS OF EFFECTIVENESS AND ADVERSE EFFECTS BY AGE

As indicated in the "Introduction" to this guideline, FDA's "Guideline for the Format and Content of the Clinical and Statistical Sections of New Drug Applications" calls for analysis of effectiveness, adverse effects, dose response, and, if available, blood level response, with respect to the influence of demographic features such as age, sex, and race, and patient characteristics such as renal, cardiac, and hepatic status, concomitant illness, and concomitant drugs, including ethanol and nicotine. These analyses should be carried out both for individual studies and in the overall integrated analyses of effectiveness and safety. The analyses of subsets with particular characteristics can be expected to detect only fairly large age-related differences. This is not a great problem, however, as only reasonably large differences are likely to be important. The results of these analyses may suggest the need for more formal dose-response or blood level response studies in an elderly population or in other patient subsets. Depending on the significance of the findings, these additional studies might be carried out before or after marketing.

V. DEFINING THE PHARMACOKINETICS OF THE DRUG IN THE ELDERLY AND OTHER POPULATION SUBSETS

Age itself is only one factor, and not the most important one, that can alter the pharmacokinetics of a drug in the elderly. The most important influences, such as renal function for drugs excreted by the kidney, should be assessed directly. The effects of other possible influences, including age, can be assessed by a screening approach, described below in section C. If a screen is not appropriate or not carried out, or if the screen suggests an influence of age, a formal pharmacokinetic study should be performed in the elderly.

Evaluation of the effects of age or age-associated conditions on the pharmacokinetics of drugs should include:

A. Effects of Renal Impairment

Drugs that are excreted (parent drug or active metabolites) significantly through renal mechanisms should be studied to define the effects of altered renal function on their pharmacokinetics. Information should be developed to support dosing instructions that provide appropriate adjustments for varying degrees of renal impairment. Because it is often difficult to obtain accurate direct measures of creatinine clearance without hospitalizing the patient for urine collections, labeling for such drugs should include a means of calculating creatinine clearance from the serum creatinine, adjusting for weight and age. The following equation, put forth by Cockcroft and Gault [Nephron 16:31-41 (1976)], is probably the most widely accepted:

$$\text{male CCr} = \frac{\text{wt (kg)} \times (140 - \text{age})}{72 \times \text{Cr (mg/100 ml)}}$$

female CCr = 0.85 x above

B. Effects of Hepatic Impairment

Drugs subject to significant hepatic metabolism, especially drugs with metabolism by oxidative mechanisms, or that have active metabolites, require particular attention to permit proper use in all patients, including the elderly. Special pharmacokinetic studies should be carried out in these situations to explore the effects of decreased liver function and to look for possible genetic variability in metabolism or drug-drug interactions. There is, unfortunately, no recognized measure of liver function that serves as a predictor of how the excretion of compounds will be altered, as creatinine clearance does for renal function, but the presence of hepatic cirrhosis has sometimes indicated a likelihood of decreased drug clearance (e.g., for theophylline). It may ultimately prove possible, however, as marker compounds like debrisoquin and aminopyrine are studied further, to define liver function in functionally relevant ways and examine the effects of specific metabolic deficiencies on new drugs.

C. Pharmacokinetic Screen

It is important to identify as many of the factors that alter pharmacokinetics of a drug as possible, but it is practical to carry out only a limited number of specific interaction (drug-drug, drug-disease) studies, and only suspected potential interactions can be studied. A pharmacokinetic screen is a means of identifying subgroups of patients in whom the drug has unusual pharmacokinetic characteristics even where no such subgroups are suspected.

A pharmacokinetic screen consists of obtaining, for all or most patients in Phases 2 and 3 of a clinical investigation, a small number (one to several) of steady-state blood level determinations in order to determine the variability of blood concentrations of a drug under defined conditions of dosing. Discussions have been published on how such screens could be conducted and analyzed [Sheiner, L B., and Benet, L Z.: Clin. Pharm. Ther. 38:481-487 (1985)] and experience will undoubtedly refine their use.

Even a relatively crude screen, consisting of one or two steady-state trough measurements, can answer a number of simple, but important, questions so long as the trials include a full range of patients with respect to age, sex, race, weight, body composition (e.g., degree of obesity or leanness), concomitant illness, smoking and alcohol consumption, and the use of concomitant drugs. It should be possible to determine the extent of inter-individual variability of blood concentrations of drug and, using multiple linear regression (or other means such as mixed effects modeling), to determine the relationship of relevant clinical features (age, sex, race, weight, lean body mass, etc.) to trough level. Extreme individual outliers would also be readily identifiable; these patients would often require further study.

It should also be possible to learn from these studies whether the elderly differ from others in their blood concentrations and whether the differences are the result of age alone or other age-associated conditions. Under crude screening conditions, only relatively large differences would be detected but, given the variability in blood concentrations experienced with most drugs, only relatively large differences are generally important. Where small differences could be important, e.g., for relatively toxic drugs with a low ratio of toxic to therapeutic blood concentration, a more rigorous screen (Sheiner and Benet, at 14) could detect even small differences. A very important possible finding of a screen would be that for various demographic (e.g., age) or clinical (e.g., use of other drugs) subsets present in adequate numbers, no apparent effect on blood concentrations was seen.

An important virtue of a screen is that it requires no prior hypothesis and can detect the unexpected. It is inherent in the idea of a "screen" that when the screen discovers something unusual and important, further studies may need to be done. Thus, if a particular sub-population (e.g., people of a certain age or those receiving another drug) were found to have significantly higher or lower blood concentrations, particularly if this would increase toxicity or decrease effectiveness, an attempt to confirm the observation and discover the reason for it might be necessary. The importance of pursuing such differences, and determining when to pursue them (preapproval or Phase 4), would depend on the therapeutic index of the drug and the extent to which toxicity or beneficial effects are blood-concentration related.

The screen may also help to interpret clinical findings in Phase 2 and Phase 3 studies. Unusual effectiveness or adverse reaction responses might be explained in some cases by the patients' blood concentrations of drug. It should be possible to carry out crude concentration-response observations using the clinical data and screening results.

D. Pharmacokinetic Study in the Elderly

If the pharmacokinetic screen is not used, a pharmacokinetic study in elderly patients (over 65 years) should be conducted. The patients should be in reasonably good health, but should usually have the condition the drug is intended to treat. A pharmacokinetic study in the elderly might also be needed if the pharmacokinetic screen suggested age-related pharmacokinetic effects.

E. Drug-Disease and Drug-Drug Interactions

Any substantial pharmacokinetic effects of concomitant illness and therapy would be expected to be revealed by the pharmacokinetic screen. In cases where the therapeutic ratio (i.e., ratio of toxic to therapeutic dose) is low, however, and the likelihood of concomitant therapy or illness is great, specific interaction studies should be carried out. The studies needed must be determined case-by-case, but would include:

1. **Interaction Studies**
    a. *Digoxin Interaction*
        So many drugs alter serum concentrations of digoxin, which is widely prescribed in the elderly and is potentially toxic, that

evaluation of this interaction is appropriate for most drugs.
b. *Drugs That Affect Hepatic Metabolism*
For drugs that undergo extensive hepatic metabolism, the effects of hepatic-enzyme inducers (e.g., phenobarbital) and inhibitors (e.g., cimetidine) should be assessed. Of particular note is the inhibition by quinidine and other drugs (propafenone, for example) of the cytochrome P-450 debrisoquin hydroxylase enzyme, causing fast metabolizer patients receiving those drugs to exhibit the slow metabolizer phenotype. For most drugs metabolized by this enzyme, the effect of quinidine should be explored.
c. *Other Drugs*
Other drugs particularly likely to be used with the test drug should be studied for possible drug-drug interactions unless the pharmacokinetic screen or the interaction screen (described below) provides adequate assurance that important interactions do not exist.
d. *Protein Binding Studies*
Drugs that are extensively bound to plasma proteins are subject to displacement from binding sites by other drugs (e.g., displacement of warfarin by NSAID's) and other drugs that are extensively bound may be displaced by the new drug. These interactions can be readily and inexpensively explored in vitro. If a clinical interaction has been observed, binding studies can help to elucidate the underlying mechanism.

2. Concomitant Disease and Concomitant Drugs; Interaction Screen

If the drug will be used in conditions where specific concomitant diseases are likely to be present, an attempt should be made to include in the treatment population patients with the other diseases. The pharmacokinetic screen will be useful in determining whether the concomitant diseases affect blood levels of the test drug, and clinical observations should permit detection of specific adverse effects associated with the other diseases. Similarly, with respect to other medications that are used concomitantly, the screen will help evaluate whether the other medications affect the kinetics of the test drug. In some cases, where a concomitant drug is used frequently, formal interaction studies should be carried out. For example, anti-anginal drugs of different pharmacologic classes (nitrate, beta-blocker, calcium antagonist) are commonly combined and should be subjected to formal studies of their combined effectiveness and tolerance.

It is possible that the new drug will have an effect on the kinetics of other drugs. There is almost no limit to the number of studies that could be mounted to explore this question; therefore, a second screening mechanism, an "interaction screen," would be helpful. If Phase 3 clinical trials include patients on a variety of other drug therapies (held stable during introduction of the new agent), trough blood levels of the other drugs can be obtained prior to dosing with the new agent and again after the new agent has reached steady state. It should thus be possible to detect, with relatively little effort, major effects of the new drug on many concomitant medications. The principal impediment to doing so will be lack of availability of reliable blood level assays for the other agents.

VI. PHARACODYNAMIC STUDIES IN THE ELDERLY

The number of age-related pharmacodynamic differences (i.e., heightened or dampened beneficial or toxic effects at a given blood concentration of drug) discovered to date is too small to necessitate routine separate pharmacodynamic or clinical studies in the elderly. Observations made during clinical trials that include both young and old patients should make it possible to identify the important differences; indeed, these trials are more likely to detect differences than studies carried out entirely in older populations. Stratifying patients by age may allow more sensitive assessments and provide the best of both approaches.

In some cases, however, most notably sedative/hypnotic agents and other drugs with important CNS effects, separate studies of older populations may be needed. Results of analyses of other trials may also suggest the need for separate studies. These should ordinarily be directed at defining the dose-response relationships for favorable and adverse effects, particularly attempting to define the lowest useful dose and to define the CNS consequences of larger doses. Specific drug and disease interaction studies might also be indicated.

DHHS—Additional Protections Pertaining to Biomedical and Behavioral Research Involving Prisoners as Subjects

45 Code of Federal Regulations 46, Subpart C. Last revised 26 January 1981.
Contact: Office for Protection from Research Risks, National Institutes of Health, 6100 Executive Blvd., Suite 3B01, Rockville, Md. 20892-7507; Telephone: (301) 496-7005.

§46.301 Applicability.

(a) The regulations in this subpart are applicable to all biomedical and behavioral research conducted or supported by the Department of Health and Human Services involving prisoners as subjects.

(b) Nothing in this subpart shall be construed as indicating that compliance with the procedures set forth herein will authorize research involving prisoners as subjects, to the extent such research is limited or barred by applicable State or local law.

(c) The requirements of this subpart are in addition to those imposed under the other subparts of this part.

§46.302 Purpose.

Inasmuch as prisoners may be under constraints because of their incarceration which could affect their ability to make a truly voluntary and uncoerced decision whether or not to participate as subjects in research, it is the purpose of this subpart to provide additional safeguards for the protection of prisoners involved in activities to which this subpart is applicable.

§46.303 Definitions.

As used in this subpart:

(a) *Secretary* means the Secretary of Health and Human Services and any other officer or employee of the Department of Health and Human Services to whom authority has been delegated.

(b) *DHHS* means the Department of Health and Human Services.

(c) *Prisoner* means any individual involuntarily confined or detained in a penal institution. The term is intended to encompass individuals sentenced to such an institution under a criminal or civil statute, individuals detained in other facilities by virtue of statutes or commitment procedures which provide alternatives to criminal prosecution or incarceration in a penal institution, and individuals detained pending arraignment, trial, or sentencing.

(d) *Minimal risk* is the probability and magnitude of physical or psychological harm that is normally encountered in the daily lives, or in the routine medical, dental, or psychological examination of healthy persons.

§46.304 Composition of Institutional Review Boards where prisoners are involved.

In addition to satisfying the requirements in §46.107 of this part, an Institutional Review Board, carrying out responsibilities under this part with respect to research covered by this subpart, shall also meet the following specific requirements:

(a) A majority of the Board (exclusive of prisoner members) shall have no association with the prison(s) involved, apart from their membership on the Board.

(b) At least one member of the Board shall be a prisoner, or a prisoner representative with appropriate background and experience to serve in that capacity, except that where a particular research project is reviewed by more than one Board only one Board need satisfy this requirement.

§46.305 Additional duties of the Institutional Review Boards where prisoners are involved.

(a) In addition to all other responsibilities prescribed for Institutional Review Boards under this part, the Board shall review research covered by this subpart and approve such research only if it finds that:

(1) The research under review represents one of the categories of research permissible under §46.306(a)(2);

(2) Any possible advantages accruing to the prisoner through his or her participation in the research, when compared to the general living conditions, medical care, quality of food, amenities and opportunity for earnings in the prison, are not of such a magnitude that his or her ability to weigh the risks of the research against the value of such advantages in the limited choice environment of the prison is impaired;

(3) The risks involved in the research are commensurate with risks that would be accepted by nonprisoner volunteers;

(4) Procedures for the selection of subjects within the prison are fair to all prisoners and immune from arbitrary intervention by prison authorities or prisoners. Unless the principal investigator provides to the Board justification in writing for following some other procedures, control subjects must be selected randomly from the group of available prisoners who meet the characteristics needed for that particular research project;

(5) The information is presented in language which is understandable to the subject population;

(6) Adequate assurance exists that parole boards will not take into account a prisoner's participation in the research in making decisions regarding parole, and each prisoner is clearly informed in advance that participation in the research will have no effect on his or her parole; and

(7) Where the Board finds there may be a need for follow-up examination or care of participants after the end of their participation, adequate provision has been made for such examination or care, taking into account the varying lengths of individual prisoners' sentences, and for informing participants of this fact.

(b) The Board shall carry out such other duties as may be assigned by the Secretary.

(c) The institution shall certify to the Secretary, in such form and manner as the Secretary may require, that the duties of the Board under this section have been fulfilled.

§46.306 Permitted research involving prisoners.

(a) Biomedical or behavioral research conducted or supported by DHHS may involve prisoners as subjects only if:

(1) The institution responsible for the conduct of the research has certified to the Secretary that the Institutional Review Board has approved the research under §46.305 of this subpart; and

(2) In the judgment of the Secretary the proposed research involves solely the following: (i) Study of the possible causes, effects, and processes

of incarceration, and of criminal behavior, provided that the study presents no more than minimal risk and no more than inconvenience to the subjects; (ii) Study of prisons as institutional structures or of prisoners as incarcerated persons, provided that the study presents no more than minimal risk and no more than inconvenience to the subjects; (iii) Research on conditions particularly affecting prisoners as a class (for example, vaccine trials and other research on hepatitis which is much more prevalent in prisons than elsewhere; and research on social and psychological problems such as alcoholism, drug addiction and sexual assaults) provided that the study may proceed only after the Secretary has consulted with appropriate experts including experts in penology medicine and ethics, and published notice, in the Federal Register, of his intent to approve such research; or (iv) Research on practices, both innovative and accepted, which have the intent and reasonable probability of improving the health or well-being of the subject. In cases in which those studies require the assignment of prisoners in a manner consistent with protocols approved by the IRB to control groups which may not benefit from the research, the study may proceed only after the Secretary has consulted with appropriate experts, including experts in penology medicine and ethics, and published notice, in the Federal Register, of his intent to approve such research.

(b) Except as provided in paragraph (a) of this section, biomedical or behavioral research conducted or supported by DHHS shall not involve prisoners as subjects.

USAID—Procedures for Protection of Human Subjects in Research Supported by USAID

USAID/General Notice PPC and G. *19 April 1995*
Contact: *US Agency for International Development, Public Inquiries, 320 21st Street, N.W., Washington, D.C. 20523-0016: Telephone: (202) 647-1850.*

1. Introduction and Purpose

Along with many other Federal Agencies, USAID has adopted the Common Federal Policy for Protection of Human Subjects (referred to herein as the Policy—see 22 CFR Part 225). The Policy sets standards for the protection of human research subjects which must be followed when research activities supported by USAID involve human subjects. The Policy, at 22 CFR 225.101(a), permits each agency to adopt procedural modifications as may be appropriate from an administrative standpoint. In conformity with the Policy, safeguarding the rights and welfare of human subjects involved in research supported by USAID is the primary responsibility of the organization to which support is awarded. No work may be initiated for the support of research involving human subjects unless the research is approved as outlined in these procedures.

While the Policy sets forth detailed guidance, it allows for some latitude in adaptation to the specific situation of each Agency. The purpose of these procedures is to describe how the Policy is implemented and interpreted by USAID. It is intended especially to help Cognizant Technical Officers (CTOs), Technical Advisors (TAs) and Mission staff to understand and apply the Policy when supporting research involving human subjects. CTOs, TAs and Mission staff are the first line of action in determining applicability of the Policy to a particular research project and for assuring that those organizations receiving USAID funds for research are adhering to requirements set forth in the Policy. USAID's Cognizant Human Subjects Officer (CHSO or successor) assists with guidance, oversight and interpretation of the Policy. The CHSO, located in USAID/Washington, is appointed by the Assistant Administrator for the Bureau for Global Programs, Field Support and Research (AA/G). Ultimate authority for decisions regarding human subjects' protection rests with the USAID AA/G or her/his designee. (For more information, refer to the Policy itself.)

2. Background and Principles

(a) Human subjects considerations are essential in the design and implementation of research projects. USAID strongly supports vigorous efforts to protect human subjects as provided for by the Policy. The Policy itself is primarily oriented towards experimental biomedical research, but some other types of research are included (see section 5 below for application of the Policy to various other types of research and for exemptions).

(b) In considering human subjects research it is essential to recognize the following three pillars of protection:

> (1) Review by a properly constituted ethical committee or Institutional Review Board (IRB)
> (2) A meaningful assessment of risk/benefit by the IRB
> (3) A meaningful informed consent procedure.

(c) The Policy recognizes that foreign countries may often present special situations and it provides mechanisms to help deal with these {see CFR section 225.101(h)}. As provided for in the Policy, USAID will accept legitimate foreign procedural systems, for example an institution which complies with the guidelines of the World Medical Assembly Declaration, as long as they are determined to provide protection "at least equivalent" to the Policy. Substantive application of the "three pillars" should generally satisfy this requirement. As noted in 22 CFR section 225.101(g), the policy does not affect any laws or regulations in foreign countries regarding protection of human research subjects, and overseas research activities, in addition to adhering to the Policy, must also conform to legal and other requirements governing research with human subjects in the country where they are conducted.

(d) USAID's implementation of the Policy seeks to avoid undue burden that might be imposed by its application, while seeking to protect human subjects. It emphasizes practicality, flexibility and common sense. Because USAID conducts no research itself directly, no need is foreseen for an subjects. It emphasizes practicality, flexibility and common sense. Because USAID conducts no research itself directly, no need is foreseen for an USAID IRB per se to review research proposals. For research other than experimental biomedical research, generally the primary issue is protection of privacy rather than direct physical harm. This guidance takes that into account.

Applicability in Various Research Settings

Whether procedures for protection of human subjects must adhere to the Policy or whether some alternative may be applied depends on where the research will be conducted.

(a) Research in the U.S. When research takes place in the U.S. it must conform to all aspects of the Policy. In cases where all or part of the research is subcontracted to another institution, the prime recipient is responsible for complying in detail with the Policy. Recipient institutions may be of two categories: (i) Many U.S.-based institutions will have an ongoing Department of Health and Human Services (HHS) "multiple project assurances" (MPAs), indicating they have an HHS-approved system for human subjects' protection in place which can be applied to USAID-supported research by reference; or (ii) If no MPA exists, the institution must provide an acceptable "assurance" to USAID describing how it will comply with the Policy (see section 8 below).

(b) Research in Foreign Countries—There are generally three mechanisms by which USAID supports research in foreign countries:

(1) The recipient is a U.S.-based institution, with the research carried out in another country. In this situation, the primary recipient will be responsible for complying or assuring compliance in detail with the Policy as described above including either an HHS or USAID approved assurance governing the research. As part of its institution building mandate, USAID encourages, but does not require the host-country collaborators of U.S.-based institutions to use an in-country IRB;

(2) The recipient is an international organization or institution (e.g. WHO, UNICEF, UNDP, and certain non U.S.-based PVOs/NGOs); and

(3) The recipient is a host country government or non-government institution.

In the last two cases, for non-U.S.-based institutions, there are three ways acceptable standards can be applied:

(i) An acceptable assurance complying with the Policy can be developed directly with USAID.

(ii) Access can be made to appropriate U.S. or other internationally accepted bodies such as an HHS-approved or WHO/CIOMS-approved IRB/Ethical Committee {see section 4(a) below} either directly or through a collaborative arrangement.

(iii) An alternative human subjects system can be employed if it can be determined (by the AA/G or her/his designee) to be "at least equivalent" to the Policy {as delineated in section 4(b) below}.

4. Determination that Alternative Protection Procedures are "at Least Equivalent" to the Policy

(a) 22 CFR section 225.101(h) describes the use of alternative protection of human subjects systems when research is conducted outside the U.S. It specifically cites the example of "... a foreign institution which complies with guidelines consistent with the World Medical Assembly Declaration (Declaration of Helsinki amended 1989) issued either by sovereign states or by an organization whose function for the protection of human subjects is internationally recognized." Research supported through or adhering to the standards established by United Nations agencies is considered to qualify as affording such "at least equivalent" protection.

(b) To make a determination that another system provides "at least equivalent" protection, a justification memorandum is required for an individual or class of research activities which is cleared by the Agency's CHSO (designee or successor) and is signed by the AA/G (or designee). Such a justification memorandum must describe how the alternative system provides the "three pillars" of protection described above under section 2(b)(1-3). An additional tool available for the determination of equivalency is a checklist of considerations which are common components of such systems (available from the CHSO). In assessing equivalency, the general concept should be whether protection under the system is for all practical purposes the same when viewed in toto and not whether any specific component (e.g. the precise make-up of the IRB equivalent) is identical. Each determination of "at least equivalent" protection, including the determination of a class of activities will be published in the Federal Register in accordance with 22 CFR 225.101(h).

5. Applicability to Various Types of Activities

As defined in the Policy [22 CFR section 225.102(d)], "Research means a systematic investigation, including research development, testing and evaluation designed to develop or contribute to generalizable knowledge. Activities which meet this definition constitute research for purposes of this policy, whether or not they are conducted or supported under a program which is considered research for other purposes." The Policy applies only to research involving living human subjects (including samples derived from living subjects). The following listed activities are guidelines for helping to assist in determining applicability of the Policy to a particular research activity. They are by no means intended to be totally inclusive. It is expected that questions will arise and when this occurs guidance should be sought from the CHSO.

(a) Experimental Biomedical Research
The Policy clearly applies to experimental biomedical research related to prevention, transmission, treatment, or curing human diseases and to prevention of pregnancy; including vaccine and drug development; clinical trials of new drugs, devices, and vaccines; and experimental studies of disease transmission involving human subjects.

(b) Survey Research\Demographic Data Collection.
(1) Survey research in which no individual identifiers are collected or in which the data collected are not highly sensitive is exempt [see CFR section 225.101(b)(2)&(3)]. Research involving issues of privacy and confidentiality are not exempt, for example, surveys of high-risk sexual behavior and of HIV infection. Surveys generally considered exempt would include typical censuses, general reproductive surveys such as the demographic and health surveys (DHS), and standard nutrition surveys.

(2) Studies such as surveys involving anthropometry and the gathering of human material through defined "minimal risk" activities are treated as survey research and may be exempt as described in section 5(b)(1)

above. Examples of "minimal risk" activities include collection of hair, nail clippings, external secretions, data via physical sensors applied to the surface of the body, etc. In and of itself, collection of such materials would not require coverage. However, if such gathering of human material exceeds these defined "minimal risk" activities, such as collection of blood samples, then this research is not exempt. A listing of activities defined as "minimal risk" is available from the CHSO.

(3) Anthropologic/ethnographic research is considered survey research as broadly defined and the same rules apply. Clearly, informed consent in this context is often unnecessary, impractical and may be waivable [see section 6(a) & (b) below].

(c) Epidemiologic Research
Depending on methodology, epidemiologic studies may be classified as survey research and treated accordingly [22 CFR section 225.101(b)(2)]. As described above [section 5(b)(1)], when no individual identifiers are collected or when data are not highly sensitive, this research is exempt. Epidemiologic studies include:

(1) Standard Case-Control and Cohort Studies. Generally treat as survey research.

(2) Surveillance. 22 CFR section 225.101(b)(4) exempts research involving existing publicly available data, records and specimens or if the investigator does not record data in an identifiable manner.

(3) Other epidemiologic studies utilizing existing data or specimens. Generally exempt under 22 CFR section 225.101(b)(4). and

(4) Outbreak Investigations. Treat as survey research, but recognize the need for expedited procedures (see section 6(b) below).

(d) Operational or Operations Research
Operational/operations research or service delivery research includes research on service delivery systems for the purpose of understanding how they function and how to improve efficiency and effectiveness. It includes making alterations in how services are provided among acceptable alternatives (e.g. comparing differences in clinic hours or evaluating the impact of adding new services). It is generally exempt under 22 CFR

section 225.101(b)(5) which exempts research on public benefit or service programs. Nevertheless, operations research in highly sensitive areas involving issues of privacy such as HIV prevention, may need special attention regarding matters such as confidentiality and there may be instances where the formal protection procedures should be applied.

(e) Research on Diagnostic Tests
Research to develop or assess diagnostic tests on blood, urine, etc. is not well delineated in the Policy and spans several research categories.

(1) Research on existing specimens is generally exempt if sources are publicly available or subjects cannot be identified.

(2) Research on newly collected materials may be treated as survey research unless collection activities exceed "minimal risk."

(3) Research on existing standard of care diagnostic methods (e.g. comparing two techniques for diagnosing Chlamydia, both of which are commonly used in programs) may be treated as operations research.

(4) Other diagnostic research may be considered experimental biomedical research.

(f) Education Research
Education research involving special subjects, such as children and mentally disabled individuals, is covered by the Policy. Much educational research is exempted under 22 CFR section 225.101(b)(1) including research in educational settings involving normal educational practices.

6. Balancing Protection with Burden

(a) Implementation of the Policy at USAID is intended to comprise the steps necessary for providing adequate protection of human research subjects, while avoiding imposition of undue burden to USAID staff and program personnel. Common sense, practicality, and flexibility are essential, especially in areas other than experimental biomedical research where there is no issues of causing physical harm. In the area of epidemiologic research, for example, informed consent may not be necessary nor practical and might pose a major impediment to conducting the research. 22 CFR sections 225.116 and 225.117 describe the appropriate mechanisms for altering or waiving the informed consent procedure, which requires IRB approval. It might also well be reasonable in many instances of survey research for the informed consent procedure to consist simply of a legitimate statement that participation is voluntary and that information will be kept confidential. In unusual circumstances, where consent is required but written consent is inappropriate in a given culture or population, verbal consent may be appropriate, but it must be witnessed and documented in writing.

(b) Additional situations calling for practicality can be foreseen. For example, there may be instances where a number of surveys or other similar research activities are highly standardized or systematized. Review and approval of such research as a group by an IRB may be appropriate. Likewise, it may be reasonable to approve outbreak investigations as a class in advance because of the emergency nature of such research.

7. Right of Access of USAID Officials to Records

To implement and monitor human subjects research activities properly, it is essential that USAID reserve the right to audit and inspect subjects and other relevant records and to prohibit research which presents unacceptable risks. Appropriate language to that effect must be included in contracts, grants and other support documents as well as in informed consent documents.

8. Implementation

(a) All research activities involving human subjects that are funded by USAID (central or Mission funds) must adhere to the standards set forth in the Policy, or have a system that provides "at least equivalent" protection which has been approved by the AA/G or designee. Compliance with USAID's human subjects procedures is the primary responsibility of the organization receiving USAID support. To help ensure observance of USAID's human subjects procedures by such recipients appropriate language will be included in funding documents when appropriate.

(b) Unless the research is conducted under application of an HHS-approved Multiple Project Assurance, or qualifies as affording "at least equivalent" protection as described in section 4 above, the recipient must proved USAID with a satisfactory written "assurance" that it will comply with the requirements set forth in the Policy. As described in 22 CFR section 225.103(b)(1), the assurance must include: a statement of principles governing the institution's responsibilities, designation of one or more IRBs, a list of IRB members, written procedures which the IRB will follow, and written procedures for ensuring prompt reporting of unanticipated problems to the IRB. Assurances may be for a single research project or for multiple projects. USAID must accept the application of existing HHS-approved multiple project assurance in lieu of a separate assurance.

(c) Within USAID the CTO, TA, or Mission personnel have the first line responsibility for implementation of procedures for the protection of human subjects including an initial determination of the applicability of the procedures. In addition, the CHSO (or successor) located at USAID/Washington, is available to provide additional guidance, oversight and interpretation. In some circumstances (for example if an assurance is especially complicated or if there is a specific concern about risk) it may be reasonable to call on expertise from outside of USAID such as the Office for Protection from Research Risks (OPRR) at the National Institutes of Health. Copies of the Policy, a list of those procedures which qualify as "minimal risk" activities and other guidance are available upon request from the CHSO. Questions and concerns that arise regarding interpretation and applicability of the Policy should be directed to the CHSO, USAID/Washington.

CIOMS—International Ethical Guidelines for Biomedical Research Involving Human Subjects

Prepared by the CIOMS in collaboration with the WHO (Geneva 1993)

Reprinted in part with permission from the Council for International Organizations of Medical Sciences. Contact: CIOMS c/o World Health Organization, avenue Appia, CH-1211 Geneva 27, Switzerland; Telephone: (41 22) 791 21 11; Fax: (41 22) 791 07 46.

General Ethical Principles

All research involving human subjects should be conducted in accordance with three basic ethical principles, namely respect for persons, beneficence and justice. It is generally agreed that these principles, which in the abstract have equal moral force, guide the conscientious preparation of proposals for scientific studies. In varying circumstances they may be expressed differently and given different moral weight, and their application may lead to different decisions or courses of action. The present guidelines are directed at the application of these principles to research involving human subjects.

Respect for persons incorporates at least two fundamental ethical considerations, namely:

(a) respect for autonomy, which requires that those who are capable of deliberation about their personal choices should be treated with respect for their capacity for self-determination; and

(b) protection of persons with impaired or diminished autonomy, which requires that those who are dependent or vulnerable be afforded security against harm or abuse.

Beneficence refers to the ethical obligation to maximize benefits and to minimize harms and wrongs. This principle gives rise to norms requiring that the risks of research be reasonable in the light of the expected benefits, that the research design be sound, and that the investigators be competent both to conduct the research and to safeguard the welfare of the research subjects. Beneficence further proscribes the deliberate infliction of harm on persons; this aspect of beneficence is sometimes expressed as a separate principle, nonmaleficence (do no harm).

Justice refers to the ethical obligation to treat each person in accordance with what is morally right and proper, to give each person what is due to him or her. In the ethics of research involving human subjects the principle refers primarily to distributive justice, which requires the equitable distribution of both the burdens and the benefits of participation in research. Differences in distribution of burdens and benefits are justifiable only if they are based on morally relevant distinctions between persons; one such distinction is vulnerability. "Vulnerability" refers to a substantial incapacity to protect one's own interests owing to such impediments as lack of capability to give informed consent, lack of alternative means of obtaining medical care or other expensive necessities, or being a junior or subordinate member of a hierarchical group. Accordingly, special provisions must be made for the protection of the rights and welfare of vulnerable persons.

PREAMBLE

The term "research" refers to a class of activities designed to develop or contribute to generalizable knowledge. Generalizable knowledge consists of theories, principles or relationships, or the accumulation of information on which they are based, that can be corroborated by accepted scientific methods of observation and inference. In the present context "research" includes both medical and behavioral studies pertaining to human health. Usually "research" is modified by the adjective "biomedical" to indicate that the reference is to health-related research.

Progress in medical care and disease prevention depends upon an understanding of physiological and pathological processes or epidemiological findings, and requires at some time research involving human subjects. The collection, analysis and interpretation of information obtained from research involving human beings contribute significantly to the improvement of human health.

Research involving human subjects includes that undertaken together with patient care (clinical research) and that undertaken on patients or other subjects, or with data pertaining to them, solely to contribute to generalizable knowledge (non-clinical biomedical research). Research is defined as "clinical" if one or more of its components is designed to be diagnostic, prophylactic or therapeutic for the individual subject of the research. Invariably, in clinical research, there are also components designed not to be diagnostic, prophylactic or therapeutic for the subject; examples include the administration of placebos and the performance of laboratory tests in addition to those required to serve the purposes of medical care. Hence the term "clinical research" is used here rather than "therapeutic research".

Research involving human subjects includes:

—studies of a physiological, biochemical or pathological process, or of the response to a specific intervention—whether physical, chemical or psychological—in healthy subjects or patients;

—controlled trials of diagnostic, preventive or therapeutic measures in larger groups of persons, designed to demonstrate a specific generalizable response to these measures against a background of individual biological variation;

—studies designed to determine the consequences for individuals and communities of specific preventive or therapeutic measures; and

—studies concerning human health-related behavior in a variety of circumstances and environments.

Research involving human subjects may employ either observation or physical, chemical or psychological intervention; it may also either generate records or make use of existing records containing biomedical or other information about individuals who may or may not be identifiable from the records or information. The use of such records and the protection of the confidentiality of data obtained from these records are discussed in *International Guidelines for Ethical Review of Epidemiological Studies* (CIOMS, 1991).

Research involving human subjects includes also research in which environmental factors are manipulated in a way that could affect incidentally-exposed individuals. Research is defined in broad terms in order to embrace field studies of pathogenic organisms and toxic chemicals under investigation for health-related purposes.

Research involving human subjects is to be distinguished from the practice of medicine, public health and other forms of health care, which is designed to contribute directly to the health of individuals or communities. Prospective subjects may find it confusing when research and practice are to be conducted simultaneously, as when research is designed to obtain new information about the efficiency of a drug or other therapeutic, diagnostic or preventive modality.

Research involving human subjects should be carried out only by, or strictly supervised by, suitably qualified and experienced investigators and in accordance with a protocol that clearly states: the aim of the research; the reasons for proposing that it involve human subjects; the nature and degree of any known risks to the subjects; the sources from which it is proposed to recruit subjects; and the means proposed for ensuring that subjects' consent will be adequately informed and voluntary. The protocol should be scientifically and ethically appraised by one or more suitably constituted review bodies, independent of the investigators.

New vaccines and medicinal drugs, before being approved for general use, must be tested on human subjects in clinical trials; such trials, which constitute a substantial part of all research involving human subjects, are described in Annex 2.

The Guidelines

[In the original document, comments are provided following each guideline. For brevity, they have been deleted here.—THE EDITORS]

Informed Consent of Subjects

Guideline 1: Individual informed consent
For all biomedical research involving human subjects, the investigator must obtain the informed consent of the prospective subject or, in the case of an individual who is not capable of giving informed consent, the proxy consent of a properly authorized representative.

Guideline 2: Essential information for prospective research subjects
Before requesting an individual's consent to participate in research, the investigator must provide the individual with the following information, in language that he or she is capable of understanding:
—that each individual is invited to participate as a subject in research, and the aims and methods of the research;
—the expected duration of the subject's participation;
—the benefits that might reasonably be expected to result to the subject or to others as an outcome of the research;
—any foreseeable risks or discomfort to the subject, associated with participation in the research;
—any alternative procedures or courses of treatment that might be as advantageous to the subject as the procedure or treatment being tested;
—the extent to which confidentiality of records in which the subject is identified will be maintained;

—the extent of the investigator's responsibility, if any, to provide medical services to the subject;

—that therapy will be provided free of charge for specified types of research-related injury;

—whether the subject or the subject's family or dependents will be compensated for disability or death resulting from such injury; and

—that the individual is free to refuse to participate and will be free to withdraw from the research at any time without penalty or loss of benefits to which he or she would otherwise be entitled.

Guideline 3: Obligations of investigators regarding informed consent
The investigator has a duty to:

—communicate to the prospective subject all the information necessary for adequately informed consent;

—give the prospective subject full opportunity and encouragement to ask questions;

—exclude the possibility of unjustified deception, undue influence and intimidation;

—seek consent only after the prospective subject has adequate knowledge of the relevant facts and of the consequences of participation, and has had sufficient opportunity to consider whether to participate;

—as a general rule, obtain from each prospective subject a signed form as evidence of informed consent; and

—renew the informed consent of each subject if there are material changes in the conditions or procedures of the research.

Guideline 4: Inducement to participate
Subjects may be paid for inconvenience and time spent, and should be reimbursed for expenses incurred, in connection with their participation in research; they may also receive free medical services. However, the payments should not be so large or the medical services so extensive as to induce prospective subjects to consent to participate in the research against their better judgment ("undue inducement"). All payments, reimbursements and medical services to be provided to research subjects should be approved by an ethical review committee.

Guideline 5: Research involving children
Before undertaking research involving children, the investigator must ensure that:

—children will not be involved in research that might equally well be carried out with adults;

—the purpose of the research is to obtain knowledge relevant to the health needs of children;

—a parent or legal guardian of each child has given proxy consent; the consent of each child has been obtained to the extent of the child's capabilities;

—the child's refusal to participate in research must always be respected unless according to the research protocol the child would receive therapy for which there is no medically-acceptable alternative;

—the risk presented by interventions not intended to benefit the individual child-subject is low and commensurate with the importance of the knowledge to be gained; and

—interventions that are intended to provide therapeutic benefit are likely to be at least as advantageous to the individual child-subject as any available alternative.

Guideline 6: Research involving persons with mental or behavioral disorders
Before undertaking research involving individuals who by reason of mental or behavioral disorders are not capable of giving adequately informed consent, the investigator must ensure that:

—such persons will not be subjects of research that might equally well be carried out on persons in full possession of their mental faculties;

—the purpose of the research is to obtain knowledge relevant to the particular health needs of persons with mental or behavioral disorders;

—the consent of each subject has been obtained to the extent of that subject's capabilities, and a prospective subject's refusal to participate in non-clinical research is always respected;

—in the case of incompetent subjects, informed consent is obtained from the legal guardian or other duly authorized person;

—the degree of risk attached to interventions that are not intended to benefit the individual subject is low and commensurate with the importance of the knowledge to be gained; and

—interventions that are intended to provide therapeutic benefit are likely to be at least as advantageous to the individual subject as any alternative.

Guideline 7: Research involving prisoners
Prisoners with serious illness or at risk of serious illness should not

arbitrarily be denied access to investigational drugs, vaccines or other agents that show promise of therapeutic or preventive benefit.

Guideline 8: Research involving subjects in underdeveloped communities
Before undertaking research involving subjects in underdeveloped communities, whether in developed or developing countries, the investigator must ensure that:

—persons in underdeveloped communities will not ordinarily be involved in research that could be carried out reasonably well in developed communities;

—the research is responsive to the health needs and the priorities of the community in which it is to be carried out;

—every effort will be made to secure the ethical imperative that the consent of individual subjects be informed; and

—the proposals for the research have been reviewed and approved by an ethical review committee that has among its members or consultants persons who are thoroughly familiar with the customs and traditions of the community.

Guideline 9: Informed consent in epidemiological studies
For several types of epidemiological research individual informed consent is either impracticable or inadvisable. In such cases the ethical review committee should determine whether it is ethically acceptable to proceed without individual informed consent and whether the investigator's plans to protect the safety and respect the privacy of research subjects and to maintain the confidentiality of the data are adequate.

Selection of Research Subjects
Guideline 10: Equitable distribution of burdens and benefits
Individuals or communities to be invited to be subjects of research should be selected in such a way that the burdens and benefits of the research will be equitably distributed. Special justification is required for inviting vulnerable individuals and, if they are selected, the means of protecting their rights and welfare must be particularly strictly applied.

Guideline 11: Selection of pregnant or nursing (breastfeeding) women as research subjects
Pregnant or nursing women should in no circumstances be the subjects of non-clinical research unless the research carries no more than minimal risk to the fetus or nursing infant and the object of the research is to obtain new knowledge about pregnancy or lactation. As a general rule,

pregnant or nursing women should not be subjects of any clinical trials except such trials as are designed to protect or advance the health of pregnant or nursing women or fetuses or nursing infants, and for which women who are not pregnant or nursing would not be suitable subjects.

Confidentiality of Data
Guideline 12: Safeguarding confidentiality
The investigator must establish secure safeguards of the confidentiality of research data. Subjects should be told of the limits to the investigators' ability to safeguard confidentiality and of the anticipated consequences of breaches of confidentiality.

Compensation of Research Subjects for Accidental Injury
Guideline 13: Right of subjects to compensation
Research subjects who suffer physical injury as a result of their participation are entitled to such financial or other assistance as would compensate them equitably for any temporary or permanent impairment or disability. In the case of death, their dependents are entitled to material compensation. The right to compensation may not be waived.

Review Procedures
Guideline 14: Constitution and responsibilities of ethical review committees
All proposals to conduct research involving human subjects must be submitted for review and approval to one or more independent ethical and scientific review committees. The investigator must obtain such approval of the proposal to conduct research before the research is begun.

Externally Sponsored Research
Guideline 15: Obligations of sponsoring and host countries
Externally sponsored research entails two ethical obligations:

—An external sponsoring agency should submit the research protocol to ethical and scientific review according to the standards of the country of the sponsoring agency, and the ethical standards applied should be no less exacting than they would be in the case of research carried out in that country.

—After scientific and ethical approval in the country of the sponsoring agency, the appropriate authorities of the host country, including a national or local ethical review committee or its equivalent, should satisfy themselves that the proposed research meets their own ethical requirements.

Part 2: Selected Major Policies

World Medical Association Declaration of Helsinki
Recommendations Guiding Physicians in Biomedical Research Involving Human Subjects

Adopted by the 18th World Medical Assembly
Helsinki, Finland, June 1964

and amended by the
29th World Medical Assembly, Tokyo, Japan, October 1975
35th World Medical Assembly, Venice, Italy, October 1983
41st World Medical Assembly, Hong Kong, September 1989
and the
48th General Assembly,
Somerset West, Republic of South Africa, October 1996

See "World Medical Association Declaration of Helsinki," page 14 above.

DHHS—Waiver of Informed Consent Requirements in Certain Emergency Research

61 Federal Register 51531. 2 October 1996.
Contact: *Office for Protection from Research Risks, National Institutes of Health, 6100 Executive Blvd., Suite 3B01, Rockville, Md. 20892-7507; Telephone: (301) 496-7005.*

Waiver

Pursuant to Section 46.101(i) of title 45 of the Code of Federal Regulations, the Secretary of Health and Human Services (HHS) has waived the general requirements for informed consent at 45 CFR 46.116 (a) and (b), and at 46.408, to be referred to as the "Emergency Research Consent Waiver," for a class of research consisting of activities[1], each of which have met the following strictly limited conditions detailed under either (a) or (b) below:

(a) The Institutional Review Board (IRB) responsible for the review, approval, and continuing review of the research activity has approved both the activity and a waiver of informed consent and found and documented:

(1) that the research activity is subject to regulations codified by the Food and Drug Administration (FDA) at Title 21 CFR part 50 and will be carried out under an FDA investigational new drug application (IND) or an FDA investigational device exemption (IDE), the application for which has clearly identified the protocols that would include subjects who are unable to consent; and

(2) that the requirements for exception from informed consent for emergency research detailed in title 21 CFR section 50.24 have been met relative to those protocols, or

(b) The IRB responsible for the review, approval, and continuing review of the research has approved both the research and a waiver of informed consent and has found and documented that the research is not subject to regulations codified by the FDA at title 21 CFR part 50 and found and documented and reported to the Office for Protection from Research Risks, Department of Health and Human Services, that the following conditions have been met relative to the research:

(1) The human subjects are in a life-threatening situation, available treatments are unproven or unsatisfactory, and the collection of valid scientific evidence, which may include evidence obtained through randomized placebo-controlled investigations, is necessary to determine the safety and effectiveness of particular interventions;

(2) Obtaining informed consent is not feasible because:

(i) The subjects will not be able to give their informed consent as a result of their medical condition;

(ii) The intervention involved in the research must be administered before consent from the subjects' legally authorized representatives is feasible; and

(iii) There is no reasonable way to identify prospectively the individuals likely to become eligible for participation in the research;

(3) Participation in the research holds out the prospect of direct benefit to the subjects because:

(i) Subjects are facing a life-threatening situation that necessitates intervention;

(ii) Appropriate animal and other preclinical studies have been conducted, and the information derived from those studies and related evidence support the potential for the intervention to provide a direct benefit to the individual subjects; and

(iii) The risks associated with the research are reasonable in relation to what is known about the medical condition of the potential class of subjects, the risks and benefits of standard therapy, if any, and what is known about the risks and benefits of the proposed intervention or activity;

(4) The research could not practicably be carried out without the waiver;

(5) The proposed research protocol defines the length of the potential therapeutic window based on scientific evidence, and the investigator has committed to attempting to contact a legally authorized representative for each subject within that window of time and, if feasible, to asking the legally authorized representative contacted for consent within that window rather than proceeding without consent. The investigator will summarize efforts made to contact representatives and make this information available to the IRB at the time of continuing review;

(6) The IRB has reviewed and approved informed consent procedures and an informed consent document in accord with Sections 46.116 and 46.117 of title 45 of the Code of Federal Regulations. These procedures and the informed consent document are to be used with subjects or their legally authorized representatives in situations where use of such procedures and documents is feasible. The IRB has reviewed and approved procedures and information to be used when providing an opportunity for a family member to object to a subject's participation in the research consistent with paragraph (b)(7)(v) of this waiver; and

(7) Additional protections of the rights and welfare of the subjects will be provided, including, at least:

(i) Consultation (including, where appropriate, consultation carried out by the IRB) with representatives of the communities in which the research will be conducted and from which the subjects will be drawn;

(ii) Public disclosure to the communities in which the research will be conducted and from which the subjects will be drawn, prior to initiation of the research, of plans for the research and its risks and expected benefits;

(iii) Public disclosure of sufficient information following completion of the research to apprise the community and researchers of the study, including the demographic characteristics of the research population, and its results;

(iv) Establishment of an independent data monitoring committee to exercise oversight of the research; and

(v) If obtaining informed consent is not feasible and a legally authorized representative is not reasonably available, the investigator has committed, if feasible, to attempting to contact within the therapeutic window the subject's family member who is not a legally authorized representative, and asking whether he or she objects to the subject's participation in the research. The investigator will summarize efforts made to contact family members and make this information available to the IRB at the time of continuing review.

In addition, the IRB is responsible for ensuring that procedures are in place to inform, at the earliest feasible opportunity, each subject, or if the subject remains incapacitated, a legally authorized representative of the subject, or if such a representative is not reasonably available, a family member, of the subject's inclusion in the research, the details of the research and other information contained in the informed consent document. The IRB shall also ensure that there is a procedure to inform the subject, or if the subject remains incapacitated, a legally authorized representative of the subject, or if such a representative is not reasonably available, a family member, that he or she may discontinue the subject's participation at any time without penalty or loss of benefits to which the subject is otherwise entitled. If a legally authorized representative or family member is told about the research and the subject's condition improves, the subject is also to be informed as soon as feasible. If a subject is entered into research with waived consent and the subject dies before a legally authorized representative or family member can be contacted, information about the research is to be provided to the subject's legally authorized representative or family member, if feasible.

For the purposes of this waiver "family member" means any one of the following legally competent persons: spouses; parents; children (including adopted children); brothers, sisters, and spouses of brothers and sisters; and any individual related by blood or affinity whose close association with the subject is the equivalent of a family relationship.

Background

It had come to the attention of HHS that there are proposals to conduct certain research, including National Institutes of Health (NIH) funded research, which could not go forward in the context of the current HHS regulations for the protection of human subjects (45 CFR part 46), unless certain informed consent requirements of those regulations were waived in accord with the waiver provisions provided at 45 CFR 46.101(i). HHS carefully reviewed the need for the exercise of the Section 46.101(i) waiver authority in these circumstances, and the requirements for informed consent were waived by the Secretary in the instance of only one specific multi-site study of head injuries which is currently underway (60 FR 38353).

The Secretary is now waiving the informed consent requirements for the class of research activities and no longer restricting the waiver to a single research project. This waiver provides clear instruction as to when research in emergency circumstances may proceed without obtaining an individual subject's informed consent. Elsewhere in this edition of the Federal Register, the FDA is publishing a final rule which amends FDA regulations to authorize a nearly identical waiver of informed consent in research which is regulated by FDA. The joint publication of these actions permit harmonization of the HHS and FDA regulations regarding research in emergency circumstances. The HHS waiver, just as the FDA regulatory change, provides a narrow exception to the requirement for obtaining and documenting informed consent from each human subject or his or her legally authorized representative prior to initiation of research if the waiver of informed consent is approved by an IRB. The waiver authorization applies to a limited class of research activities involving human subjects who are in need of emergency medical intervention but who cannot give informed consent because of their life-threatening medical condition, and who do not have available a legally authorized person to represent them. The Secretary, HHS is authorizing this waiver in response to growing concerns that current regulations, absent this waiver, are making high quality research in emergency circumstances difficult or impossible to carry out at a time when the need for such research is increasingly recognized.

HHS notes testimonies to this effect delivered to: (i) the Subcommittee on Regulation, Business Opportunities, and Technology, Committee on Small Business, U.S. House of Representatives (Washington DC, May 23, 1994); (ii) the Coalition Conference of Acute Resuscitation Researchers (Washington DC, October 25, 1994); (iii) the meeting of Applied Research Ethics National Association (Boston MA, October 30, 1994); (iv) the meeting of Public Responsibility in Medicine & Research (Boston MA, November 1, 1994); and (v) the Food and Drug Administration/National Institutes of Health Public Forum on Informed Consent in Clinical Research Conducted in Emergency Circumstances (Rockville MD, January 9-10, 1995).

Periodic Review

A periodic review of the implementation by IRBs of this Section 101(i) waiver will be conducted by the Office for Protection from Research Risks, National Institutes of Health, to determine the adequacy of the waiver in meeting its intended need or if adjustments to the waiver might be necessary and appropriate.

Notes

1. Because of special regulatory limitations relating to research involving prisoners (subpart C of 45 CFR part 46), and research involving fetuses, pregnant women, and human in vitro fertilization (subpart B of 45 CFR part 46), this waiver is inapplicable to these categories of research.

FDA—Waiver of Informed Consent in Certain Emergency Research*

* *Actual title: Protection of Human Subjects; Informed Consent*
61 Federal Register *51498. 2 October 1996. Codified at 21* CFR *Parts 50, 56, 312, 314, 601, 812, and 814.*
Contact: *Office of Health Affairs (HFY-20), Food and Drug Administration, 5600 Fishers Lane, Rockville, Md. 20857; Telephone: (301) 827-1685.*

Summary

The Food and Drug Administration (FDA) is amending its current informed consent regulations to permit harmonization of the Department of Health and Human Services' (DHHS) policies on emergency research and to reduce confusion on when such research can proceed without obtaining an individual subject's informed consent. This regulation provides a narrow exception to the requirement for obtaining and documenting informed consent from each human subject, or his or her legally authorized representative, prior to initiation of an experimental intervention. The exception would apply to a limited class of research activities involving human subjects who are in need of emergency medical intervention but who cannot give informed consent because of their life-threatening medical condition, and who do not have a legally authorized person to represent them. FDA is taking this action in response to growing concerns that current rules are making high quality acute care research activities difficult or impossible to carry out at a time when the need for such research is increasingly recognized."

[The text of the FDA regulation concerning waiver of informed consent in certain emergency research amended many sections of the FDA's regulations. For relevant text, the reader should refer to sections

50.3 (n), 50.24, 56.109 (c) and 56.109(d) of title 21 of the *CFR*, reproduced in this volume, see "FDA—Protection of Human Subjects," page 74, and "FDA—Institutional Review Boards," page 86. Regulatory amendments related to emergency waiver that are not reproduced in this volume concern investigational new drug applications (21 *CFR* part 312), applications for FDA approval to market a new drug or an antibiotic drug (21 *CFR* part 314), licensing (21 *CFR* part 601), and investigational device exemptions (21 *CFR* part 812), and premarket approval of medical devices (21 *CFR* part 814). Relevant changes to the foregoing parts are detailed in 61 *Federal Register* 51498, 2 October 1996.—*THE EDITORS*]

FDA—Determinations that Informed Consent is not Feasible for Military Exigencies*

* Actual title: *Informed Consent for Human Drugs and Biologics; Determination that Informed Consent Is Not Feasible*
Excerpted from 55 Federal Register 52814. 21 December 1990. Codified at 21 CFR 50.23 (d).
Contact: Office of Health Affairs (HFY-1), Food and Drug Administration, 5600 Fishers Lane, Rockville, Md. 20857; Telephone: (301) 443-6143.

[Revocation or amendment of this interim final rule is under consideration by the FDA. See 62 Fed. Reg. 40996, 1997.—*The Editors*]

Summary

The Food and Drug Administration (FDA) is issuing an interim regulation to amend its current informed consent regulations. This will permit the Commissioner of Food and Drugs to make the determination that obtaining informed consent from military personnel for the use of an investigational drug or biologic is not feasible in certain battlefield or combat-related situations. The amendment authorizes the Commissioner to make such a determination when the physician(s) responsible for the medical care of the military personnel involved and the investigator(s) named in the investigational new drug application (IND) provide written justification for their conclusions that, in the use of specific investigational drugs or biologics in a specific combat-related situation, obtaining informed consent is not feasible and withholding treatment would be contrary to the best interests of the military personnel because of military combat exigencies and that the waiver of informed consent is ethically justified. Military combat (actual or threatened) circumstances in which the health of the individual or the safety of other military personnel, may require that a particular drug or biologic for prevention or treatment be provided to a specified group of military personnel, without regard to any individual's personal preference for no treatment or for some alternative treatment. The Department of Defense (DOD) must also provide a written statement that the use of the investigational drug or biologic and the waiver of informed consent has been reviewed and approved by a duly constituted institutional review board (IRB). In determining whether obtaining informed consent is not feasible in these circumstances, the Commissioner must also consider certain other criteria. This action is being issued as an interim rule with an immediate effective date because of the urgency created by current military operations in Operation Desert Shield.

SUPPLEMENTARY INFORMATION

I. Informed Consent Regulations

Sections 505(i) and 507(d) of the Federal Food, Drug, and Cosmetic Act (the act) *(21 U.S.C. 355(i) and 357(d))* require FDA to publish regulations governing the use of human drugs, including certain biologics and antibiotics, in clinical investigations (hereafter "investigational drugs"). Sections 505(i) and 507(d) provide that such regulations must include, among other requirements, a requirement that investigators who use investigational drugs inform the subjects of their investigations that the drugs are investigational and "obtain the consent of such human beings or their representatives, except where they deem it not feasible, or in their professional judgment, contrary to the best interests of such human beings."

FDA issued its current regulations governing informed consent in the Federal Register of January 27, 1981 (46 FR 8942). Those regulations, codified in 21 CFR part 50, apply to all clinical investigations regulated by FDA under sections 505(i), 507(d), and 520(g) *(21 U.S.C. 360j(g))* of the act, as well as to clinical investigations that support applications for research or marketing permits for products regulated by FDA. The regulations require that investigators obtain informed consent from the subjects of clinical investigations. The only circumstance in the current regulations in which obtaining informed consent is deemed not to be feasible is for emergency use of an investigational article, where both the investigator and a physician who is not otherwise participating in the clinical investigation certify in writing that: (1) The subject is confronted by a life-threatening situation necessitating the use of the test article; (2)

informed consent cannot be obtained because of an inability to communicate with or obtain legally effective consent from the subject; (3) there is insufficient time to obtain consent from the subject's legal representative; and (4) there is no available approved or generally recognized therapy that provides an equal or greater likelihood of saving the life of the subject. The current regulations do not permit a determination that obtaining informed consent is otherwise not feasible or is contrary to the best interest of the subject.

II. DOD's Request

The Assistant Secretary of Defense (Health Affairs) set forth DoD's request in his October 30, 1990 letter to the Assistant Secretary for Health of the Department of Health and Human Services as follows:

This is to follow up on discussions of DoD and HHS personnel over the past weeks. As you know, the memorandum of understanding between DoD and the Food and Drug Administration recognizes "special DoD requirements to meet national defense considerations." Operation Desert Shield presents such special DoD requirements.

Our contingency planning in Desert Shield has had to take into account endemic diseases in the area and the well-publicized capabilities of the Iraqi military with respect to chemical and biological weapons. For some of these risks, we have determined that the best preventive or therapeutic treatment calls for the use of products now under "investigational new drug" (IND) protocols of the FDA.

These are not exotic new drugs; these drugs have well-established uses (although in contexts somewhat different from our requirements) and are believed by medical personnel in both DoD and FDA to be safe. For example, one product consists of a very commonly used drug packaged in a special intramuscular injector to make it readily useable by soldiers on the battlefield. Another example involves a vaccine long recognized by the Centers for Disease Control as the primary preventive treatment available for a particular disease, but the relative infrequency of its use has slowed the accumulation of sufficient immunogenicity data to yet support full licensing of the product. Still another example involves a drug in common use at a particular dosage level, but to preserve alertness of the soldiers, we prefer a lower-dosage tablet, which is not an FDA approved product. FDA personnel have been extremely cooperative and supportive in reviewing our proposed protocols for these products, quickly providing favorable responses to all of our submissions to date.

FDA assistance is also needed on the issue of informed consent. Under the Federal Food, Drug and Cosmetic Act, the general rule is that, regardless of the character of the medical evidence, any use of an IND, whether primarily for investigational purposes or primarily for treatment purposes, must be preceded by obtaining informed consent from the patient. The statute authorizes exceptions, however, when the medical professionals administering the product "deem it not feasible" to obtain informed consent.

Our planning for Desert Shield contingencies has convinced us that another circumstance should be recognized in the FDA regulation in which it would be consistent with the statute and ethically appropriate for medical professionals to "deem it not feasible" to obtain informed consent of the patient—that circumstance being the existence of military combat exigencies, coupled with a determination that the use of the product is in the best interest of the individual. By the term "military combat exigencies," we mean military combat (actual or threatened) circumstances in which the health of the individual, the safety of other personnel and the accomplishment of the military mission require that a particular treatment be provided to a specified group of military personnel, without regard to what might be any individual's personal preference for no treatment or for some alternative treatment.

In all peacetime applications, we believe strongly in informed consent and its ethical foundations. In peacetime applications, we readily agree to tell military personnel, as provided in FDA's regulations, that research is involved, that there may be risks or discomforts, that participation is voluntary and that refusal to participate will involve no penalty. But military combat is different. If a soldier's life will be endangered by nerve gas, for example, it is not acceptable from a military standpoint to defer to whatever might be the soldier's personal preference concerning a preventive or therapeutic treatment that might save his life, avoid endangerment of the other personnel in his unit and accomplish the combat mission. Based on unalterable requirements of the military field commander, it is not an option to excuse a non-consenting soldier from the military mission, nor would it be defensible militarily—or ethically— to send the soldier unprotected into danger.

To those familiar with military command requirements, this is, of course, elementary. It is also very solidly established in law through a number of Supreme Court cases establishing that special military exigencies sometimes must supersede normal rights and procedures that apply in the civilian community. Consistent with this, long-standing military regulations state that military members may be required to submit to medical care determined necessary to preserve life, alleviate suffering or protect the health of others.

Such special military authority carries with it special responsibility for the well-being of the military personnel involved. Thus, we propose specific procedural limitations on the "not feasible" waiver of informed consent based on military combat exigencies. We propose that decisions on waiving informed consent be made on a case-by-case basis by the Commissioner, assuring an objective review outside of military channels of all pertinent information and an independent validation of the special circumstances presented. Further, we propose the following specific limitations: (1) That drug-by-drug requests for waiver be accompanied by written justification based on the intended uses and the military circumstances involved; (2) that no satisfactory alternative treatment is available; (3) that available safety and efficacy data support the proposed use of the drug or biologic product; (4) that each such request be approved by the applicable DoD Institutional Review Board; and (5) that the waivers be time-limited.

To recap, we have nothing exotic in the works. We are methodically planning for a range of medical treatment contingencies in Operation Desert Shield corresponding to the predictable medical problems that might arise. Some of these contingencies require the availability of products now under IND protocols. For products that will be in the best interests of the patients, military combat exigencies may justify deeming it not feasible to obtain informed consent. FDA's regulation should provide the mechanism, subject to appropriate limitations, for DoD to request on a drug-by-drug basis, and the Commissioner to decide, that a waiver be granted in cases in which it is established that military combat exigencies make that necessary.

Your cooperation and assistance in this regard is appreciated.

III. Provisions of This Regulation

FDA continues to recognize its responsibility in protecting the human subjects exposed to investigational drugs and the central role that informed consent plays in ensuring that protection. Because of the paramount importance of informed consent, only the narrowest exceptions to this requirement are consistent with FDA's responsibilities and consistent with the best interests of human subjects. Nevertheless, FDA has determined that, in the special circumstances that may be created by the use of troops in combat and consistent with its obligations under sections 505(i) and 507(d), FDA may narrowly expand the circumstances in which the Commissioner may determine that obtaining informed consent is not feasible. FDA agrees with DOD's judgment that, in certain combat-related situations, it may be appropriate to conclude that obtaining informed consent from military personnel for the use of investigational drugs is not feasible and withholding treatment would be contrary to the best interests of military personnel involved. DOD has the right and responsibility to make command decisions that expose troops to the possibility of combat and has the concomitant responsibility to protect the welfare of these troops both individually and as a group. DOD has stated that traditional informed consent, based on the right of the individual to choose his or her own treatment, may not be appropriate under the circumstances of specific combat-related conditions. FDA respects DOD's obligation and commitment to do everything possible to protect military personnel who may be exposed to potentially hazardous conditions. FDA further appreciates that this protection may include medical treatment or prevention with an investigational drug considered necessary to protect not only the health of individual soldiers but to ensure the welfare of the remaining forces. FDA will consider investigational products proposed for military use on a case-by-case basis, and the agency is prepared to waive the requirement of informed consent where it can be documented that use of these agents in combat-related situations serves the best interests of individual soldiers and the military combat units in which they serve. Since these individual soldiers may be required to be exposed to combat, permitting them to choose whether to receive an investigational product that is the only available satisfactory protection against life-threatening conditions, is contrary to their individual best interests and to the welfare of the other soldiers involved. FDA therefore believes that such an exercise of the Commissioner's discretion is ethically justified. Moreover, all the products at issue would be reviewed by FDA for safety and expanded availability, and their use would be monitored by DOD and reported to and reviewed by FDA. DOD and FDA do not expect that all combat-related situations will create a situation of the kind that would obviate obtaining informed consent. DOD and FDA must determine that there is justification for a waiver of informed consent for a particular drug, following the approval of the use and the waiver by a duly constituted IRB, and a conclusion that the circumstances surrounding the anticipated distribution and use of the drug meet the limited circumstances recognized in the regulations. DOD and FDA also emphasize that accepted ethical principles permit waiver of informed consent only where the preventive or treatment is in the best interests of the individuals involved. Therefore, it is not sufficient as an ethical matter to waive informed consent in the military context where obtaining informed consent is "not feasible," unless it is also the case that withholding the treatment would be contrary to the best interests of the individuals involved. FDA is therefore amending 21 CFR 50.23 to add limited conditions under which the Commissioner may find that it is not feasible to obtain informed consent in the proposed use of an investigational drug. Under the amended regulation, the Commissioner will make any such determination on a product-by-product basis. In determining whether obtaining informed consent is not feasible and withholding treatment would be contrary to the best interests of the military personnel, the Commissioner must find that there is no available satisfactory alternative therapy for the intended diagnosis, prevention, or treatment of the disease or condition. The Commissioner will also consider other factors, including the extent and strength of the evidence of the safety and effectiveness of the investigational drug for the intended use. Other factors that the Commissioner will consider include the nature of the information provided to the recipients of the investigational drug concerning the potential risks and benefits of the drug, known adverse effects of the drug, and risks of not taking such a product in combat-related situations, whether the disease or condition to be treated is life-threatening or highly contagious and debilitating, and the setting in which the drug is to be administered. For example, it may be more feasible to obtain informed consent in a hospital than on the battlefield or when it is administered by a health professional rather than self-administered. FDA recognizes, however, that there may be combat-related circumstances in which obtaining informed consent is not feasible and withholding treatment would be contrary to the best interests of military personnel even outside battlefield conditions.

When DOD seeks a determination by FDA that obtaining informed consent would not be feasible in the proposed use of a specific investigational drug and withholding treatment would be contrary to the best interest of the military personnel, DOD must submit a written request. The request must be for use of a specific investigational drug in a specific protocol under an IND sponsored by DOD, in a specific combat-related setting. The request will also include a written justification supporting the conclusions of the physician(s) responsible for the medical care of the military personnel involved and the investigator(s) identified in the IND that a military combat exigency exists because of special military combat (actual or threatened) circumstances in which, in order to facilitate the accomplishment of the military mission, preservation of the health of the individual and the safety of other personnel require that a particular treatment be provided to a specified group of military personnel, without regard to what may be any individual's personal preference for no treatment or for some alternative treatment.

The request must further contain a statement that the duly constituted IRB has reviewed and approved the proposed use of the investigational drug and concluded that it may be administered without obtaining informed consent under the criteria set forth in this document. The request must be submitted with the original IND submission or as an amendment to the IND.

The Commissioner may consult with appropriate experts, including those responsible for the protection of human subjects, before reaching a determination on a DOD request under this regulation.

To ensure that the period in which informed consent is not obtained does not exceed that necessary to deal with the actuality or threat of combat, the Commissioner's determination regarding informed consent will automatically expire at the end of 1 year or when DOD informs FDA that the specific military operation creating the need for the investigational drug has ended, whichever is earlier. If, at the end of 1 year, United States military forces are still engaged in the military operations, DOD may seek to renew the determination. This provision does not preclude the Commissioner from revoking or otherwise modifying the determination at any time based upon changed circumstances. In particular, consistent with DOD's responsibilities under the IND's under which these products will be administered, DOD will collect data on any use of these products without informed consent. FDA will review these data and will revoke or modify the determination if the review indicates that the determination is no longer appropriate.

This amendment applies only to the use of investigational drugs. It does not apply to other clinical investigations to which 21 CFR part 50 applies.

IV. Effective Date

FDA is issuing this amendment as an interim rule, with an effective date on publication in the Federal Register because of the urgent need to provide adequate medical support for Operation Desert Shield, a military operation involving the immediate threat of combat, which is already underway. Because of the unexpected and emergency nature of this situation, and the need for immediate action to meet the requirements of national defense, FDA finds, in accordance with section 553(b) of the Administrative Procedure Act *(5 U.S.C. 553*(b)(3)(B)), that it would be impracticable and contrary to the public interest to provide for notice and public comment. For these reasons, FDA also finds, in accordance with section 553(d) of the Administrative Procedure Act *(5 U.S.C. 553*(d)), that it has good cause to make this rule effective on publication in the Federal Register and that this rule relieves a restriction, an independent basis for an immediate effective date under the Administrative Procedure Act. As an additional independent basis for an effective date on publication in the Federal Register, this rule involves a military affairs function of the United States within the meaning of section 553(a)(1) of the Administrative Procedure Act *(5 U.S.C. 553*(a)(1)). FDA is, however, allowing 30 days for public comment on the interim rule in accordance with its procedural regulations (21 CFR 10.40(e)). FDA believes that the same emergency conditions described above justify shortening its usual comment period from 60 to 30 days.

[Sections V through VI and filing information have been omitted. Full text of the rule is at §50.23 (d) of 21 *CFR* Part 50, reproduced in this volume, see "FDA—Protection of Human Subjects," page 74.—*THE EDITORS*]

Part Three:
Selected Bibliography

Overview of Part 3

This selected bibliography is designed to provide information about some of the ethical issues related to research with human subjects that may (1) provide insight into the application and analysis of relevant research policies, and (2) prove useful in describing some of the important considerations in designing, conducting or evaluating research with human subjects where formal policies currently do not exist. It is not intended to be a comprehensive bibliography on the ethics of research with human subjects; the quantity of available resources would make such a compendium unwieldy and inaccessible. Rather, we hope that this selection will prove useful to those seeking direction and further understanding regarding the ethical conduct of this research.

The selection process for inclusion in this bibliography consisted of several steps. We first identified material that we have found particularly useful in our research and teaching. This was followed by electronic searches in the Bioethicsline database. From these additional citations, we reviewed and selected materials based on the following criteria. Materials needed to be: (1) on point, related to the scope of the bibliography as described in the paragraph above, (2) directive in nature, rather than simply providing background information, (3) accessible in most university libraries, (4) not redundant, to the extent possible, with other material in the bibliography, and (5) forward-thinking rather than an historical review. These criteria obviously eliminate many materials that may be important to a full understanding of issues in the ethics of research with human subjects, such as reports and background papers of governmental committees and professional bodies. For readers who are interested in more information, the general resources and the topic-specific citations listed in the bibliography can serve as starting points for locating additional materials. In addition, focused electronic searches in Bioethicsline should prove useful. For those unfamiliar with searching this database or performing a complex search, it is possible to telephone the National Reference Center for Bioethics Literature (NRCBL) at

Georgetown University for assistance (1-800-med-ethx). In addition, NRCBL staff will currently provide a free search service of Bioethicsline.

We hope that the materials listed here offer a foundation for understanding the policy environment of the ethical conduct of research with human subjects. Such a foundation enhances the likelihood that the rights and interests of research subjects will continue to be served.

The Selected Bibliography generally follows the organization of the previous parts of this volume, with additional sections where major policies do not exist. For instance, under "Subject Populations," we first include references to areas in which policies have been reprinted in this volume, followed by sections on students and healthy volunteers. Similarly, under "Research in Particular Settings," references regarding research in prisons and international research, we included a section on research within institutions. In the final section, we include references for other issues such as genetic research, research on those with diminished capacity, and compensation (both as incentives to participate and research injury). The table of contents can be used to facilitate finding these sections.

Selected Bibliography

General Resources

Kahn, J.P, A.C. Mastroianni, and J. Sugarman, eds. *Beyond Consent: Seeking Justice in Research.* New York: Oxford University Press, 1998.

Levine, R.J. *Ethics and Regulation of Clinical Research.* 2nd ed. New Haven, Conn.: Yale University Press, 1988.

Vanderpool, H.Y., ed. *The Ethics of Research Involving Human Subjects: Facing the 21st Century.* Frederick, Md.: University Publishing Group, 1996.

Office for Protection from Research Risks (OPRR) Web Site: <http://www.nih.gov/grants/oprr/oprr.htm>

History

Advisory Committee on Human Radiation Experiments. *The Human Radiation Experiments*. New York: Oxford University Press, 1996.
———. "Research Ethics and the Medical Profession: Report of the Advisory Committee on Human Radiation Experiments." *Journal of the American Medical Association* 276, no. 5 (1996): 403-09.
Annas, J.G. and M.A. Grodin. *The Nazi Doctors and the Nuremberg Code: Human Rights in Human Experimentation*. New York: Oxford University Press, 1992.
Beecher, H.K. "Ethics and Clinical Research." *New England Journal of Medicine* 274, no. 24 (1966): 1354-60.
Caplan, A.L. *When Medicine Went Mad: Bioethics and the Holocaust*. Totowa, N.J.: Humana Press, 1992.
Faden, R.R. and T.L. Beauchamp. *A History and Theory of Informed Consent*. New York: Oxford University Press, 1986.
Gray, B.H. "The Regulatory Context of Social Research: The Work of the National Commission for the Protection of Human Subjects." In *Deviance and Decency: The Ethics of Research with Human Subjects*, edited by C.B. Klockars and F.W. O'Connor, 197-223. Beverly Hills, Calif.: Sage, 1979.
Jones, J.H. *Bad Blood: The Tuskegee Syphilis Experiment, New and Expanded Edition*. New York: Free Press, 1993.
Jonsen, A.B., R.M. Veatch, and L.B. Walters, eds. *Source Book in Bioethics*. Washington, D.C.: Georgetown University Press, 1998.
Katz, J. *Experimentation with Human Beings: The Authority of the Investigator, Subject, Professions and State in the Human Experimentation Process*. New York: Russell Sage Foundation, 1972.
———. "The Regulation of Human Experimentation in the United States: A Personal Odyssey." *IRB* 9, no. 1 (1987): 1-6.
Lederer, S.E. *Subjected to Science: Human Experimentation in America Before the Second World War*. Baltimore, Md.: Johns Hopkins University Press, 1995.
Levine, R.J. *Ethics and Regulation of Clinical Research*. 2nd ed. New Haven, Conn.: Yale University Press, 1988.

———. "Research Ethics Committees." In *Encyclopedia of Bioethics*, revised edition, edited by W.T. Reich, 2266-70. New York: Simon and Schuster Macmillan, 1995.

McCarthy, C.R. "The Evolving Story of Justice in Federal Research Policy." *In Beyond Consent*, edited by J.P. Kahn, A.C. Mastroianni, and J. Sugarman, 11-31. New York: Oxford University Press, 1998.

McNeill, P.M. *The Ethics and Politics of Human Experimentation*. New York: Cambridge University Press, 1993.

Pappworth, M.H. "Human Guinea Pigs: A History." *British Medical Journal* 301, no. 6766 (1990): 1456-60.

Rothman, D.J. "Ethics and Human Experimentation: Henry Beecher Revisited." *New England Journal of Medicine* 317, no. 19 (1987): 1195-99.

———. "Research, Human: Historical Aspects." In *Encyclopedia of Bioethics*. Revised edition, edited by W.T. Reich, 2248-58. New York: Simon and Schuster Macmillan, 1995.

———. *Strangers at the Bedside: A History of How Law and Bioethics Transformed Medical Decision Making*. New York: Basic Books, 1991.

Savitt, T.L. "Minorities as Research Subjects." In *Encyclopedia of Bioethics*. Revised edition, edited by W.T. Reich, 1776-80. New York: Simon and Schuster Macmillan, 1995.

Sherman, M. and J.D. VanVleet. "The History of Institutional Review Boards." *Regulatory Affairs Journal* 3 (1991): 615-27.

U.S. Congress, Office of Technology Assessment. *Biomedical Ethics in U.S. Public Policy—Background Paper*, OTA-BP-BBS-105. Washington, D.C.: U.S. Government Printing Office, June 1993.

Subject Populations

Racial and Ethnic Groups

Caplan, A.L. "When Evil Intrudes: [Twenty Years After: The Legacy of the Tuskegee Syphilis Study]." *Hastings Center Report* 22, no. 6 (1992): 29-32.

Dula, A. "Bearing the Brunt of the New Regulations: Minority Populations." *Hastings Center Report* 27, no. 1, (1997): 11-12.

El-Sadr, W. and L. Capps. "The Challenge of Minority Recruitment in Clinical Trials for AIDS." *Journal of the American Medical Association* 267, no. 7 (1992): 954-57.

Gamble, V.N. "Under the Shadow of Tuskegee: African Americans and Health Care." *American Journal of Public Health* 87, no. 11 (1997): 1773-78.

Gamble, V.N. and B.E. Blustein. "Racial Differentials in Medical Care: Implications for Research on Women." In *Women and Health Research: Ethical and Legal Issues of Including Women in Clinical Studies.* Vol. 2, Workshop and Commissioned Papers, edited by A.C. Mastroianni, R. Faden, and D. Federman, 174-91. Washington, D.C.: National Academy Press, 1994.

Jones, J.H. *Bad Blood: The Tuskegee Syphilis Experiment, New and Expanded Edition.* New York: Free Press, 1993.

King, P.A. "The Dangers of Difference. [Twenty Years After: The Legacy of the Tuskegee Syphilis Study]." *Hastings Center Report* 22, no.6 (1992): 35-38.

———. "Race, Justice and Research," In *Beyond Consent,* edited by J.P. Kahn, A.C. Mastroianni, and J. Sugarman, 88-110. New York: Oxford University Press, 1998.

Lex, B.L. and J.R. Norris. "Health Status of American Indian and Alaska Native Women." In *Women and Health Research: Ethical and Legal Issues of Including Women in Clinical Studies.* Vol. 2, Workshop and Commissioned Papers, edited by A.C. Mastroianni, R. Faden, and D. Federman, 192-215. Washington, D.C.: National Academy Press, 1994.

Mitchell, J.L. "Recruitment and Retention of Women of Color in Clinical Studies." In *Women and Health Research: Ethical and Legal Issues of Including Women in Clinical Studies.* Vol. 2, Workshop and Commissioned Papers, edited by A.C. Mastroianni, R. Faden, and

D. Federman, 52-56. Washington, D.C.: National Academy Press, 1994.

Osborne, N.G. and M.D. Feit. "The Use of Race in Medical Research." *Journal of the American Medical Association* 267, no. 2 (1992): 275-79.

Yu, E.S.H. "Ethical and Legal Issues Relating to the Inclusion of Asian/Pacific Islanders in Clinical Studies." In *Women and Health Research: Ethical and Legal Issues of Including Women in Clinical Studies.* Vol. 2, Workshop and Commissioned Papers, edited by A.C. Mastroianni, R. Faden, and D. Federman, 216-31. Washington, D.C.: National Academy Press, 1994.

Zambrana, R.E. "The Inclusion of Latino Women in Clinical and Research Studies: Scientific Suggestions for Assuring Legal and Ethical Integrity." In *Women and Health Research: Ethical and Legal Issues of Including Women in Clinical Studies.* Vol. 2, Workshop and Commissioned Papers, edited by A.C. Mastroianni, R. Faden, and D. Federman, 232-40. Washington, D.C.: National Academy Press, 1994.

Women

American College of Clinical Pharmacy, "Women as Research Subjects (ACCP White Paper)." *Pharmacotherapy* 13, no. 5 (1993): 534-42.

Bush, J.K. "The Industry Perspective on the Inclusion of Women in Clinical Trials." *Academic Medicine* 69, no. 9 (1994): 708-15.

Charo, R.A. "Protecting Us to Death: Women, Pregnancy, and Clinical Research Trials." *Saint Louis University Law Journal* 38 (1993): 135-87.

Dresser, R. "Wanted: Single White Male for Medical Research." *Hastings Center Report* 22, no. 1 (1992): 24-29.

Kass, N.E. "Gender and Research." In *Beyond Consent*, edited by J.P. Kahn, A.C. Mastroianni, and J. Sugarman, 67-87. New York: Oxford University Press, 1998.

Kass, N.E., H.A. Taylor, and P.A. King. "Harms of Excluding Pregnant Women from Clinical Research: the Case of HIV-Infected Pregnant Women." *Journal of Law, Medicine and Ethics* 24, no. 1 (1996): 36-46.

Mastroianni, A.C., R. Faden, and D. Federman, eds. *Women and Health Research: Ethical and Legal Issues of Including Women in Clinical Studies.* Vol. 1 and Vol. 2. Washington, D.C.: National Academy Press, 1994.

Merkatz, R.B., et al. "Women in Clinical Trials of New Drugs: A Change in Food and Drug Administration Policy." *New England Journal of Medicine* 329, no. 4 (1993): 292-96.

Merton, V. "Ethical Obstacles to the Participation of Women in Biomedical Research." In *Feminism and Bioethics*, edited by S. Wolf. New York: Oxford University Press, 1996.

——. "The Exclusion of Pregnant, Pregnable, and Once-Pregnable People (a.k.a. Women) from Biomedical Research." *American Journal of Law and Medicine* 19, no. 4 (1993): 369-451.

Minkoff, H., J.D. Moreno, and K.R. Powderly. "Fetal Protection and Women's Access to Clinical Trials." *Journal of Women's Health* 1, no. 2 (1992): 137-40.

Rothenberg, K.H. "Gender Matters: Implications for Clinical Research and Women's Health Care." *Houston Law Review* 32, no. 5 (1996), 1201-72.

Embryos and Fetuses

American College of Obstetricians and Gynecologists Committee Opinion: Committee on Ethics. "Preembryo Research: History, Scientific Background, and Ethical Considerations, no. 136, April 1994." *International Journal of Gynecology & Obstetrics* 45, no. 3 (1994): 291-301.

Andrews, L.B. "State Regulation of Embryo Research." in *Papers Commissioned for the NIH Human Embryo Research Panel*. Vol. 2, 297-322. Bethesda, Md.: National Institutes of Health, 1994. Publication No. 95-3916.

Andrews, L.B. and N. Elster. "Cross-Cultural Analysis of Policies Regarding Embryo Research." In *Papers Commissioned for the NIH Human Embryo Research Panel*. Vol. 2, 51-64. Bethesda, Md.: National Institutes of Health, 1994. Publication No. 95-3916.

American Medical Association Board of Trustees, "Frozen Pre-Embryos," *Journal of the American Medical Association* 263, no. 18 (1990): 2484-87.

Eisenberg, V.H. and J.G. Schenker. "Preembryo Research: Medical Aspects and Ethical Considerations." *Obstetrical and Gynecological*

Survey 52, no. 9 (1997): 565-74.

Ethics Committee of the American Society for Reproductive Medicine. "Informed Consent and the Use of Gametes and Embryos for Research." *Fertility and Sterility* 68, no. 5 (1997): 780-81.

Fletcher, J.C. "Fetal Therapy, Ethics and Public Policies." *Fetal Diagnosis & Therapy* 7, no. 2 (1992): 158-68.

Green, R.M. "The Human Embryo Research Panel: Lessons for Public Ethics," *Cambridge Quarterly of Healthcare Ethics* 4, no. 4 (1995): 502-515.

Human Embryo Research Panel. *Report of the Human Embryo Research Panel.* Bethesda, Md.: National Institutes of Health, 27 September 1994. Publication number 95-3916.

Levine, R.J. "The Fetus and the Embryo," In *Ethics and Regulation of Clinical Research.* 2d ed., 297-320. New Haven, Conn.: Yale University Press, 1988.

National Bioethics Advisory Commission. *Cloning Human Beings: Report and Recommendations of the National Bioethics Advisory Commission.* Rockville, Md.: National Bioethics Advisory Commission, 1997.

Pechura, C.M. "Fetal and Embryo Research: A Changing Scientific, Political, and Ethical Landscape." In *The Ethics of Research Involving Human Subjects: Facing the 21st Century,* edited by H.Y. Vanderpool, 371-400. Frederick, Md.: University Publishing Group, 1996.

Singer, P. et al. *Embryo Experimentation.* Cambridge, England: Cambridge University Press, 1990.

Steinbock, B. "Ethical Issues in Human Embryo Research." In *Papers Commissioned for the NIH Human Embryo Research Panel.* Vol. 2, 1-25. Bethesda, Md.: National Institutes of Health, 1994. Publication No. 95-3916.

Van Blerkom, J. "The History, Current Status and Future Direction of Research Involving Human Embryos," in *Papers Commissioned for the NIH Human Embryo Research Panel.* Vol. 2, 1-25. Bethesda, Md.: National Institutes of Health, 1994. Publication No. 95-3916.

Walters, L. "Ethics and New Reproductive Technologies: An International Review of Committee Statements." *Hastings Center Report* 17, no. 3 (1987): S3-S9.

Warnock, M. *A Question of Life: The Warnock Report on Fertilisation and Embryology.* New York: Basil Blackwell, 1985.

Minors

General

American Academy of Pediatrics Committee on Drugs. "Guidelines for the Ethical Conduct of Studies to Evaluate Drugs in the Pediatric Population." *Pediatrics* 95, no. 2 (1995): 286-94.

Bartholome, W.G. "Ethical Issues in Pediatric Research." in *The Ethics of Research Involving Human Subjects: Facing the 21st Century*, edited by H.Y. Vanderpool, 339-370. Frederick, Md.: University Publishing Group, 1996.

Choudhry, S. "Review of Legal Instruments and Codes on Medical Experimentation with Children." *Cambridge Quarterly of Healthcare Ethics* 3, no. 4 (1994): 560-73.

Cooke, R.E. "Vulnerable Children." In *Children as Research Subjects: Science, Ethics, and Law*, edited by M.A. Grodin and L.H. Glantz, 193-214. New York: Oxford University Press, 1994.

Freeman, W.L. "Research with Radiation and Healthy Children: Greater than Minimal Risk." *IRB* 16, no. 5 (1994): 1-5.

"Does Radiation Research in Healthy Children Pose Greater than Minimal Risk? (Replies to Freeman)." *IRB* 16, no. 5 (1994): 5-9.

Freedman, B., A. Fuks, and C. Weijer. "In Loco Parentis: Minimal Risk as an Ethical Threshold for Research upon Children." *Hastings Center Report* 23, no. 2 (1993): 13-19.

Gidding, S.S. et al. "A Policy Regarding Research in Healthy Children (Special Article)." *Journal of Pediatrics* 123, no. 6 (1993): 852-5.

Grodin, M.A. and L.H. Glantz. *Children as Research Subjects: Science, Ethics and Law*. New York: Oxford University Press, 1994.

Koren, G. ed. *Textbook of Ethics in Pediatric Research*. Malabar, Fla.: Krieger, 1993.

Leikin, S. "Ethical Issues in Epidemiologic Research with Children." In *Ethics and Epidemiology*, edited by S.S. Coughlin and T.L Beauchamp, 199-218. New York: Oxford University Press, 1996.

Levine, R.J. "Children." In *Ethics and Regulation of Clinical Research*. 2d ed., 235-256. New Haven, Conn.: Yale University Press, 1988.

National Commission for the Protection of Human Subjects of Biomedical and Behavioral Research. *Research Involving Children: Report and Recommendations*. Washington, D.C.: U.S. Government Printing Office, 1977. Publication number (OS) 77-0004.

Nelson, R.M. "Children as Research Subjects." In *Beyond Consent*, edited by J.P. Kahn, A.C. Mastroianni, and J. Sugarman, 47-66. New York: Oxford University Press, 1998.

Adolescents

Brooks-Gunn, J. and M.J. Rotheram-Borus. "Rights to Privacy in Research: Adolescents Versus Parents." *Ethics & Behavior* 4, no. 2 (1994): 109-21.

Hoagwood, K. "The Certificate of Confidentiality at the National Institutes of Mental Health: Discretionary Considerations in its Applicability in Research on Child and Adolescent Mental Disorders." *Ethics & Behavior* 4, no. 2 (1994): 123-31.

Kopelman, L.M. "When is the Risk Minimal Enough for Children to be Research Subjects?" In *Children and Health Care: Moral and Social Issues*, edited by L.M. Kopelman and J.C. Moskop, 89-99. Boston: Kluwer Academic, 1989.

Levine, R.J. "Children as Research Subjects." In *Children and Health Care: Moral and Social Issues*, edited by L.M. Kopelman and J.C. Moskop, 73-87. Boston: Kluwer Academic, 1989.

Murray, T.H. "Research on Children and the Scope of Responsible Parenthood." In *The Worth of a Child*, 70-95. Berkeley, Calif.: University of California Press, 1996.

Oberman, M. "Minor Rights and Wrongs." *Journal of Law, Medicine & Ethics* 24, no. 2 (1996): 127-38.

Phillips, S.R. "Asking the Sensitive Question: the Ethics of Survey Research and Teen Sex." *IRB* 16, no. 6 (1994): 1-7.

Rogers, A.S., L. D'Angelo, and D. Futterman. "Guidelines for Adolescent Participation in Research: Current Realities and Possible Resolutions." *IRB* 16, no. 4 (1994): 1-6.

Stanley, B. and J.E. Sieber, eds. *Social Research on Children and Adolescents: Ethical Issues*. London: Sage, 1992.

Weir, R.F. and J.R. Horton. "Genetic Research, Adolescents, and Informed Consent." *Theoretical Medicine* 16, no. 4 (1995): 347-73.

Zinner, S.E. "The Elusive Goal of Informed Consent by Adolescents," *Theoretical Medicine* 16, no. 4 (1995): 323-31.

Older Persons

McGloin, J. M. and A.M. Ostfeld. "The Ethics of Epidemiologic Research with Older Populations." In *Ethics and Epidemiology*, edited by S.S. Coughlin and T.L. Beauchamp, 219-38. New York: Oxford University Press, 1996.

Reich, W.T. "Ethical Issues Related to Research Involving Elderly Subjects." *Gerontologist* 18, no. 4 (1978): 326-37.

Sugarman, J., D.C. McCrory, and R.C. Hubal. "Getting Meaningful Informed Consent from Older Adults: A Structured Literature Review of Empirical Research." *Journal of the American Geriatrics Society* 46, no. 4 (1998): 517-24.

Weiss Lane, L., C.K. Cassel, and W. Bennett. "Ethical Aspects of Research Involving Elderly Subjects: Are We Doing More than We Say?" *The Journal of Clinical Ethics* 1, no. 4 (1990): 278-85.

Wicclair, M.R. "Research with Elderly Subjects." In *Ethics and the Elderly*, 160-200. New York: Oxford University Press, 1993.

Students

Christakis, N. "Do Medical Student Research Subjects Need Special Protection?" *IRB* 7, no. 3 (1985): 1-4.

Miller, B.L. "Students as Research Subjects." In *Encyclopedia of Bioethics*. Rev. ed. Edited by W.T. Reich, 2413-15. New York: Simon and Schuster Macmillan, 1995.

Healthy Volunteers

Phillips, M. and A.J. Vazquez. "Abnormal Findings in 'Normal' Research Volunteers." *Controlled Clinical Trials* 8 (1987): 338-42.

"Research on Healthy Volunteers: A Report of the Royal College of Physicians," *Journal of the Royal College of Physicians of London* 20, no. 4 (1986): 243-57.

Research in Particular Settings

Prisons

Levine, R.J. "Prisoners." In *Ethics and Regulation of Clinical Research*, 2d ed., 277-95. New Haven, Conn.: Yale University Press, 1988.

Moreno, J.D. "Convenient and Captive Populations." In *Beyond Consent*, edited by J.P. Kahn, A.C. Mastroianni, and J. Sugarman, 111-30. New York: Oxford University Press, 1998.

International

Bankowski, Z. "International Ethical Considerations for Research on Human Subjects." In *Ethical Issues in Research*, edited by D. Cheney, 177-88. Frederick, Md.: University Publishing Group, 1993.

Christakis, N.A. "The Distinction between Ethical Pluralism and Ethical Relativism: Implications for the Conduct of Transcultural Clinical Research." In *The Ethics of Research Involving Human Subjects: Facing the 21st Century*, edited by H.Y. Vanderpool, 261-80. Frederick, Md.: University Publishing Group, 1996.

Christakis, N.A. and M.J. Panner. "Existing International Ethical Guidelines for Human Subjects Research: Some Open Questions." *Law, Medicine & Health Care* 19, nos. 3-4 (1991): 214-21.

Dommel, F.W. Jr., and D. Alexander. "The Convention on Human Rights and Biomedicine of the Council of Europe." *Kennedy Institute of Ethics Journal* 7, no. 3 (1997): 259-76.

Ijsselmuiden, C.B. and R.R. Faden. "Medical Research and the Principle of Respect for Persons of Non-Western Cultures." In *The Ethics of Research Involving Human Subjects: Facing the 21st Century*, edited by H.Y. Vanderpool, 281-301. Frederick, Md: University Publishing Group, 1996.

———. "Research and Informed Consent in Africa—Another Look (Sounding Board)." *New England Journal of Medicine* 326, no. 12 (1992): 830-34.

Levine, R.J. "International Codes and Guidelines for Research Ethics: A Critical Appraisal." In *The Ethics of Research Involving Human Subjects: Facing the 21st Century*, edited by H.Y. Vanderpool, 235-60. Frederick, Md.: University Publishing Group, 1996.

Macklin, R. "International Research: Ethical Imperialism or Ethical Pluralism." *Accountability in Research* 6, no. 4 (1998), forthcoming.
———. "Justice in International Research." In *Beyond Consent*, edited by J.P. Kahn, A.C. Mastroianni, and J. Sugarman, 131-46. New York: Oxford University Press, 1998.
Newman, A.M. "Drug Trials, Doctors, and Developing Countries: Toward a Legal Definition of Informed Consent (Special Section: Rejuvenating Research Ethics)." *Cambridge Quarterly of Healthcare Ethics* 5 (1996): 387-99.
Wichman, A., et al. "Collaborative Research Involving Human Subjects: A Survey of Researchers Using International Single Project Assurances." *IRB* 19, no. 1 (1997): 1-6.

Institutions

Levine, R.J. "Proposed Regulations for Research Involving Those Institutionalized as Mentally Infirm: A Consideration of Their Relevance in 1996." *IRB* 18, no. 5 (1996): 1-5.
———. "Those Institutionalized as Mentally Infirm." In *Ethics and Regulation of Clinical Research*. 2d ed., 257-76. New Haven, Conn.: Yale University Press, 1988.

Waivers of Informed Consent

Emergency Research

Brody, B.A. "New Perspectives on Emergency Room Research." *Hastings Center Report* 27, no. 1, (1997): 7-9.

———. "Research on the Vulnerable Sick." In *Beyond Consent*, edited by J.P. Kahn, A.C. Mastroianni, and J. Sugarman, 32-46. New York: Oxford University Press, 1998.

Dula, A. "Bearing the Brunt of the New Regulations: Minority Populations." *Hastings Center Report* 27, no. 1 (1997): 11-12.

Katz, J. "Blurring the Lines: Research, Therapy, and IRBs." *Hastings Center Report* 27, no. 1 (1997): 9-11.

Military Settings

Fotion, N.G. "Getting Consent from the Troops?" In *Biomedical Ethics Reviews: 1992*, edited by J.M. Humber and R.F. Almeder, 7-29. Totowa, N.J.: Humana, 1993.

Howe, E.G. "Ethical Issues Regarding Mixed Agency of Military Physicians." *Social Science Medicine* 23, no. 8 (1986): 803-15.

Levine, C. "Military Medical Research: 1. Are There Ethical Exceptions?" *IRB* 11, no. 4 (1989): 5-7.

Moreno, J.D. "Convenient and Captive Populations." In *Beyond Consent*, edited by J.P. Kahn, A.C. Mastroianni, and J.Sugarman, 111-30. New York: Oxford University Press, 1998.

Other Issues

Genetics

American Society of Human Genetics. "ASHG Report: Statement on Informed Consent for Genetic Research." *American Journal of Human Genetics* 59, no. 2 (1996): 471-74.

American Society of Human Genetics Ad Hoc Committee on DNA Technology. "DNA Banking and DNA Analysis: Points to Consider." *American Journal of Human Genetics* 32, no. 5 (1988): 781-83.

Andrews, L.B., et al., eds. *Assessing Genetic Risks: Implications for Health and Social Policy*. Washington, D.C.: National Academy Press, 1994.

Clayton, E.W. et al., "Informed Consent for Genetic Research on Stored Tissue Samples." *Journal of the American Medical Association* 274, no. 22 (1995): 1786-92.

Glass, K.C. et al. "Structuring the Review of Human Genetics Protocols: Gene Localization and Identification Studies." *IRB* 18, no. 4 (1996): 1-9.

Glass, K.C. et al. "Structuring the Review of Human Genetics Protocols Part II: Diagnostic and Screening Studies." *IRB* 19, no. 3, 4 (1997): 1-12.

Juengst, E.T. "Respecting Human Subjects in Genome Research: A Preliminary Policy Agenda." In *The Ethics of Research Involving Human Subjects: Facing the 21st Century,* edited by H.Y. Vanderpool, 401-29. Frederick, Md.: University Publishing Group, 1996.

Mastroianni, A.C. and J.P. Kahn, "Ethical Issues in Genetic Research." *Accountability in Research* 6, no. 4 (1998): forthcoming.

Powers, M. "Publication-Related Risks to Privacy: Ethical Implications of Pedigree Studies." *IRB* 15, no. 4 (1993): 7-11.

President's Commission for the Study of Ethical Problems in Medicine. *Screening and Counseling for Genetic Conditions: A Report on the Ethical, Social and Legal Implications of Genetic Screening, Counseling and Education Programs*. Washington, D.C.: U.S. Government Printing Office, 1983.

Walters, L. and J.G. Palmer. *The Ethics of Human Gene Therapy*. New York: Oxford University Press, 1997.

Weir, R.F. and J.R. Horton. "DNA Banking and Informed Consent, Part 1." *IRB* 17, no. 4 (1995): 1-4.

Weir, R.F. and J.R. Horton, "DNA Banking and Informed Consent,

Part 2." *IRB* 17, no. 5,6 (1995): 1-8.
———. "DNA Banking and Informed Consent, Part 2." *IRB* 17, nos. 5-6 (1995): 1-8.
———. "Genetic Research, Adolescents, and Informed Consent." *Theoretical Medicine* 16, no. 4 (1995): 347-73.

Subjects with Diminished Capacity

American College of Physicians. "Cognitively Impaired Subjects." *Annals of Internal Medicine* 111, no. 10 (1989): 843-48.
Bonnie, R.J. "Research with Cognitively Impaired Subjects." *Archives of General Psychiatry* 54, no. 2 (1997): 105-11.
Candilis, P.J., R.W. Wesley, and A. Wichman. "A Survey of Researchers Using a Consent Policy for Cognitively Impaired Human Research Subjects." *IRB* 15, no. 6 (1993): 1-4.
DeRenzo, E.G. "Decisionally Impaired Persons in Research: Refining the Proposed Refinements." *Journal of Law, Medicine & Ethics* 25, nos. 2-3 (1997): 139-49.
Haimowitz, S., S.J. Delano, and J.M. Oldham. "Uninformed Decisionmaking: The Case of Surrogate Research Consent." *Hastings Center Report* 27, no. 6 (1997): 9-16.
High, D.M. "Research with Alzheimer's Disease Subjects: Informed Consent and Proxy Decision Making." *Journal of the American Geriatrics Society* 40, no. 9 (1992): 950-57.
High, D.M. et al. "Guidelines for Addressing Ethical and Legal Issues in Alzheimer Disease Research: A Position Paper." *Alzheimer Disease and Associated Disorders* 8, suppl. 4 (1994): 66-74.
National Bioethics Advisory Comittee. *Research Involving Subjects with Mental Disorders Affecting Decisionmaking Capacity.* Rockville, Md.: National Bioethics Advisory Comittee, 1998. [A draft version is available at < http://bioethics.gov > —*THE EDITORS*]
Shamoo, A.E. and D.N. Irving. "Accountability in Research Using Persons with Mental Illness." *Accountability in Research* 3, no. 1 (1993): 1-17.
Sunderland, T. and R. Dukoff. "Informed Consent with Cognitively Impaired Patients: An NIMH Perspective on the Durable Power of Attorney." *Accountability in Research* 4, nos. 3-4 (1996): 217-26.
Wichman, A. and A.L. Sandler. "Research Involving Subjects with Dementia and Other Cognitive Impairments: Experience at the NIH, and Some Unresolved Ethical Considerations." *Neurology* 45, no. 9 (1995): 1777-78.

Compensation

Incentives

LaPuma, J. "Physicians' Conflicts of Interest in Post-Marketing Research: What the Public Should Know, and Why Industry Should Tell Them." In *The Ethics of Research Involving Human Subjects: Facing the 21st Century,* edited by H.Y. Vanderpool, 203-22. Frederick, Md.: University Publishing Group, 1996.

Lind, S.E. "Financial Issues and Incentives Related to Clinical Research and Innovative Therapies." In *The Ethics of Research Involving Human Subjects: Facing the 21st Century,* edited by H.Y. Vanderpool, 185-202. Frederick, Md.: University Publishing Group, 1996.

———. "Finder's Fees for Research Subjects." *New England Journal of Medicine* 323, no. 3 (1990): 192-95.

Macklin, R. "On Paying Money to Research Subjects: 'Due' and 'Undue' Inducements." *IRB* 13, no. 5 (1981): 1-6.

Wilkinson, M. and A. Moore. "Inducement in Research," *Bioethics* 11, no. 5 (1997): 373-89.

Injury

"Compensation Systems for Research Injuries (Appendix D)." In *Women and Health Research: Ethical and Legal Issues of Including Women in Clinical Studies.* Vol. 2. Workshop and Commissioned Papers, edited by A.C. Mastroianni, R.R. Faden, and D. Federman, 243-252. Washington, D.C.: National Academy Press, 1978.

Ladimer, I. "Protection of Human Subjects: Remedies for Injury." In *The Use of Human Beings in Research,* edited by S.F. Spicker et al., 261-71. Boston: Kluwer Academic, 1988.

Mariner, W.K. "Compensation for Research Injuries." In *Women and Health Research: Ethical and Legal Issues of Including Women in Clinical Studies.* Vol. 2. Workshop and Commissioned Papers, edited by A.C. Mastroianni, R.R. Faden, and D. Federman, 113-26. Washington, D.C.: National Academy Press, 1994.

President's Commission for the Study of Ethical Problems in Medicine and Biomedical and Behavioral Research. *Compensating for Research Injuries: A Report on the Ethical and Legal Implications of Programs to Redress Injuries Caused by Biomedical and Behavioral Research.* Vol. 1 and Vol. 2. Washington, D.C.: U.S. Government Printing Office, 1982.

Appendices

List of Abbreviations

ADAMHA	Alcohol, Drug Abuse, and Mental Health Administration
ATSDR	U.S. Agency for Toxic Substances and Disease Registry
CDC	Centers for Disease Control and Prevention
CDER	FDA Center for Drug Evaluation and Research
CFR	*Code of Federal Regulations*
CIOMS	Council of International Organizations of Medical Sciences
DHHS	U.S. Department of Health and Human Services
DOD	U.S. Department of Defense
FDA	U.S. Food and Drug Administration
Fed. Reg.	*Federal Register*
FR	*Federal Register*
GPO	U.S. Government Printing Office
HHS	U.S. Department of Health and Human Services
IND	investigational new drug application
IRB	institutional review board
MPA	multiple project assurance
NDA	new drug application
NIH	National Institutes of Health
OPRR	NIH Office for Protection from Research Risks
P.L.	public law
USAID	U.S. Agency for International Development
U.S.C.	*United States Code*
US GPO	U.S. Government Printing Office
WHO	World Health Organization

Relevant Web Sites

ARENA and PRIM&R: Applied Research Ethics National Association and Public Responsibility in Medicine and Research
http://www.aamc.org/research/primr/arena

Centers for Disease Control and Prevention
http://www.cdc.gov

Food and Drug Administration
http://www.fda.gov

GPO Access (U.S. Goverment Printing Office)
http://www.access.gpo.gov

National Institutes of Health
http://www.nih.gov

Office for Protection from Research Risks (NIH)
http://www.nih.gov:80/grants/oprr/library_human.htm
http://www.nih.gov:80/grants/oprr/irb/irb_guidebook.htm
[IRB Guidebook]

THOMAS: Legislative Information on the Internet
http://thomas.loc.gov